Through the Moongate

The Story of Richard Garriott, Origin Systems Inc. and Ultima

---

Part 1

From Akalabeth to Ultima VI

ANDREA CONTATO

Page Layout by Progetto Iskandar

Imprint: Independently published

ISBN 9781071006856

Dedicated to my Mother,
        my first Player Two.

For Martina,
        forever my Player Two.

For Diego and Alessandro,
        That as adults, reading it, they can
        understand the games of my generation.

Preface

My first meeting with the world of Ultima took place relatively late, in 1994, when I was able to get a copy of the special edition EA Compilation, bundled with the Discovery CD 16, a Creative Labs kit containing a CD-ROM drive, a Sound Blaster 16 bit and a set of 2.0 speakers.

Having been, for years, a passionate and avid gamer, especially of RPGs, I had the opportunity to come across such champions as Wizardry, Bard's Tale, Dungeon Master and Eye of the Beholder. Obviously, I already knew about Wing Commander, a game included in the Compilation and a title so successful that it even made its way into a town in the province of Bergamo, Italy until finding a place on the shelf of a small computer store where I used to loiter and window shop for long periods of time.

The Origin Systems Inc. brand was not new to me, but Ultima was.

Managers at Creative Labs had chosen to bundle software with the media kit to give their customers an instant chance to appreciate the power of their sound card and CD player. It was a clever idea and in my case, it worked: the emergence of the red face of the Guardian from the iridescent screen and his deep, mocking voice made me shake. And they conquered me.

I played The Black Gate in one go, writing down notes in a notebook borrowed from a stack of school materials. When I got to the end, I wanted more. I could only satisfy my thirst with Ultima Underworld: The Stygian Abyss and then, ravenously, look for other titles in the series in the first stores of a well-known commercial chain dedicated to computer science and technology. I wasn't aware at the time, but I was experiencing the Ultima series at the peak of its popularity. First, playing the finest installments, innovative and ingenious, and then, proceeding backwards in time, consuming the chapters that I had missed out on when I had been busy playing BurgerTime, Raid over Moscow and Double Dragon.

Studying, out of passion, the story of Origin Systems Inc. and its co-founder, Richard Garriott, I realized how it was intimately intertwined with the role-playing genre and the career of many of the most influential personalities in the video game and computer industries. It was a story that deserved to be told.

My research began in magazines and newspapers of the period, starting from reviews, fragmentary news reported by the press, interviews of Garriott to promote his products and company. Always pushing the envelope, has never wavered. The more I studied and collected data however, the more I felt dissatisfied because I became restless that I was working on material already published, known, and that the answers to the questions formulated in my mind after this long research, could not be found without accessing new information: I needed to go to the source, to talk to the witnesses and protagonists of the story I wanted to tell. What's more, I wanted them to tell it to me first.

The subsequent search, this time not for data, but for people, was not easy yet less difficult than I had feared. Most of Garriott's colleagues and companions in the adventure were young and original programmers with a flair for video games. Although a few decades had passed, many were still in business, some retired, and a few remained engaged in the video game industry. Once they were contacted, their response was enthusiastic. Almost everyone wanted to contribute to my research, generously giving me their memories, their time, and even sending me photographs, drafts, notes and memories of when they were Originites, part of the Origin Systems Inc. family. Some did so openly while others asked to remain anonymous.

In the hundreds of e-mails exchanged over more than six months of work, in the very long conversations via Skype or instant messaging, I managed to ask thousands of questions and received as many — if not more — answers. With thirty-three interviews "on the records" and others confidential, I was able to listen for the first time to the story I wanted to tell. Thanks to the generosity and availability of many, I had collected all the elements I needed to get to work.

When I first installed an Ultima game on my PC, like many others before me, I wondered who this Lord British was that appeared in the manual's instructions, as an author, and even as an NPC in the game. It was the first in a long series of questions that took me very far.

It is an honor for me to have been able to write this book, made possible only by the testimonies of all the special people I met along the way and who believed in my project.

Andrea Contato

Introduction

On October 12, 2008 at 07:01 UTC, the Soyuz TMA-13 space mission launched from the Russian cosmodrome in Baikonur. The crew consisted of three people: Commander Yury Lonchakov, a Russian cosmonaut on his third space mission, flight engineer Michael Fincke, a NASA astronaut from Pittsburgh, Pennsylvania, and a Texan passenger, the sixth "space tourist" in history, a wealthy video game developer.

The mission that brought Richard Garriott into space was the fulfillment of a long cultivated dream and the culmination of a career that had seen him excel in popularity and success, as a rock star in the video game industry. Being the son of a NASA astronaut, he had lived with the hope of following in his father's footsteps and going into space, becoming one of the first second-generation astronauts.

The occasion was also used to ensure a return to popularity for Tabula Rasa, the science fiction MMORPG Garriott had long worked on. Ever since the Texan developer was able to regain a place on the exclusive list of "space tourists" at a high price, his future adventure had been used as a showcase to bring his latest and most ambitious work to the public's attention.

The programmer remained in orbit for 11 days and 20 hours, during which he carried out some educational experiments proposed and designed by British schools, shot the first science fiction short-film made in space, and started his activity as an amateur radio host from the international space station ISS. With constant audiovisual connections in addition to radio chats, he clearly showed the enthusiasm he felt for his experience, which cost him no less than 30 million dollars. Back on Earth, and still in quarantine, he signed a press release dated November 11, 2008, which NCsoft immediately issued, explaining how the journey had changed him and his priorities, pushing him to seek new interests and leave the development of video games.

It was painful and unexpected news for his fans and difficult to accept, but in a certain sense understandable, at least for the most sensitive or empathetic. However, the ranks of those much less indulgent, were more numerous. Industry journalists, game enthusiasts and players openly criticized, ridiculed and ranted about the millionaire who had bought a ticket to the stars and abandoned his latest creation upon return from space. With the harsh opinions and the poor results achieved by the advertising campaign of Tabula Rasa, which had used the space adventure of its designer in an attempt to increase publicity for the game, were immediately annihilated; and everything turned against the already worn-out image of Garriott's MMORPG.

The belief that Tabula Rasa would not survive the departure of its creator for long immediately spread. It didn't take long for fears to materialize in an official statement. On November 24, 2008 NCsoft announced the closure of Tabula Rasa for the end of February and the public's amazement and disappointment with Garriott quickly turned into resentment. In the eyes of many, the decision of the Korean software house could only be the direct consequence of the abandonment of its creative director and executive producer. A MMOPRG, more than any other game, requires a considerable investment of resources by its players, not only monetary, but especially in time spent to level-up their characters. Richard's departure made the Tabula Rasa players feel abandoned and the shutdown of the MMORPG made them feel betrayed.

From a professional point of view, his dismissal from NCsoft and the closure of Tabula Rasa was a painful debacle. The worst part of the story was that Garriott's already opaque image had suffered a very hard blow from which it was difficult to recover. The video game industry is often anonymous, focused on companies, hardware platforms and brands. Nonetheless, in Richard's case, the public had a close connection to a face and name, and this relationship had become sour. For better or for worse, Richard was now about to come to terms with the disappointment of his fans. From a prodigy, a rich and lucky entrepreneur, then to an innovator in the video gaming industry, a creator of worlds and new ways of playing and understanding RPGs, and finally an astronaut, Richard Garriott's career had been marked by great victories and difficult moments. In orbit around the Earth, he had reached the personal and professional peak of his existence. Similar to the trajectory of the rocket that brought him into space, after the apex Garriott experienced the descent, but without brakes nor parachutes.

What really happened during the days he spent on board the ISS and during his short stay in the Russian quarantine institution? What drove him to turn his back on his creation and let it shut down? What other interests would he want to pursue? How was it that he had to sell his home, Britannia Manor, in order to cope with sudden economic hardship? Did he really want to leave the video game industry, to which he made such an important contribution?

The poor success of Tabula Rasa had contributed to the idea that he had lost his acumen, the magic touch that made his works special, unique, successful and memorable. After contributing to the birth of a billion dollar industry, he caused and rode at the same time the boom of computer role-playing games [CRPG]. During that process, he created a historical company whose name survived in Electronic Arts' digital distribution platform, and anticipated, with brilliant intuition, the Internet revolution; creating a new subgenre that for over a decade had dominated undisputed above all the others. Garriott seemed to have really lost interest in the development of video games.

Was this really the case, though?

The true story of Richard Garriott, how he contributed to the boom of the video game industry and changed the way we play, founded one of the most influential software houses, met some of the most skillful developers, did business and clashed with companies well known in the history of video games, begins on Independence Day in 1961.

First steps

THROUGH THE MOONGATE

D&D in the shadow of the Space Center

"We both traveled in the Geek and Nerd crowds and within a short period of time our circle of players grew."

Robert White

"I was normally a B/C student, but I competed successfully at science fairs so the school knew I was a good independent student, and even though there was no such thing as independent work projects, they let me have my own class. No teacher, no curriculum. Every semester I said, 'I'm going to make some games and I'll show them to you when I'm done,' and they said, 'Go for it.' I wrote 28 games throughout high school."

Richard Garriott, Explore/Create

Richard Garriott was born on July 4, 1961 in Cambridge, England, to Helen Mary Walker and Owen Key Garriott. The third of what would later be four children, Richard had two brothers, Robert and Randall, and a younger sister, Linda. His parents were both American citizens and when Richard was a few months old, they decided to move and settle permanently in the United States. However, his birth in the United Kingdom would later play a significant role in Richard's life.

In the early 1960s his father, Owen, was promoted from assistant professor to associate professor at the Department of Electrical Engineering at Stanford University in California. Through a bizarre series of coincidences, a handful of years later, a young student named Nolan Bushnell, future co-founder of Atari and designer of Pong, had in the Stanford AI lab a fateful and dazzling encounter with Spacewar!, one of the very first video games.

In 1965, Garriott was selected by NASA from a very small group of six scientists to become an astronaut. Owen's work forced the whole family to move to Nassau Bay, Texas near the Johnson Space Center, the mission control center of all manned expeditions. 1973 was the year of the Skylab mission, which, for a short time, made Richard's father the astronaut with the record of longest time spent in space, about 60 days. Upon his return to the Earth, the astronaut was interviewed publicly with his family as per the political conventions of the time due to the Cold War and Space Race. Richard was twelve, when he was immortalized on film playing with a miniature replica of the Skylab 3, the small metal shell that had kept his father alive in space for two months.

The boy grew up in close contact with Science and Technology. The world around him began to change at an ever-increasing pace, while the computer revolution taking place in research institutes made its way into universities and then into higher education. In 1964, a couple of teachers at Dartmouth college in New England, John George Kemeny and Thomas Eugene Kurtz, found that technology and teaching had made giant strides, and for the first time it was possible to offer their students programming courses. They also decided that the programming languages available were too difficult for young people as a first experience.

For this reason, inspired by Fortran and ALGOL, Kemeny and Kurtz laid the foundations for a new programming language. They had just finished installing a new time-sharing system based on a General Electric mainframe (the Dartmouth Time-Sharing System) and called their language BASIC (Beginner's All purpose Symbolic Instruction Code). Students designed their own programs, writing lines of BASIC code into their notebooks, then storing them on hand-punched tapes. By operating teletypewriters wired to the main computer, in some cases from remote sites using modems — they would run their own programs on the mainframe and see the output printed on paper.

To spread their language as widely as possible, Kemeny and Kurtz decided not to sell it and distributed the compiler to numerous schools in New Hampshire, working to promote it and add new functions over the years. Thanks to this approach, by the mid-1970s BASIC had spread throughout the United States, including to Clear Creek High School, Richard's school, where in 1975, he began to attend some programming courses for BASIC.

Garriott, at least initially, was not very interested in computer science. Unlike the majority of his peers, given the daily contact with new technologies as well as scholars, researchers, scientists and even astronauts, he gave little importance to computers. To Richard, they were simply part of the environment in which he lived and were nothing special. What really interested him were the works of J.R.R. Tolkien, in particular The Lord of the Rings, of which he was an avid fan.

In the summer of 1977, parents Owen and Helen decided to send Richard to a summer camp at the University of Oklahoma. At the end of the season, their son would begin his final year of high school and his parents, especially his father, had high expectations of him. The main purpose of the summer course was for Richard to learn programming skills in Fortran. As useful as that may have been, the courses were less influential on Richard's future than other experiences he had in Oklahoma. In fact, in the few weeks he spent at the campus, two events occurred that would mark his life forever. Contained and shy, for the first time Richard found himself having to deal with his own difficulties in settling into a new environment, in contact with strangers. Luckily, some of his peers broke the ice: when a small group of boys gathered around him, Richard greeted them with a formal "Hello" that caught everyone by surprise.

"No one from around here says 'hello' ", they challenged. The discussion that followed helped the boys get to know each other better. When Richard explained that he was born in England, the boys connected this curious circumstance with the greeting. It didn't matter that Richard had only spent a couple of months in the UK and had a Texan accent: as a joke, they called him "Lord British" and the young man liked the nickname so much that he kept it forever.

The nickname alone would have changed nothing if Richard hadn't had an unexpected encounter with destiny. After entering one of the campus recreation rooms, the young man saw his peers talking about monsters, swords and spells. When he asked what they were doing, the explanation dazzled him: it was a game that allowed anyone to relive the adventures that he had enjoyed so much while reading the works of Tolkien.

It was Dungeons & Dragons,[1] the role-playing game created by Gary Gygax and Dave Arneson.

After timidly witnessing his first adventure, Richard became a regular player, devoting a large part of his free time to D&D. His enthusiasm and passion for the game helped him break down the barriers and shyness that had initially blocked him.

"It was a summer of programming and girls. It was one of those pivotal momen-

---

1   Designed by two fans of war games and published for the first time in 1974, Dungeons & Dragons (D&D) was one of the first role-playing games in history, most likely the first marketed. Over the decades, D&D's popularity only increased, reaching 20 million players in 2004 for a total turnover of over a billion dollars in books and various merchandise, while its mechanics have been a reference point for all subsequent generations of role-playing games. Its influence crossed the limits of its genre, pushing itself into video games, literature, films, music and, in general, into popular culture.

ts. A lot of firsts happened there", he recounted years later.[2] At the end of summer 1977, Richard had changed in a sense. A new world had opened up before his eyes after the abrupt change of environment, and the first thing he did was to try to bring some of the experience he had gained in Oklahoma to Texas.

The first to get involved in D&D was Robert White, a longtime friend of Richard. Both had parents involved in science and technology as White's father was a flight technician while Richard's was an astronaut. Moreover, both men were colleagues at NASA in Houston, and had known each other for a long time. Robert, a year older, had met Richard for the first time in 1971 at a Webelos event, an intermediate class between the Cub Scouts and the Boy Scouts. White: "Richard and I were participating in the High School science fair, both of us had been participating every year since we were in kindergarten, both with a big passion for science, when during one of the down times he showed me these three little game pamphlets he had picked up. These were the three original D&D books [...] I didn't have much time to view them, but the next day he and I and a couple of other friends tried a little game with Richard as the first DM."

In addition to the two friends, the group that was formed included Elizabeth Froebel, Chuck Bueche, Rene Hans and Keith Zabalaoui, a young boy who lived in the house next to the Garriott family. None of Richard's friends knew about D&D, but the promise of a lot of fun was enough to drag the geeky teenagers to the table, where Garriott staged his first adventure as Dungeon Master (the storyteller of a role-playing game).

The D&D session was so satisfying, that the group asked to meet more often. Word spread quickly at school and more and more kids asked to join, to the point that Garriott's house was literally invaded by aspiring young players. White: "Things kind of snowballed from there. We soon had games every Friday night over at Richard's house with about 8–10 people. His mother made cake every game session and both parents laughed and encouraged our creativity in this story-telling game. It became apparent quickly that our games were too big to manage so we ended up splitting them into two. I became the other chief DM and Richard continued his game."

Richard's mother, Helen, in addition to constantly baking cakes, had to leave the studio where she worked as an artist at their disposal. She transferred her equipment to the garage outside the house, a move that she would have to repeat but backwards a few years later, to leave her son the garage space to complete one of his greatest exploits.

By his own admission, Richard was initially not one of the best DMs. His adventures resulted in brief introductions to the game's background story in preparation for his favorite activity: the fights, challenging the players with increasingly

---

2   King, Brad; Borland, John (2014) Dungeons and Dreamers: The Rise of Computer Game Culture from Geek to Chic

dangerous and fearsome opponents. Robert was rather skillful at creating dark adventures and demonic environments where players would face his diabolical machinations. According to White, the style of the two DMs was closely linked to each other's literary tastes: "Richard was more into much lighter fantasy reading (outside of LOTR) than I was. I was reading lots of Burroughs (Tarzan, Mars), Howard (Conan), Lovecraft, and the new fantasy kid Stephen R. Donaldson (Chronicles of Thomas Covenant) at the time. My games became more complicated, interconnected, and darker. The two game system became a success and we would often play in each others realms when the crowd was light, but that became less and less as more people began to play."

The group grew to about thirty participants, a real invasion of the Garriott house, which forced the boys to find other venues for their games and ease pressure off of Richard's family. Observing the other Dungeon Masters at work, over time, the young Garriott was able to improve the quality of his stories and create more interesting twists. One of them written by him around the age of 17, described the ascent and fall of the fearsome magician Mondain in the lands of Sosaria.

Role-playing had become a very important part of Richard's daily life as he went to school and in his spare time between classes. He enjoyed reliving and talking about previous adventures with his fellow players, and trusty black notebook under his belt, the young student took notes and drew maps endlessly; to the point that Richard decided to combine the useful with the enjoyable.

As mentioned, Clear Creek High School had a BASIC course. Through terminals, students could connect to a DEC (Digital Equipment Corporation) PDP-11 minicomputer and thanks to a time-sharing system, use its resources. In a world where even the most important companies bought machine time from giants like General Electric, rather than equipping themselves with heavy, bulky and expensive mainframes, the teletypewriters Richard had access to were state of the art. The quick rise of the microcomputer [3] had already begun and would soon set foot in the homes of millions of families and schools.

Curiously, just a handful of years earlier, a young man named William Henry Gates III had also learned BASIC using a Teletype Model 33. Nicknamed "Bill", he had already gained recognition as a child for his innate ability to crash the systems he put his hands on[4] and would soon show that he could commercially exploit the language that its creators, professors Kemeny and Kurtz, had decided to freely distribute.

Despite Richard's lack of interest in computer science, thanks to the summer

---

3   Microcomputer was the then-term used to describe computers made with microprocessors, which were smaller and cheaper than mainframes or minicomputer but also less capable. It was soon replaced with the term Personal Computer.

4   KWallace, James; Erickson, Jim (2005) Hard Drive - Bill Gates and the Making of the Microsoft Empire

camp at the University of Oklahoma, his programming skills were now more advanced than those needed to follow the lessons organized at school, to the point that even teachers had little to offer him. For this reason, Richard came up with a bold idea that would allow him to work independently on computers and combine his passion for role-playing with school demands. The boy asked to the principal for permission to customize his curriculum towards computer science: he would try to program a computer game for the end of each semester and this would be worth an A. Recognizing his enthusiasm, the principal accepted. Bending the rules a bit, the computer course was recorded as a course in foreign languages, in which Richard would participate alone. Soon, Richard found himself writing notes on his first program[5], DND1,[6] while waiting patiently for his turn on the computer.

It is difficult nowadays to imagine how the prototypes written by the young Garriott would work. The teletypewriters he had access to were without monitors: they were typewriters operated remotely from the mainframe to which they were connected and the output of the program was printed on continuous paper. Lacking graphic capabilities of any kind, the teletypewriters were limited to printing a small set of individual characters and capital letters only, even more restricted than their typewriter ancestors.

Young Richard and Robert had already contact with the very first video games. White: "We held meetings at the TRW building across from NASA and they gave us access to the mainframes and taught us how to program. We actually got pretty good, focusing mostly on Fortran and some basic programming. We even tried our hand at wireframe graphics. We would often dial into the University of Houston computers and play an ASCII Star Trek game."

Programmed by Mike Mayfield, Star Trek was inspired by the epic television series featuring crew members from the Enterprise spaceship. The idea behind the game was the result of a collaboration between Mayfield and some of his schoolmates, but it was Mike who wrote the program in the summer of 1971 by him-

---

5   The source code of the first prototype — made available in a contest for the launch of Shroud of the Avatar — reveals a curious feature: at the beginning the player was given the option to read the instructions but a confirmation would immediately end the game with a curt reply "WHO SAID YOU COULD PLAY". The same result was achieved when choosing 'SHAV' as character name. Richard Garriott: "SHAVS was a name my high school girlfriend would call me. She told me she would tell me what it meant when I turned 40 or got married. I was (and am) pissed off at her to find out it had no meaning. Yes, was because no one but ME played it, so if you needed instructions… there weren't any!"

6   The series of games programmed by Garriott at school is often called D&D, with individual versions named D&D 1, D&D 2, etc. Although used by Garriott in Explore/Create, this notation is incorrect since the names of these prototypes were DND1, DND2 etc., as teletypes were unable to represent ampersands (&).

self. By irregularly connecting to the University of California mainframes, Mayfield had scheduled everything in a few weeks.

Mike Mayfield: "Back in 1971 I was a senior in high school. My school didn't have any computers, but I had managed to 'use' (read 'steal') an account on a Sigma 7 at University of California, Irvine. I was trying to teach myself BASIC from a book. At the time there was a program that ran on a vector graphics terminal on the Sigma 7 that was a simple 'shoot-em-up' space war game. I wanted to make a game like that, but I only had access to an ASR-33 Teletype non-video terminal (hey, there is only some[sic] much I could 'use' in high school)." [7]

Mayfield was also inspired by Spacewar!, the same game that influenced Bushnell and prompted him to enter the arcade market. However, Mayfield's approach was different because his Star Trek was a turn-based game in which the player had to manage their resources (Photon Torpedoes and energy) and defeat a number of enemy vessels in a randomly generated map.

His experiment would have been unknown if Mike hadn't bought a small but innovative portable computer, the HP-35, and hadn't gone to Hewlett-Packard's local offices to ask for some tips on how to use his new hardware. On one of these visits, office staff offered Mayfield to implement a version of his Star Trek game on their HP 2000C minicomputer. The latter was also a BASIC-based time-sharing system and Mayfield's work was included in a library of software publicly distributed by HP under the name of STTR1 and later published in the book 101 BASIC Computer Games.

As was common in the early days of video game history, the Mayfield program passed from hand to hand, and ended up attracting the attention of passionate programmers.[8] They delighted in translating it and bringing it to other systems, adding features, modifying the gameplay and in general, trying to improve it according to their tastes. The first step was taken thanks to David H. Ahl and Mary Cole, who rewrote it for DEC systems and then distributed it in newsletters. It became very popular and a version of Star Trek by Mayfield arrived to the computer systems of Houston University, where Richard and Robert White had the chance to try it out in late 1977.

The Star Trek game used only text for graphics and the user interface. The space map, on which the battles took place between the player-guided spaceship (E) and the enemy Klingons (K), was a grid of ten rows by ten columns. The player interacted with the program by using single character commands, such as W for Warp Engine, or T to launch a deadly Photon Torpedo towards the enemies.

---

7   Mayfield, Mike (2000) https://gamesoffame.wordpress.com/star-trek/

8   Steve "Slug" Russell's Spacewar! had a similar fate, shared between enthusiastic players and aspiring programmers, it spread throughout most of the American research institutes until it became a source of inspiration for the Nolan Bushnell's first video game

```
------------ Star Trek (sample output) ------------
STAR TREK


DO YOU WANT INSTRUCTIONS (THEY'RE LONG!)? N


YOU MUST DESTROY 8 KLINGONS IN 28 STARDATES WITH  3
STARBASES

ENTERPRISE IN QUADRANT - (2 1) SECTOR (4 4)


. . . . . . . . . .
. . . . * . . . . *
. . . . . . . . . .
. . . E . . K . . .
. . . . . . . * . .
. . . . . . . . . .
. . . . . . . . . .
. . . . . K . . . .
. . . * . . . . . .
. . . . . . . . . .


COMMAND? T

TORPEDO COURSE (1-9)? 1

TRACK: 4 - 5  4 - 6  4 - 7

KLINGON DESTROYED!

-------------------------------------------------------
```

Richard decided to follow the same concept and represent the monsters or objects of his role-playing game with simple letters: the goblins, for example, were represented by a G, while an A indicated giant ants.[9] The result was similar to that of other programmers, such as Rogue's,[10] and others that will be discussed later, based on a top-down view and the use of ASCII characters to draw maps and dungeons.

The player typed in commands which the terminal transmitted to the mainframe and once the program was executed it created the output on paper, reprinting the updated map. The game system was therefore turn-based and each turn was marked by the execution of a single action that took often more than ten seconds to be computed and for the result to be printed by the teletypewriter.

Garriott: "You had to wait 10-30 seconds for each new 'frame'... very low 'frame-rate'. 'Hulking' is the right word... by today's standards, unbelievably slow. Coupled with that 300 baud accoustic modem!" [11]

For the first time, the student was facing the difficulty of creating a game in BASIC, while computer technology suddenly accelerated. Charles Ingerham Peddle was a brilliant U.S. engineer who had made his mark at General Electric in the golden years of selling time-sharing services. Noting that the market was changing and the services that had made GE's fortune were less in demand year after year, Peddle left the company to join Motorola, where he was part of Thomas H. Bennett's team that developed the MC6800, the first chip in the 6800 family, which was used in numerous products such as POS systems, CRTs, some arcade and pinball machines, as well as in some computer kits and microcomputers.

In the mid-1970s, microprocessors were very expensive, limiting their use. Peddle was convinced that a low-cost chip could revolutionize the market, but his intuition was not shared by Motorola's management. He decided to leave Motorola and joined MOS Technology,[12] along with many other members of the MC6800 team. Here, the team led by Peddle managed to create a new chip, the MOS 6502, which not only could be sold profitably for $25 (compared to $170 for the MC6800 and over $200 for the Intel 8080), but could compete on equal terms with the competition's chips and, in some cases, boast even better performance.

MOS' secret for providing low cost products lay in its production process which allowed for a much lower rate of defective chips than the competition. This made

---

9   Early versions of DND had a similar user interface to Star Trek and other BASIC games of the time: commands were executed by typing in a character, number or simple words (pressing enter only or typing an invalid command displayed a list of possible actions with their associated codes)

10   The progenitor of the Roguelike genre, characterized by random maps, permanent death of the playing characters and turn-based movements

11   Garriott, Richard (2011) interview with Robert Kosarko "Bladed Edge", http://www.hardcoregaming101.net

12   MOS is the acronym for Metal Oxide Semiconductor, referencing MOSFETs, a type of transistors

it an important driver of the microcomputer revolution. The entry of the MOS 6502 forced other semiconductor manufacturers to drastically reduce the prices of their products, fueling the birth of a new industry. With prices in free fall, it suddenly became possible for average consumers to afford products with micro-processors; creating a new market for all those who were interested in owning a computer themselves. Prior to the introduction of microcomputers, early adopters would build simple computers from assembly kits designed and sold by creative and capable innovators. Among this rare breed, was one especially talented engi-neer, Steve Wozniak, who was designing his own computer around the Motorola 6800. Unlike many other computer enthusiasts who believed the Intel 8008 would win, he preferred the competitor; and thanks to its low price, could afford buying a sample of the MOS 6502 from Peddle himself, and adapted his microcomputer design from the 6800 to the very similar 6502. When he showed the result to his friend Steve Jobs, the latter was enthusiastic and suggested starting a business to sell assembly kits akin to many other companies such as MOS, MITS and IMSAI.

The leap from these first experiments to commercial prototypes was very short. Peddle himself realized the possibility, but MOS management was reluctant to ven-ture into the niche market of microcomputers and Motorola soon moved to crush the competition on their 6800 market, bringing MOS to court and forcing it into an extra-judicial agreement. The purchase of MOS by calculator company Commo-dore, founded and led by Jack Tramiel, a Polish naturalized American entrepreneur, gave the engineer Peddle a chance to take a big step. Although, in truth, Tramiel had bought MOS only to cheapen the production of calculators and thus be able to compete on equal terms with Texas Instruments. When Peddle tried to explain to the CEO of Commodore that the calculators market was in a declining phase and that microcomputers could be a new market in which to reposition themselves (with the enormous advantage of having the lowest cost chip on the market), the entrepreneur was impressed and agreed on the production of a microcomputer.

To beat the competition to the market with a finished product, Peddle proposed buying an already available system to Tramiel. Recalling his experience helping Wozniak and Jobs during their development of the Apple II, Peddle advised Tra-miel to contact them and see if it was possible to buy their prototype, as well as improve and produce it en masse. The negotiations started, but Jobs was very ambi-tious and couldn't agree with Tramiel on the terms: Apple could have been bought by Commodore, but things didn't go that direction.

Therefore, Peddle had to do without the Wozniak prototype and created the Commodore PET, a powerful and relatively inexpensive microcomputer, equipped with a magnetic tape reader and keyboard very similar to those of the calculators that Tramiel insisted on producing, but which were having ever greater problems because of competition with Texas Instruments. Realizing that a microcomputer sold without an adequate operating system would not have many possibilities, at the last minute Peddle decided to include in the ROM of the PET a version of BA-SIC written by a small software house called Micro-Soft. The product of Paul Allen and Bill Gates was already known and appreciated in the computer world, even by users who had not purchased the expensive software license. [13]

Meanwhile, the adventure of Jobs and Wozniak had not reached its conclusion. The two succeeded to get some funds from venture capitalists, including Don Valentine and Mike Markkula, and managed to launch their Apple II. This microcomputer was also based on the MOS 6502 and had characteristics very similar to the PET, both in terms of available memory and support for a magnetic tape drive.

Both founders of Apple had a relationship with Nolan Bushnell of Atari. Jobs had worked there as a repairman, while Wozniak had designed the hardware layout for Atari's game Breakout (1976). When Wozniak went to work on the Apple II, he foremost aimed at making a platform that had the tools needed to create games. Wozniak wrote a dialect, Integer BASIC, with graphics capabilities and color functionality (16 in low resolution mode, 6 in high), but lacked the capabilities to perform floating point calculations.

At the same time, Radio Shack also wanted to offer a similar product and contacted Commodore. Once again, Tramiel was unwavering in his demands and the deal fell through, forcing RS to do it on their own. Tandy Corporation technicians led by Steve Leininger, quickly developed the TRS-80, a microcomputer based on the Zilog Z-80, another low-cost chip designed by a member of the Intel 8008 development team, Federico Faggin. This chip would be used extensively in video games, such as arcade favorites like Pac-Man, Galaxian and Galaga, and on consoles such as the Sega Master System and GameBoy.

In 1977, therefore, three different microcomputers were marketed: the Apple II by the Steves, the TRS-80 by Tandy Corporation (sold by Radio Shack), and Chuck Peddle's Commodore PET (The first step into the IT market of the company founded by Jack Tramiel). All three computers had BASIC as a common feature, as the TRS-80 also had its own dialect based on Tiny BASIC, which was written specifically for machines with little RAM. Commodore's choice of BASIC proved to be a wise decision and within a year of releasing the PET, Apple II and TRS-80,[14] all were shipped with a version of BASIC written by Micro-Soft. Wozniak, to his disappointment, had to give up on his own version of BASIC in favor of the one written by Paul Allen and Bill Gates, with the help of Monte Davidoff. The latter wrote the floating-point math component of MS BASIC, which made it superior to all other versions.

---

13   Gates, Bill (1976) Open Letter to Hobbyists because of the rampant piracy of BA-SIC on the Altair 8800

14   at the time, these machines were referred to as the Trinity computers and 1977 branded as "The Year of the Trinity"

Like his fellow students at Dartmouth, Richard had to organize his thoughts by writing down code in his notebook before later transferring it to the minicomputer during his hours of access to the teletype. Once he had typed the whole program, he could run it, study its behavior and make changes, although he was limited by the slowness of the machine's connection (each action could take minutes before the user could continue with the next step) and printable characters. During the long waits, Richard imagined the possibility of having a computer all to himself, so that he could proceed more quickly and not be bound by school schedules.

Among the Trinity machines, the Apple II was the most interesting to make games on. It was equipped with graphic capabilities that neither the PET nor the TRS-80 had, and a much more comfortable keyboard than Commodore's, which was recycled from their calculators. Steve Wozniak, one of the first developers of video games, designed the Apple II to run them, while PET and TRS-80 microcomputers were more appreciated by businesses and schools. For Garriott, an Apple II was the ideal choice, but its most basic model cost $1,298,[15] which in today's dollars, is the equivalent of $4,200. Meanwhile, his father Owen did not have a favorable opinion on video games but was relieved to see his son finally interested in computer science and programming.

With the summer of 1979 approaching along with the end of the school year, Richard began anxiously considering his own situation: the end of his studies implied the loss of access to the school's computer and therefore the suspension of his experiments, which had by now exceeded 20 revisions beyond its initial prototype. Only the purchase of a microcomputer could allow him to continue working throughout the summer break, but this would not be possible without the permission of his parents. As he had done at the beginning of the school year when entering the principal's office, Richard took courage and approached his father to propose a pact: he would continue to obtain good grades at school while completing his game and making it free of bugs. In return, his parents would buy him a microcomputer.

Owen accepted and his son did not disappoint. His grades remained high and allowed him to enroll at the University of Texas, following in his father's footsteps and becoming a freshman in the Electrotechnics program. Even more important to Richard was that his game had reached its 28th and final version; having withstood testing without any signs of bugs or malfunctions.

Richard had kept his word and now it was his father's turn: young Garriott got his first microcomputer.

A new Apple II Plus, of course.

---

15   Recommended retail price for the starter system with 16K and a cassette player in June 1979

Whiz kids

"On one eventful evening [..] at one of the large game sessions, Richard showed up with his first computer and a little program he was working on (we were at another friend's house that eve). It was a bit of what would eventually become Akalabeth."

Robert White

"I had seen an early low-resolution graphics game called Escape[!]. It was a simple maze game, but it inspired me to figure out how 3-D graphics worked. I spent that summer working on high-resolution 3-D graphics and adapting them to yet another version of my little role-playing game — and wrote what was never intended to be published, Akalabeth."

Richard Garriott, The Official book of Ultima by Shay Addams.

In June 1979, Jobs and Wozniak's company launched the first revision of its workhorse to the market: the Apple II Plus. While fully compatible with the previous one, the basic version of the Apple II Plus was sold with 48K compared to the mere 4K of the previous models, thanks to a sharp drop in the cost of RAM. Apple had a problem with the FCC[16] for the electromagnetic emissions of the basic model and

---

16   Federal Communications Commission, an independent federal agency responsible for managing and regulating radio, television and cable communications in the United States.

would even have been forced to withdraw from the market the paddles bundled with the Apple II within a few months. The Plus version was designed with a special plastic case inside which contained a brass mesh to shield the equipment and keep electromagnetic emissions low. The real novelty of the Plus was the inclusion of Applesoft, the BASIC dialect created by Microsoft for Apple (hence the compound name) directly in the ROM. Already available in 1977 as a paid expansion, Applesoft was more powerful and equipped with the mathematical capabilities that Wozniak's Integer BASIC lacked. This made it easier to create financial and scientific applications. More powerful and with more functionality, but at the same time considerably slower than Integer BASIC, Applesoft ended up definitively replacing the Wozniak dialect, after the launch of the Apple II Plus.

Like its big brother, Apple II Plus could not display lowercase characters and therefore did not have a key to switch from upper to lowercase but was equipped with a REPEAT key used to make up for the inability of the keyboard to repeat the same character several times when the key remained pressed. Users who needed lowercase characters had to resort to special expansions or switch to the much slower high-resolution mode. This lack was advantageous to their most direct competitor, Commodore's PET, especially in school and office environments, resulting in a curious consequence: Richard and other programmers had to write the texts of their first programs using capital letters only.

Having a microcomputer all for himself was a turning point for the boy. The system allowed him to view and modify code in real-time, save it on tape instead of punch cards, as well as run the program and immediately notice its output without the waiting time due to time-sharing and slow printing on paper. The Apple II also had remarkable graphics capabilities, including being able to show colors (something Garriott did not take advantage of).

Apple II also had remarkable graphics capabilities, for the period, and was the only Trinity one not to be monochrome .

Richard's latest prototype DND28, developed in Clear Creek High School's labs, was designed for the available output at the time, teletype printing. Richard's first venture was to simply port DND28 from the minicomputer to his Apple II. It was an essential operation which did not exploit in any way the true potential of the microcomputer, apart from displaying on the monitor what was previously printed on paper, and saving his code on a floppy disk instead of undergoing the painstaking process of writing it on paper and punching it into paper rolls.

Owning an Apple II Plus not only freed him from depending on the school's computer systems, providing him with a much more powerful and personal tool, but also gave him the chance to experience some of the games that began to spread quickly among students with the exchange of floppies. One of the most significant games for the young programmer was undoubtedly Escape![17] by Silas S. Warner, a little-known American programmer, whose games were published by the small, but very popular, North American software house: M.U.S.E. Software.

Silas Sayers Warner is one of the most interesting and least known characters in the history of video games. A skilled programmer who discovered his innate talent for computer science accidentally and found employment as a computer technician at the University of Indiana in the early 70s. In this position, Warner contributed to the creation of a network of terminals for the PLATO (Programmed Logic for Automatic Teaching Operations) system, a didactic software that allowed students to create multi-user "lessons" using the TUTOR programming language.

Based on a platform from Control Data Corporation, one of the most important companies in the mainframe market and in the business of selling time-sharing services, the PLATO system underwent a rapid development. With the release of the fourth version, powerful graphics capabilities were implemented, a prerequisite for people to consider when using the new technology to create a game. Another of the first student developers was John Daleske from the University of Iowa, who in order to have the necessary resources (called "Lesson space", a name that clearly indicated the didactic designation of the PLATO system), asked Silas Warner for help.

The resulting game was Empire (1973), the first multi-player arena shooter in the history of video games and the source of a massive drop in student performance and of the PLATO system, overloaded with countless game sessions. Silas liked Empire so much that he asked and obtained permission from Daleske to create a derivative game, more tactical and reflective, which he called Conquest. But this was only the beginning of his career as a game creator.

With the release of the Trinity computers, Ed Zaron, an acquaintance of Warner, decided to buy an Apple II and trusted his friend. On the evening of the same day as the purchase, Silas paid Ed a surprise visit, sat down in front of the microcomputer, and started programming. By one O'clock in the morning, his first Apple II game was ready. The name was Apple Tree and the aim of the game was to collect apples that fell from a tree. It was little more than an experiment, but the experience was so striking for Silas that, the next day he enthusiastically went to buy an Apple II too, which had the serial number 234.

Ed Zaron took his friend's passion for computer science very seriously and decided to found a software house to sell programs for the Apple II; he called it M.U.S.E. Software and started personally developing a fighting video game called Tank War. Given Silas' skill, Ed convinced him to write games that the small company would sell and they started doing serious business, with Jim Black, a newcomer.

Silas had a natural talent for programming and one of his first experiments was Maze, a game with rudimentary 3D graphics. The target was to get out of a pro-

---

17   Garriott, Richard, Space Gamer number 39, May 1981

cedurally generated maze, with the ability to use a map, a compass or leaving fo-
otprints (all options were disabled at the start of the game). Advanced and innovative, Maze was just a technical test for a much more ambitious project.

Immediately after Maze's publication, Silas developed Escape!, another much
more complex and interesting game, in which the maze was randomly generated
at the beginning and inhabited by guards who obstructed the passage, asking the
player for a pass, and other non-player characters who could give information (correct or wrong) or give the player a pass, a compass or the map with a pinch of luck.

As with Empire, Escape! was responsible for a drastic drop in productivity in any
laboratory where a copy of it arrived. Even at Steve Jobs' company headquarters,
Escape! did not take any prisoners: when David Gordon (an Apple employee at
that time) introduced it to his colleagues, the mania spread and soon a large number of staff found themselves engaged in solving puzzles and crafting maps of the
labyrinth, rather than do work. Apple lost about 60 weeks of productivity due to
the jewel of M.U.S.E. Software.[18]

Silas Warner's programming career did not end with Escape!, but continued
with RobotWar (1981), a fighting game in which the player used a programming
language and had 256 lines of code to program a robot and observe it fighting in
an arena with three other automatons. Next were Castle Wolfenstein (1981) and
Beyond Castle Wolfenstein (1984),[19] two of the first stealth games in history, as
well as the innovative program The Voice (1983), one of the first pieces of software capable of capturing the human voice and reproducing it with the rudimentary audio system of the Apple II. We will hear more about these very skilled
programmers and their creations later.

Richard, like many other players before him, found himself trapped in the nar-
row corridors of the labyrinths of Escape!, forced to solve puzzles, craft maps and
draw logical schemes to understand if passers-by had lied or told the truth. This
experience profoundly changed his instinctive way of creating games. Until then, influenced only by his experience with Mayfield's Star Trek and the long role-playing
sessions in which, sitting at the table with his friends, he had used pen and paper to
draw the world from above and his imagination to visualize it in his mind. Escape!
had shown him a different way to play and visualize the world using a computer.

The latest version of his DND used ASCII characters to represent monsters and
objects from above. After experimenting with Escape!, Richard decided to comple-

18   Gorgon, David (1984) Creative Computing Magazine (November 1984)
Volume 10 Number 11

19   The brand was reused in the early 90s by ID, whose developers were fans of the
two games from Silas Warner. They contacted him to ask for a license to use the name,
but discovered M.U.S.E.'s failure and that the trademark on Wolfenstein had expired, thus
allowing for registering and using it for their famous FPS Wolfenstein 3D.

tely review the graphical representation of his game. The ability to draw objects and monsters in a first-person view rather than representing them with symbols such as asterisks, brackets and percentages, made possible by Apple II's innovative hardware, was an opportunity he had to exploit.

In order to draw corridors, forks and objects in perspective, Richard had to master instruments he had not used up until then. The first person to help him was his mother Helen who taught him the techniques of representation and perspective. Without proper help in math, however, Richard couldn't have created the routines needed for his Apple II to draw a maze like Warner had done in Escape!. Once again his Father Owen came to his rescue and helped laying down the necessary trigonometric foundation. Drawing the contours of the objects according to the wireframe model, which Richard and Robert had already started experimenting with in 1977, he transformed his prototype once again and divided the game into two parts. When the player was moving on the surface of the world, it was represented the usual way with the map seen from above, but when the action moved into the dungeons, the rudimentary graphics drawn with a few lines would reconstruct the basements with long corridors, doors and monsters, in a first-person view.

Since this was the only novelty from the previous version, Richard decided to call the latest version DND28B, a simple evolution of the previous prototype.

During the summer break of 1979, Richard started looking for a job and found one at John Prosper Mayer's shop. The latter had been a scientist at NACA,[20] later NASA, and had participated in the Bell XI flight (the plane with which Colonel Chuck Yeager had broken the sound barrier), as well as in several projects on the Mercury, Gemini and Apollo programs. In the mid-70s, however, NASA began a policy of cost reduction and encouraged senior staff to take early retirement.

Understanding the scope of the ongoing revolution, Mayer decided to accept the challenge and try his luck selling computers in Houston, where he expected the concentration of technology and science generated by the Space Center would help to create local demand. Mayer opened a shop in the ComputerLand franchise chain with the help of two colleagues, Stan Mann and Kenneth Wetcher, and his wife Geraldine Couch, whom he met at NACA, where she worked as a "human computer" performing complex calculations with the sole aid of a Friden electromechanical calculator. To assist him, he chose a young and talented programmer he had met at a social event hosted by the Houston Amateur Microcomputer Club; one of the first clubs for computer enthusiasts. The boy's name was Kenneth Wayne Arnold.

A music and computer enthusiast, Arnold was twenty years old (a few years older than Richard) and made his own experiences not on microcomputers, like Garriott, but on a much simpler product built around one of the early microprocessors: a single board computer, sold commonly to engineers as an affordable way

---

20   National Advisory Committee for Aeronautics, federal body, precursor of NASA, established in 1915.

to learn a specific machine language. Those with the affordable MOS 6502 sold surprisingly well to hobbyists too, who added a power supply, a terminal and a cassette tape drive to get a full computer on the cheap. The first hardware Kenneth occupied himself with was the Familiarizor produced by an Oklahoma company called EBKA, a single board computer based on the MOS 6502, like many computer kits of the time. Kenneth Arnold: "For input, the Familiarizor had a 20-key keypad, which included four control keys and 16 hexadecimal keys. For output, it had two display devices… each of which could display a single hexadecimal digit. It had a mere 1 kbyte of main memory, and no storage memory. You keyed in your programs by hand in hexadecimal, and when the power was turned off, the program was forgotten. The machine was far too small for a high-level language. It was even too small for an Assembly language."

Having such a modest machine at his disposal, Kenneth had to learn to program the 6502 in hexadecimal. This fact, as we will see, would be of fundamental importance.

During his first year at Houston University in 1977, Arnold learned about the Houston Amateur Microcomputer Club. Hosting it was Joe Ellis, a technology enthusiast and locally known jazz musician. At the behest of Joe, Arnold was invited to show the club his first musical experiments and the young man involved two of his friends, James VanArstsdalen and Gary Morrison. The former was an owner of a Commodore PET, while the latter had an Electrocomp, one of the first commercial synthesizers. The demonstration was called "The Singing Computer", and even attracted the attention of the Houston Post, as well as that of Mayer, who invited Arnold to work at his store.

Arnold: "One day I arrived at work and began my day as normal, assembling computers and so on. At some point I needed to take some empty boxes to the trash bin behind the store. When I got behind the store, I found a young man breaking down boxes. No one had told me we had a new employee, but I introduced myself. It was Richard Garriott."

The two soon became friends and Arnold was invited to D&D sessions at Garriott's home, where he met many of Richard's cohorts. On such an occasion, Garriott showed Arnold a program he had written to keep track of the progress of his D&D adventures: the Dungeon Master's Assistant. The two talked at length about computers and programming. Richard enjoyed programming with his Apple II in BASIC. Arnold, on the contrary, had meanwhile saved enough to buy an Apple II and tried BASIC, however he remained tied to the machine code of the MOS 6502: it was much more powerful and faster than any interpreted language such as the one from Kemeny and Kurtz.

As John Mayer learned about DND28B, he wanted to try it, and was so impressed that he suggested his employee put it up for sale. His reasoning was based on the pragmatic logic of a trader: the products he sold, mainly Apple II and Commodore PET, were expensive and totally useless in the hands of a beginner. The software industry was still in its infancy and buyers of microcomputers very often had to write the software for themselves. A good game could act as a catalyst for the sales of microcomputers and convince even those who did not want to become programmers or create their own software to buy an Apple II.

Arnold: "One day John P. Mayer saw Richard's game. He told Richard he wanted 200 copies to send to ComputerLand stores nation wide. So we went in to overtime production mode copying cassette tapes, printing manuals, and stuffing it all into plastic bags."

Not being able to sell his game under the name DND28B, Richard had to invent something and he fell back onto his great passion for the works of Tolkien. With an obviously Tolkienian inspiration, Garriott decided to call his first game Akalabeth: World of Doom. Armed with many good intentions and a pinch of naivety, Richard put friends and family to work. Keith Zabalaoui, a Houston neighbor who had been taking part in the D&D sessions, designed the title screen (which earned him accreditation for the game's graphics), Richard's mother the cover, while the programmer personally copied the instructions and took care of the packaging with Ziploc plastic bags.

Each package was numbered with a small green label on the top right corner, so Richard could keep count of sales. In the following weeks, between eight and twelve packages were purchased for $19.95, while the others remained on the shelf.[21] Garriott had barely been able to make up his costs and was preparing to leave his job at the store and move to Austin to attend university again. However, one copy came to the attention of a small publishing house called California Pacific Computer Company (CPCC). According to some accounts, it was the owner of the ComputerLand store who shipped one of the Ziploc bags to CPCC: During a telephone call with CPCC for a software reorder, Mayer mentioned the game he was selling on his shelves. Getting the attention of the other party, he committed himself to sending them a copy of it as soon as possible.[22] According to other versions, the software went from hand to hand in the form of unauthorized copies until it reached California. In any case, when the game arrived in the hands of Al Remmers, the owner of CPCC, he called Richard to try to convince him that the game could sell very well with proper distribution.

---

21   Brad King in Dungeons and Dreamers: The Rise of Computer Game Culture from Geek to Chic maintains that the number of copies sold was 15, but in 1992, in an interview at the University of Austin, Richard himself said he had only sold 8 copies. Later, in 2013, Richard offered 10 copies of Akalabeth: World of Doom created from scratch with original materials advanced in 1979. For marketing reasons he published a photo of copy number 12, the last one to be sold, and which returned to his possession years later.

22   An interview with Lord British, The Wizards Journal Volume 2, No.1 Summer 1984

Like many computer pioneers in the late 1970s, the young man had not regarded software as a marketable product and only exchanged it with other computer enthusiasts. Remmers, however, with some business flair, understood that software could, and indeed should, be sold like any other product. The market was still small, but growing rapidly; and was hungry for good programs because not all buyers of microcomputers were willing to learn BASIC and spend days creating their own custom software.

Richard had already come across Remmers' company, with the exchange of cassettes and 51/4" floppy disks in between friends and acquaintances, experiencing the first games of Bill Budge. A pioneer of microcomputers who made a name for himself by redesigning classic games such as Pong and Breakout for the Apple II (which says a lot about the perception of copyright in the early years of consumer computing, even among those who actually worked as programmers), distributed personally by Remmers store to store.[23]

Richard had never seriously considered becoming a game developer. D&D and programming were passions, but his life seemed to be routed another way. Completing the game was a challenge that earned him a great grade at school and a new Apple II. Self-publishing had been an adventure, though unprofitable, seeing one's own game on the shelves of a computer store had been of great satisfaction. Now, however, Richard could take another step forward, but he needed the approval of his parents.

Owen and Helen cautiously asked their son to contact CPCC about the proposal, so that they could better assess the opportunity offered. Richard didn't need to be told twice: as soon as possible he took the plane and traveled to California where he met Al Remmers in person who proposed a publication contract to him with generous royalties. At the request of CPCC, the manual would be rewritten to give the publication a more professional form than the sheets printed by Richard. Remmers also decided that the price would be increased by exactly $15 to $34.99.

As for the author's name, that Richard had included in the title screen of the game, Remmers had something to object to. "There's nothing wrong with Richard Garriott, but we don't think it's helpful for marketing. But we love the name Lord British".[24] They proposed to publish the game signed with Lord Briti-

---

23   "After I had traded my 'Pong' game to Apple, I decided to write more games and try to make some money. I was a graduate student in Computer Science at UC Berkeley. A friend introduced me to a computer rep who traveled to all the computer stores, selling 8" floppies for CPM systems. This rep, whose name was Al Remmers, thought he could sell some of my games, and we made a deal to split fifty-fifty. I was shocked when the first month's check was for $7000." Budge, Bill (1997) Halcyon Days: Interviews with Classic Computer and Video Game Programmers by James Hague

24   Garriott, Richard (2017) Explore/Create, Chapter 3

sh, instead of Richard's legal name or the nickname Shamino,[25] perhaps without fully understanding the long-term consequences of this choice that would have given a boost to Garriott's career.

Richard signed without hesitation and immediately returned to Houston. Summer's end was close and the young man facing the imminent publication of his school experiment, already had plans to lay the foundations for the follow-up of Akalabeth. To do so, he would ask Arnold for help. The two went to work: while Richard was trying to give his game more depth, a real story and increase the features, Ken Arnold, who knew how to program in Assembly, took care of writing the routine to update the game map, as well as dealing with the title graphics.

It took Richard two years to get to DND28B. The little time available before the start of university was not enough for the two to do more than lay down the foundation for the project, which they would complete separately via working remotely. Soon, Richard had prepared his luggage to go to the University of Texas in Austin, taking with him his trusty Apple II.

---

25   The initial screen of Akalabeth, which in the ComputerLand version was written in capital letters (like all text, given the graphics capabilities of the Apple II), "CREATED BY SHAMINO SALLE DACIL, ALIAS RICHARD GARRIOTT ©-1980 BY RICHARD GARRIOTT", will be replaced by "CREATED BY LORD BRITISH © 1980 BY CALIFORNIA PACIFIC COMPUTER"

Akalabeth: World of Doom

"Akalabeth wasn't much of a story: go kill a monster. And when the player came back to the castle after killing the monster, he would be told, go kill the next monster."

Richard Garriott, Explore/Create

"Besides the comprehensive care in design and attention to detail that characterize Akalabeth, subtle touches suggest the mysterious Lord British to be a person of droll wit and good nature. Incidentally, British apparently derives his pseudonym from the character in Akalabeth who doles out quests and confers knighthoods."

Softalk, January 1981, review of Akalabeth

There are at least four official versions of Akalabeth: World of Doom. The first and rarest of them all, is the one self-published by Richard Garriott and sold at ComputerLand. It is likely that only twelve of these were sold, making it one of the most coveted and expensive collector's items in the history of video games,[26] even

---

26   Between 2011 and 2013, two copies were sold for $4,050 and $4,900 on Ebay. Neither copy was originally sold or offered in the ComputerLand store (which were distinguishable by a green label with a number). Instead, Richard produced them much later using leftovers from the originals (labels and manuals) and new materials (he bought floppies and copied the game onto them personally), giving some to friends and shipping others to the crowdfunding supporters of Shroud of the Avatar.

more so because over the years, its creator was able to regain possession of some of the copies originally purchased in Mayer's store.

The second version is the one published by CPCC between 1980 and 1981. There are two reprints: the first is very similar to Garriott's self-published one, also known as the Castle edition because of the artwork featuring the front of a large castle, while the second came with Denis Loubet's artwork, the so-called Demon painting, and an eight-page manual containing a concise introduction, a brief explanation of the character's attributes, and a list of game commands. Of these two editions, 10,000 to 30,000 were sold, still making them a collector's item of high value. [27]

The third version was the most widespread and advanced, created by Corey Roth for the IBM PC. Originally intended for the launch of Ultima IX, it was finally included in the Ultima Collection (1998), due to continuous development delays.

There is also a fourth, lesser known version. It is a PC port of the CPCC edition, in monochrome, without audio or the ability to save and all the improvements made by Corey Roth.

All of them have in common that the game begins with character creation, except for the 1998 PC port, which includes an initial menu allowing the player to see the credits, to continue a saved game and see the ending (if they already completed the game at least once). As soon as the game starts the player is faced with a question, "Tipe thy magic number...?" which requires the user to enter a seed for the pseudo-random generation of the entire game world.[28]

Like many games of this early generation, Akalabeth did not offer an option to save; thus finishing the game could take quite some time. When Richard completed the DN-D28B version, he still didn't have a floppy drive and therefore could not implement a save system. Once he had one, he found that there was not enough memory left, which would require rewriting a good part of the game, freeing space, to fit in a save routine.

Therefore, Richard decided the game world should be procedurally generated,

---

27   Richard Garriott has repeatedly stated sales reached 30,000 units, earning him $150,000 in revenue. However, when analyzing the sales rankings of Softalk magazine, as well as those of Computer Gaming World's issue 2.5 of September-October 1982 (in which Akalabeth does not appear at all), and comparing the position of Akalabeth, the numbers indicated by Garriott appear to be inaccurate. E.g K-Byte's K-Razy Shoot-Out sales of 35,000 copies by June 1982, as well as Akalabeth's relative lack of collectibles in its CPCC version and Remmers' company's high royalty policy, do not support Garriott's claim. Akalabeth was sold in a third reissue in 1981, included in the special packaging of Ultima, also by CPCC. Ultima probably acted as a catalyst for the sales of Akalabeth, prompting Garriott to remember having sold 30,000 copies, including the two separate editions by CPCC, as well as more copies sold together with the first installation of Ultima.

28   The procedural generation algorithm written by Richard Garriott for Akalabeth was deterministic, i.e. it received as input a number called seed and always generated the same output.

as in Star Trek, based on the input of the user. The result allowed more clever and determined players to draft a map of the world and be able to play the next games with a perfect knowledge of where the dungeons and cities are.[29] Provided, of course, they used the same lucky number.

The player then had to choose whether to accept the traits of his randomly generated character or try his luck. As all dice rolls behind these stats and all consequent dice rolls were derived from the "lucky number", the sequence of "random" numbers was identical for each play-through with the same lucky number and similarly exploitable.

Once the character was created, the game started in one of its many cities and asked the player to choose their equipment using money earned from the previous dice roll. In the shop, which is always the same, regardless of the city, one could buy either a shield, a magic amulet, food or one of three types of weapons: sword, axe, or bow and arrow.

Many mechanics were clearly derived from D&D and the gaming sessions that Richard used to organize and tried to recreate on a computer. The introduction of food was one of the most innovative aspects of the game as it required the user to plan ahead, without going too far from the shops or spending large amounts of money to have enough food with them. During each game, the player had to keep an eye on the amount of food remaining because when the counter reached zero, the game ended immediately.

Akalabeth: World of Doom was an amateur product made by a young, novice programmer, who was clearly a fan of Tolkien. Like many adventures written by the Dungeon Masters that Richard had seen at work, Akalabeth began with acquiring equipment. After a very brief introduction on the boot screen, curiously only present in the Apple II version of CPCC and removed in the PC one, some explanations were given in the manual. Until DND28 became DND28B on his Apple II, Richard had always been the main user and tester of his game and never felt the need to create an introductory section to present his own game to himself.

The manual filled this gap and explained to the player the setting of the game. Wizard Mondain, Wolfgang's son, envious of his firstborn brother, had used magic to fill Akalabeth's world with evil creatures. In the higher levels of the dungeons, Mondain had placed goblins, skeletons and hordes of thieves, while in the bowels of the earth, at the deepest levels of the tunnels, demons and fearsome Balrogs, another reference from Tolkien, were set up as guards. Mondain's era was to end at the

---

29   In a contest for the launch of Shroud of the Avatar, Garriott made the source code of DND1 available using a scanned printout dated February 28, 1979. In this version, the game world was premade and stored in user-selectable data files. In between DND1 and DND28, Garriott modified the graphical representation of the game world from digits only to letters for the map, and implemented the pseudo-random generation system of the world, improving it beyond the release of Akalabeth.

hands of Lord British, the Champion of Light. The hero had defeated his opponent and driven him out of Akalabeth. Like in Tolkien's The Silmarillion, Mondain's fall wasn't enough to free the world from the evil the Dark Lord had spread: it was up to the player to do their part and free the realm of Lord British from evil creatures.

Following the only suggestion in the manual, the player had to find Lord British's castle and introduce themselves to the King, who would then issue a series of quests the player had to solve in order to advance to the final victory. However, outside of quests, the world could still be freely explored and enemies were generated in either case.

When entering the castle for the first time, Lord British introduced himself to the player: "Welcome peasant into the halls of the mighty Lord British. Herein thou may choose to dare battle with the evil creatures of the depths, for great reward! What is thy name peasant?" The text for the entire game was written in capital letters because of Apple II's inability to display lowercase characters, unless one was using expansions or the much slower high-resolution mode and give up valuable memory.

Another thing that stood out immediately, was the pompous Elizabethan language with which Richard had decided to give voice to Lord British. This choice, a clear reflection of the young man's experiences of live role-playing, was destined to become one of the characteristic traits of Garriott's work.

In front of Lord British, the player then had to answer the question, choosing the name of his virtual alter ego. The game behaved in an agnostic way towards the player's character, not asking about his sex or age but, after generating the parameters of strength, dexterity, endurance, wisdom and life points, only his profession (fighter or mage) and name.

Finally, Lord British asked the player if he was ready to embark on a great adventure. Having obtained a positive answer, the sovereign delivered his commands.[30] Lord British's missions were always the same: entering dungeons and defeating a creature in the bestiary of ten monsters (which Richard's self-produced cover defined ambitiously as "hi-res").

After leaving the castle, the player had to find a dungeon (marked on the world map with an X) and enter by pressing the correct key. Up to this point, the game had nothing special, even by the modest industry standards of the time. After entering the dungeon, however, the entire gaming experience changed.

Extremely original, and technically avant-garde, the representation of the dungeons from the player's point of view elevated Akalabeth from a scholastic experiment to a commercial phenomenon; determining its success and giving rise to the game development career of its creator.

With just a few lines, Richard designed corridors, rooms, doors, ladders and trapdoors for the dungeons in a very effective manner. The Apple II was a pri-

---

30   It was possible to answer with a No. In this case, the player would be kicked out of the castle but still able to return and repeat the entire sequence as if nothing had happened.

mitive machine and BASIC had limited capabilities that Richard would learn to exploit to the fullest before moving on to a more sophisticated and powerful language. Despite all this, with the modest tools available and his brilliant intuition, the young man was able to effectively recreate the experience of board games, bringing it to the microcomputer.

Richard had spent long hours with checkered paper to calculate the coordinates and format in Wozniak's obtuse graphic system for his schematic monster representations. Yet, these monsters in "high resolution" were much more detailed than the one game that had preceded Akalabeth and many of those who would follow on microcomputers.[31]

Players moved in steps, rotating at 90 or 180 degrees and going up or down where possible, using the keys only.

The author perfected the engine that generated the game world with each version, and arrived with Akalabeth at a high level of complexity. It was able to generate three-dimensional dungeons with walls and doors, starting from the lucky number. The generated dungeons were fully explorable and never led to dead ends. As Richard had taken his cues from studying Star Trek's BASIC code (published in numerous newsletters and in the book 101 BASIC Computer Games) while working on Akalabeth, he ended up writing a more complex and advanced code, making full use of Applesoft's capabilities.

When the player came across a monster, a fight began. As in DND1 and its other predecessors, the fight was turn-based, always allowing for a single action, usually pressing the A key to "attack". At this point, the program asked "With which weapon?" the character was preparing their blow, forcing them to remember the hotkeys used to buy weapons (R for Rapier, A for Axe and B for Bow and Arrow). Complicating matters was the possibility that thieves could steal equipment, which actually happened quite frequently, leaving the character weaponless. In such cases, the player had no choice but to resort to using another weapon, if available, or fighting with their bare hands.

Having killed the required monster, the player would return to Lord British and receive a new mission of increasing difficulty. After completing their final assignment of defeating the Balrog, the game's most fearsome monster, Lord British would extend his congratulations: "Thou hast accomplished thy quest! Thou hast proved thyself worthy of knighthood, continue play if thou dost wish, but thou hast accomplished the main objective of this game... Call california pacific computer at (415)-569-9126 to report this amazing feat!"

The last sentence (replaced by "Report thy amazing feat to Lord British today!"

---

31   The powerful PLATO system had been successfully used for the creation of extremely advanced games such as dnd (1975), a precursor of rogue-like games, Moria (1975-78), a crawl dungeon with wireframe graphics and first-person visuals, and the already mentioned Empire multi-player game.

in the PC version) had been included by Richard in preparation of the edition sold at the ComputerLand store. "The game was so personal, and our expectations so small, that I included my home address and phone number and asked players to call me when they finished the game" explained Richard. When switching from the self-produced version to the CPCC marketed one, the number had changed, but players could still call and get a certificate signed by Lord British in person.[32]

The whole game was written in Applesoft BASIC, which was notoriously slow, as with every move in the dungeons or on the surface, the microcomputer took a few seconds to redraw the map or the dungeon view. This also made the source code accessible to anyone: simply interrupt the loading to see the entire listing of the program on the screen. For the more curious, this was a good way to see the operation of a fairly complex software from the inside. For others, it was a source of further leisure: being able to change any parameter, a capable player was able to customize their adventure by modifying parts of the program.

One of the more bizarre aspects of the game was the magic amulet available at the beginning, but it could only be used safely by players choosing the mage character (and thus giving up the use of a sword and shield). Activated at any time during the exploration of dungeons, the magical amulet could make the character rise to the upper level of the underground, bring them down to the lower level, create a magic dart (thus performing an attack) or try their luck with the spell "Bad?".

The latter option was considered destabilizing against the balance and mechanics of the game, as it could be easily exploited by the pseudo-random generation of each electronic dice roll. By selecting "Bad?", the player ran the risk of being transformed into a toad (resulting in a lowering of all characteristics to 3), lose half their life points, or, at best, be transformed into a lizard-man resulting in a 150% increase of all characteristics. This could be repeated several times, bestowing incredibly high capabilities upon the player within a few minutes and making everything much easier.[33]

Another quirk of Akalabeth was the complete lack of a cure system or a maximum limit of life points. These could be lost during combat or gained only when leaving a dungeon, through a mechanism that gave the player a number of life points depending on the monsters defeated. Although peculiar and counterintuitive, the system worked and forced the player running out of life points to enter a

---

32   Garriott, Richard (2017) Explore/Create, Chapter 3

33   For example, Jason Kuntz, a fan of Akalabeth and many other role-playing games, wrote a very detailed guide on how to exploit its pseudo-random sequence of dice rolls to their own advantage, providing a lucky number and suggesting to the readers to perform 9 actions, whose failure was, so to speak, predestined and attempting luck with the amulet at the tenth dice roll, when success was assured. "Attack 10 times, then cast the 'Bad??' spell. Again, the Lizard Man! Keep doing this until you are strong enough to kill anything in one blow with your bare hands — 1000+ in the Strength and Dexterity departments should be plenty, 5000 tops."

dungeon and earn them by defeating monsters. Another consequence of this setup was that Richard managed to avoid implementing an experience and leveling system borrowed from D&D and thus reduce the complexity of the program.

Therefore, life points (or Hit Points, HP) were a resource that could, and indeed should, be collected, rationed and used in the best way, and preferably accumulated for challenging situations. There was no theoretical limit to HP due to the level mechanics (while being displayed on the monitor with a 4-digit counter, they could have reached a maximum of 9,999 points, much more than actually needed to complete the adventure), the game pushed the user to save them for the most difficult fights.

Akalabeth: World of Doom was the second officially commercialized computer role-playing game in the world, beaten in time only by Jon Freeman's and Jeff Johnson's Temple of Apshai, published by Automated Simulations (later renamed to Epyx) in August 1979 for the TRS-80, being the first episode of the Dunjonquest series.

The latter, in fact the first RPG for microcomputers, was equipped with even rougher graphics because of the very limited capabilities of the machine on which it was programmed. Tandy's microcomputer had a monochrome video output and, like the Commodore PET, used semigraphical characters to make up for the inability to visualize rasterized graphics.

In Temple of Apshai the player was assigned a character at random, with a series of dice rolls, after which the user had to choose the name of his alter ego and buy equipment using the starting money. Curiously, the first opponent of the player was the always haggling dealer who had to provide the equipment.

Next, the player could finally venture into the dungeon by selecting a starting level, a feature made necessary by the absence of a saving system. Compared to Akalabeth, the initial impact was decidedly disappointing. Due to the graphical limitations of the TSR-80, the player's character was represented by a ">" shaped sign linked to the players movement, treasures with white rectangles and enemies with crosses.

To overcome the significant memory limitations of early machines, the programmers had set up a gaming system using the provided paper material. The dungeons were made up by rooms, which are described in detail in the manual. Even the treasures that players could find while wandering around Apshai's dungeons were generically described in the game as "Treasure #" followed by a number. The player then had to cross-reference the manual's index to find out what they had just obtained. Each level had a list of room and treasure descriptions. For the first level, the most frequently found treasure was No. 20: "Nothing of value."

The combat system was a hybrid of turn-based and real-time, unlike Akalabeth's turn-based one (a result of the time-sharing and teletype-based system on which Garriott started programming DND). Each action required a turn and the computer recalculated the entire scene, making the character and the monster act (never more than one at a time but, in the rooms with the best treasures, defeating the first, could generate more monsters). If the player did not make a choice within a time limit, the system would consider the turn lost and continue with the next turn.

Temple of Apshai players could engage in melee combat using various controls. With A (Attack) the player character attacked the enemy with a normal blow, with T (Thrust) he carried out a special attack, more powerful but fatiguing and requiring Stamina, while with P (Parry), the character chose the defense, doing less damage, but recovering a bit of breath. It was also possible to engage in combat at a distance with bow and arrows.

Despite the game's limitations, Temple of Apshai was the first to give the microcomputer user an opportunity to experience the typical situations of role-playing board games and face important tactical choices. Success was not that far away.

Freeman and Johnson discovered that the small software house they had founded exclusively to sell programs written to recoup the costs of buying the microcomputer (as an aid to their favorite hobby D&D), could be a significant source of income.

Freeman and Johnson had bought the microcomputer mainly as an aid to their favorite hobby D&D. To recoup the high costs, they started writing games, and to this end they had founded a small software house.

Having discovered that selling games could be a great source of income, the two soon started work on ports for PET, Apple II and, from 1982, also for Commodore 64 and IBM PC. In total, on all platforms, Temple of Apshai sold almost 30,000 copies in less than three years before its withdrawal from the market. It gave rise to a successful series of titles that reached ten chapters and served as the engine for the young Automated Simulations, pushing it to become a famous software house in the microcomputer industry under the name of Epyx.

One of the reasons the game sold so many copies was that the next two chapters, Upper Reaches of Apshai and Curse of Ra, were expansions, as they required the first game in order for the user to resume the game where they'd left off.

Unfortunately, the first magnetic tape versions of Temple of Apshai had no saving mechanism: the player had to note the status of their character, magic potions, equipment, money, and answer (sincerely or not) to the questions of the program upon restarting. One also had to indicate their exact level at the end of the previous gaming session. Similar to Akalabeth's pseudo-random generation system, Freeman and Johnson's ploy was not flawless but overcame a technological barrier and allowed the player to complete the game in multiple sessions.

As rough and limited as they appear, Temple of Apshai and Akalabeth were extraordinary cutting-edge products as the very first role-playing games for microcomputers. Before anything else, Garriott's game was created as a school experiment without the intent of being released commercially. So it was a sketchy role-playing game, while also a tech demo, as we would call it today, able to show the potential of the computer and programmer, and fortunately arrived on stores shelves with a great impact, radically changing the history of video games and the life of Richard Garriott.

The Age of Darkness

Darkness

THROUGH THE MOONGATE

Creative Anachronism

"Yeah, the Society of Creative Anachronism. I'm still a member but less active than I was. If you know any local SCA people, you'll probably recognize their names in the game, along with names of most of the employees here at Origin, close friends, whoever's walking outside in the hall…"

Richard Garriott, Lord British: A Fantasy Interview - 4/23/92 by David Taylor

"They told me to bring my Demon painting because they wanted to show it to Steve Jackson, who happened to be the local Baron at the time. When, in medieval garb, I showed the painting to Steve, he looked at it and said he wanted it for the cover of the Space Gamer magazine. And so, surrounded by knights and ladies in waiting, I made my first professional sale to Steve Jackson Games for $250.00, and began my career."

Denis Loubet, Interview With Denis Loubet, The First Artist Hired At
Steve Jackson Games, 2015

As at Oklahoma University during summer camp, Richard's first weeks in Austin were a source of frustration. Because of his shy personality, it was difficult for him to fit into a new environment and the distance from home made it challenging for him to work constructively on the new game. Although he had brought his trusty Apple II with him, programming languished. Sparse contact with Arnold required the two to work separately, without knowing what the other was doing, and this often resulted in days of work ending up as unusable.

In California, CPCC had put their staff to work and within a few months the first copies of Akalabeth: World of Doom would start to arrive in the shops thanks to Remmers' network and personal connections and the distributor Softsel Computer Products Inc. Meanwhile Richard was isolated and alone, not by his own volition, but due to having difficulty breaking the ice with his new classmates. As often as he could, he went home to Houston and tried to carry on his work but his morale

slowly began to spiral downwards. For Christmas 1979, Richard decided to temporarily put aside programming and do something to build relationships with fellow
students. He was just waiting for a good opportunity, which came in Austin in form
of a leaflet from the Society for Creative Anachronism (SCA), an association dedicated to the study and reenactment of medieval culture and life.

Today, SCA is a fairly famous international association, thanks in part to its members who participated in activities over the years and consequently, generated publicity. However, at the end of 1979, SCA was still relatively unknown and not widespread. Its origins date back to May 1st, 1966 when a costume tournament was
held with participants competing in fencing fights at a party to celebrate Dr. Diana
L. Paxson's degree in medieval studies. The event was very popular and the enthusiastic guests proposed to organize a second gathering the following year. It became
necessary to book a park to accommodate all the people who were expected to
attend. In order to book the park it was required to indicate the name of the orga-
nizing association on the form. Writer Marion Zimmer Bradley had been involved
in the group's activities from the start and proposed the name Berkeley Society for
Creative Anachronism. Her suggestion was immediately liked and accepted.

Initially, BSCA's activities were limited to the University of Berkeley's California campus. Two years later, Bradley moved to New York, where she founded a
chapter of SCA, called Kingdom of the East with the help of local enthusiasts, and
held the association's first official tournament. At this point, for obvious reasons,
BSCA's name was changed (dropping the first part, "Berkeley") and ultimately became the Society for Creative Anachronism. Increasing its popularity via word of
mouth and student associations, by the end of the 1970s SCA had spread to many
parts of the United States, including Austin. When Garriott received the leaflet, he
considered with hope and curiosity the opportunity of doing something creative,
original and meeting interesting people.

He would not be disappointed.

In 1979, the Stellar Kingdom of Ansteorra of SCA (as it would be called later,
when it began to include the International Space Station, in addition to much of
Texas) expanded to include the territory of Austin and a new barony was created
on this occasion. According to the internal rules of the association, the leading role
had to be earned through a fencing fight.

Held on May 12 1979, the first royal tournament of Ansteorra, was attended by
about thirty fighters. The chronicles of the SCA recall the final clash that decided
the fate of the competition as thus: "The final bout was between Count Jonathan
(who'd stepped down as King of Atenveldt a couple of months earlier) and a relatively new fighter from the Shadowlands, known as Otto the Merciless".[34] Having
won the competition, Count Jonathan DeLaufyson became first King of Ansteorra.

---

34   Moondragon Manor online, http://moondragon.info/wiki/Main_Page

Among the ranks of fighters was also a Viking-Celtic warrior, Vargskol Halfblood, who stood out for his skills and was named Baron of Bryn Gwlad (as the SCA called Austin). Vargskol had only recently joined the SCA via a back door: always interested in board games and role-playing, he had become involved in the activities of the association in order to practice fencing and experience for himself the deeds of which the games he wanted to create spoke. His real name was Steve Jackson.[35]

By his own words, he had attended the University of Hudson and spent much of his time there playing war games and working on the student gazette, The Thresher, being the editor for two years. Despite his many interests and distractions, in 1974 he managed to graduate and enrolled in the law program at the University of Texas in Austin, but his vocation as a game designer had finally got the better of him: Jackson threw in the towel just before the qualifying tests to practice as a lawyer and dedicated himself full-time to the creation of games. Nevertheless, his stay at university had important consequences, such as allowing him to come across the SCA, which he continued to attend even after he had decided to leave school. As Baron, and later, as National Chronicler, he found himself at the center of the SCA in Austin having many interesting encounters with people, including meeting a very promising young artist: Denis Loubet.

The novice artist was invited to an SCA activity and had brought with him his Demon Painting, an elaborate drawing with a demon inside a pentacle. Recognizing the artist's skill at once, Jackson told Loubet that he would like the demon to be on the cover of his magazine, Space Gamer, and paid him $250, starting a working relationship that would last a long time. Loubet was hired as a typographical composer at Steve Jackson Games, the company the game designer had just founded to publish his works independently.

Although he would later occupy other roles, initially the artist was assigned to the laborious and tedious preparation of typographical sets for printing. Despite their good intentions, SJG was just an adventurous enterprise housed in the barn behind Jackson's house. However, over time, it would grow and the artist would have the chance to show off his talent and grow professionally. "As a typesetter I sucked big time, but soon Steve was able to support me as a full-time staff artist. I was glad to leave the Selectric typewriter's frenzied golf ball behind and work entirely on science fiction and fantasy art."[36]

At about the same time as Loubet and Jackson's fortunate encounter, Richard received SCA's flyer: It was the second half of the year and incredibly positive rumors about Akalabeth sales were beginning to arrive from California. Garriott

---

35   The namesake of Steve Jackson, a British citizen and co-founder of Games Workshop, Fighting Fantasy and, together with Peter Molyneux, Lionhead Studios.

36   Loubet, Denis (2015) Interview With Denis Loubet, The First Artist Hired At Steve Jackson Games, http://www.sjgames.com

immediately went to Waterloo Park, the society's meeting point, and arrived just as a couple of fencers were practicing. It was David Watson, a 30-year-old craftsman, and his 20-year-old roommate Greg Dykes. The young man stayed a while to watch them and then asked to participate.

Watson: "We met in Waterloo park, in Austin, at an SCA fighter practice. He was a skinny kid with really fast reflexes, who wanted to use his fencing training on a wider field. He and my pal Greg Dykes (Dupre'[sic]) hit it off right away, the three of us went to some SCA events together (I had a reliable car)."

More than ten years older than the others, Watson was an eccentric and very interesting personality for Richard. A skilled arbalist,[37] David had chosen the name Iolo for himself in the SCA. David Watson: "[In] Spring of 1979, I was in the local park (Shoal Creek Park in Austin) and discovered local medievalists were having a spring recruiting fair. They had fencing, sword and shield combat, music, and a number of silly games. The people were friendly, and I had a lute. So we sat down and played some music. The group met in that park every Sunday afternoon, so I showed up the next Sunday for more. I was hooked. Within a few weeks I was invited to the big crown tournament,[38] being held just outside town. I went out early, helped prepare the site (a lovely little meadow beside the local creek… maybe Wilbarger Creek, I don't remember). I had fun, sent in my membership and I've been playing with SCA ever since."

Passionate about history and crossbow shooting, years earlier David Watson had begun to rediscover the art of making these medieval devices. Watson: "When I was a teenager, in the 1960s, my dad bought a WhamO Powermaster crossbow (yes, the same company that made Frisbee flying discs.) We lived on 8 acres on the edge of town, with lots of trees, so it was easy to find a safe place to shoot behind the house. Years later, when I was in graduate school (studying history at University of Texas, in Austin, @ 1972) I bought a used WhamO Powermaster at a rummage sale. I took it home and shot in my backyard. The thing was a disaster: bolts didn't fly straight, but fishtailed and whirligigged in flight. I knew that wasn't right. Being a history student, I went to the library to do some basic crossbow research. There I found 'The Crossbow, Medieval and Modern' by Ralph Payne Gallwey, published in 1907. It was a fat book full of wonderful arcane knowledge, so I invested 40 whole dollars and bought a copy. Having devoured the book, cover to cover, I discovered what was wrong with my Powermaster. Simple answer: somebody had removed the bowstave (prod) and re-installed it half an inch off, so one side was working harder than the other. I corrected that and the bow shot just fine… but the bow had a number of other design flaws. I started making modifications, each of which slightly improved performance, until I finally accepted the fact that

---

37   a person trained to use a crossbow

38   The event where Steve Jackson became Baron of Bryn Gwlad

I had pushed that particular design as far as it would go. However, there was a set of plans for a proper medieval crossbow right there in the book. I had a few tools and a neighbor had a complete wood shop. So I bought some wood and talked my way into Patrick Tucker's shop. We made a working medieval crossbow that had its own set of problems. Yes, there were errors in Payne Gallwey's pattern as well. So I set about fixing those flaws."

When he arrived at the SCA, Iolo immediately made himself known for his incredible crossbows, which led him to change his job and become a professional craftsman, a job that to date, he has yet to abandon. Watson: "Everybody there thought my crossbow was great. So I made one for a friend, then another and another. Things were getting out of hand. Next, I discovered a company from which I could mail-order inexpensive aluminum-alloy bowstaves (prods or laths) instead of the built-up fiberglass things we had been using. The cheap aluminum prods made it possible for me to make and sell crossbows to friends and at medieval fairs. So @ 1981, I quit my dayjob and started making crossbows for sale… mostly to other medieval-nuts, and New World Arbalest was born. The business has never made much money, but with my wife's job as a tech-writer for the Texas Highway Department, we made enough to get by. Eventually we found suppliers for steel bows to augment sales of the cheaper aluminum ones, and I started offering stronger bows for hunting and longer-range target practice. So here we are 38 years later, and I'm still making a few crossbows, by hand as always."

The main interest of the three was fencing with rapiers. Tivar Moondragon was a point of reference for aspiring fencers in the Austin area, also one of the most active members of the SCA and the first Don[39] of the Order of the White Scarf of Ansteorra, an organization dedicated to leading in combat, among other things. Within the White Scarf, Christian Richard Dupre was number 4, Iolo FitzOwen number 9, Gwenllian Gwalch-Gaeaf (Watson's future partner) number 14 and Shamino Salle Dacil, then cadet of Dupre, Scarf number 28.[40]

Beyond the necessary demonstrations of respect due to the ranks and functions performed by some members of the SCA, the environment of the Order of the White Scarf was very informal and amicable. There was no shortage of jokes in the friendly atmosphere in which Tivar Moondragon, despite his leadership role, summarized everything with an effective wise crack: "They think I'm important; I

---

39   From "What is a Don?" written by Don Robin of Gilwell: "There shall exist in Ansteorra an Order which may be given at the pleasure of the Crown to members of the populace of Ansteorra who have demonstrated all of the following qualities: 1. Exceptional skill and chivalry in combat with the weapons of the duello, 2. Service to Ansteorra and its people, 3. Knowledge of courtly graces, and 4. Obedience to the laws and ideals of the Kingdom of Ansteorra and of the Society for Creative Anachronism."

40   http://www.stormypetrel.org/cgi-bin/wsa/server.cgi

think I've been screwed".[41] In this environment it is easy to imagine how the Don cards could be compiled, a set of typewritten sheets dedicated to the Dons of the Order, accompanied by a photograph of the holder and a description very similar to that of a character card in role-playing games, with clearly useless characteristics, evaluated on a scale from 1 to 4. Shamino himself was portrayed in one of the Don cards with his favorite phrase: "And then he said, 'Wanna buy a duck?' ".

Dykes and Watson were interested in more than SCA's fencing, pranks or social activities. Watson was already a skilled craftsman at the time and the two came across a research of a British forensic pathologist named Bernard Knight. In the article Some Medicolegal Aspects of Stab Wounds, Dupre and Iolo discovered that the resistance of the human body to the penetration of blades was mainly due to the top layer of the skin, which is capable of withstanding between one to six pounds of force before tearing. Experimenting, the two came to the conclusion that a thin strip of leather soaked in water had a similar resistance to that of human skin.

Based on this, Iolo and Dupre built a device they called "The Machine" in order to have an instrument to measure their combat skills. It consisted of a small target with a strip of wet leather that was used to measure the force of each blow. The result was quite impressive. Watson: "We had no way of calibrating 'passant' shots... touches that seemed to slide off the 'victim' without doing any damage. The drawcut machine seemed to be good for that, so I took my sharp rapier (really sharp) and tried to just skim a shot off the rawhide on the pipe. Ooops, it actually went in. So I tried again: Ooops, went in again. I discovered I could not make the blade slide off the target if the tip actually made contact, no matter how flat the angle. Thus we proved those shots where the recipient claimed the tip just skipped off their jacket... sorry, fella, that's in there. Doesn't necessarily mean it would prove to be an incapacitating shot, but it's not nothing."

According to David, Richard was a skilled fencer, even more so than his training buddies. Watson: "Richard was a very good fencer: fast and accurate. He quickly rose to the top of the list, and was awarded a White Scarf... that made him part of the de-facto group that ran SCA fencing in Texas."

Practicing fencing wasn't only done for tournaments. Between Richard and Greg a friendly and playful rivalry was immediately born, which led them to explore the limits of their abilities by inventing increasingly bizarre ways to fight. Watson: "Richard and Dupre had a rivalry that eventually led to a set of duck feet and duck bill to be worn while fencing."

Fencing was also an excellent way of solemnly resolving, in an old-fashioned way, the playful contrasts that sometimes arose between members of the SCA. In particular, Richard had soon begun calling Greg with the nickname "Super Duper" derived from mispronouncing Dykes' battle name Dupre within the SCA. Long taunted by

---

41   Don Tivar Moondragon, The Swashbuckling Game

his friend, Dupre, now annoyed, challenged Shamino to a duel, but lost, allowing Shamino to continue calling him by the insufferable nickname for another six months. Contrary to what one might think, the three were inseparable, bound by a friendship that survived for over four decades, and any excuse was a good one for duels.

Soon Richard was completely absorbed by SCA and found himself spending countless hours immersed in its imaginative medieval world, along with trusted Dupre and Iolo. Having to choose a different name for himself to use at SCA events rather than the formal-sounding "Lord British" that Remmers liked so much, he preferred the low-key moniker "Shamino Salle Dacil". This was the name he had initially signed the Computerland version of Akalabeth with and that he had often used during role-playing sessions. As with Akalabeth, Richard had created the name Shamino inspired by an already existing name (in this case the brand of his bike Shimano), but with a typo.

Shamino also met Vargskol Halfblood or Steve Jackson, and the two discovered that they had many common interests. Both had joined the SCA out of curiosity and found inspiration for the creation of their own games. Richard was more attracted to the design of worlds and stories, while Steve was more interested in inventing mechanics to create strategy and role-playing games. Both had been D&D players but while Richard tried to bring some of the mechanics of Gygax and Arneson's game back to the computer, Steve was dissatisfied with their game system because of its numerous variety of dices, the fact that (at least in the first reissues) 20-sided dices tended to wear out quickly, and when they eventually ended up with rounded corners, it required multiple dice rolls to have a clear and unambiguous result. Steve didn't like any of this and in his mind, the idea of creating a new game system began to take shape, based only on the six-sided dice. This would become GURPS in 1986.

In one of his many conversations with Jackson, Richard first came across Loubet's Demon artwork, which was the cover of Space Gamer magazine issue 28 of May-June 1980. Loubet: "Richard liked the Demon painting when he saw it at Steve Jackson Games and bought the rights from Steve Jackson to use it as the cover to Akalabeth". Until then, Akalabeth had been printed in the so-called Castle edition and its cover art was simple, depicting a castle. However, the first print was now sold out and Richard took the opportunity to propose that CPCC use Loubet's artwork for the second print of Akalabeth.

Garriott often talked to Jackson about his computer projects. Steve was also interested in computers, but didn't have the time to follow it seriously, since he already had enough to do for the magazine and his small board games company. Very often the discussions between the two concerned topics that had little to do with SCA as they were both happy to submit their games to the other members of the club for feedback. Richard actually went much further. After a few months in the SCA, he began to ask his fellow adventurers what phrases they wanted their virtual alter egos to use and write them down in his black notebook. He had already entertained the idea of including characters in his games which were created based on the images of the SCA members he was in close contact with. In doing so, Richard believed that he could create more realistic characters.

Towards the end of the academic year, it became apparent that Akalabeth was about to become a commercial success and a generous source of income for its programmer because of the high percentage of royalties reserved for Garriott. When the money started to come in, Richard's life changed quickly. The first thing the student did was to scrap the old Subaru that his older brother Robert had left him and buy a new car that he would replace again the following year with a Mitsubishi Starion. His look also changed radically as Richard started dressing in leather jackets, a habit he would stick to for a long time. The most important effect of the unexpected and great success of his game was that he suddenly found himself having to manage more money than his father would earn in a whole year at NASA.

Richard's personality underwent a transformation that his companions at the Society didn't like very much. At one point, some of them decided to address this and told him that they felt success had gone to his head. Then came the ultimatum: Richard either had to change his behavior or be discharged.

Initially, Richard did not want to accept any judgment from his friends. His first reaction was to feel outraged: having tried to share his newfound wealth with them, Richard could not immediately understand what was wrong with his behavior. Slowly, the truth in their words began to sink in and Richard realized that he had allowed himself to get carried away. To make amends, he promised to show off less and work harder.

In reality, not everyone noticed changes in Richard's attitude, instead the birthday parties he used to organize at the time for himself (which fell on Independence Day) changed. David Watson: "I never observed any asshole-behavior on Richard's part, but I would say the really big birthday parties ramped down after Thunderdome."[42]

Meanwhile in California, despite Akalabeth's sales going well, the Remmers company started experiencing difficulties. CPCC had some great programmers under contract, like Bill Budge, who had scored several excellent titles including the "Trilogy of Games" and the "3-D Graphics System & Game Tool", which sold very profitably to universities around the world. Yet the accounts didn't add up and CPCC needed a new success to get its budget balanced. The pressure on Garriott to get to work on a new game, possibly a sequel to Akalabeth, began to grow.

The progress on Richard's project had been very poor due to several factors: his distance from collaborator Ken Arnold in Houston, spending too much time at SCA events, and leisurely enjoying his sudden wealth. The ultimatum of his closest friends in Austin, pressure from CPCC, as well as his renewed determination to give a po-

---

42   Garriott's parties often had a theme. In this case it was a reference to Mad Max Beyond Thunderdome

sitive direction to his life, helped him get back to work, but by nature Richard was, in the words of his mother Helen, a "teenage dreamer with a perfectionist streak".

His parents, still thinking that writing games was not a legitimate career path, considered the success of Akalabeth as a bizarre anomaly and advised Richard to take advantage of the opportunity, as long as it lasted, after which he would have to find a "real" job. If Akalabeth had changed from a school experiment to a commercial game by chance, Richard's next title was designed to be sold to the public. Before there was a storyline, the prototype already had a name: Ultimatum. As with many other titles, Richard chose it by chance, and also because of the fact that it sounded very "badass". Unfortunately, he later learned that Ultimatum was already registered as a trademark some years earlier for a war game set in a hypothetical clash between the United States and the Soviet Union. Without losing his enthusiasm, Richard shortened the name to Ultima and continued with his work.

Creating a microcomputer game in the early 1980s was possible for anyone with enough imagination, determination and good programming skills. No special hardware was required and very often no license was needed. The total costs were therefore limited to the purchase of the platform on which the game would be developed. These circumstances allowed for the birth of numerous home software creators. Richard Garriott, Silas Warner, Bill Budge, Jon Freeman and Jeff Johnson were just the vanguard of a multitude of software creators (recreational or not) who were about to try their luck in the rapidly expanding consumer computing market.

CPCC was pushing for a product in the shortest time possible, but this time Richard didn't want to take a risk with an amateur product and did everything to create something new. Completely rewriting the game would have taken too long, so Garriott decided to keep much of the code developed for Akalabeth, improve it, and reuse it within Ultima.

Kenneth Arnold did his best to convince his colleague to abandon BASIC and move on to Assembly, but Richard, who didn't know this language, was in a hurry to take action. The two came to an agreement. Arnold: "One day at Computer-Land I told Richard something like 'You know what Richard, with a little work your program could become a game at least as good as the ones we are selling. But you'd have to switch to assembly language to make it fast enough.' Richard's reaction was immediate: 'Blech! Assembly language? Too tedious.' But I persisted. I told him I would write the parts that needed to be fast, and he could concentrate on the game logic, which didn't have to be as fast."

With Akalabeth, Richard pushed BASIC to its limits, exploiting much of the potential of Applesoft. Since there was little room for improvement, he let Arnold take care of some sections in Assembly, writing them more efficiently to save memory and increase the speed of the game. His experience was extremely useful in writing a graphics engine that would have been impossible with BASIC, or at least too slow to be playable. Richard meanwhile started working on the plot and focused on creating the world.

He had great ambitions for the creation of the world: having filled his notebook during SCA meetings, this time he wanted to give his new game a different feel. Abandoning the random generation of the world, he wanted to create continents, rivers, cities and points of interest, populating them with characters that had names and something to say. They now faced the problem of the Apple II's poor memory, into which they had to fit the program, game data and the world that Richard wanted to draw personally. Arnold's part was much more efficient than anything Richard could devise in BASIC but, despite everything, he couldn't draw pixel by pixel the world Garriott had in mind: to be able to store so much data would require more than the entire memory of the Apple II or the two floppy disks on which he imagined to store the game.

The high-resolution and mixed mode of the Apple II was 280 by 192 pixels, with up to 6 colors. The last 32 lines of the screen were reserved for four lines of text used for the dialogue box and counters for life, gold and food as in Akalabeth. They divided the upper part in 20 by 10 tiles each 14x16 pixels and began to prepare the Ultima game world map, composed of four continents. To save space, they cleverly recycled the same shapes several times, rotating and fitting them together so as to obtain four continents that were apparently different, but essentially composed of the same elements.

At this point, all that remained was to draw the tileset to compose the surface world geography and make sure that everything worked with Ken's components. Having to do it by hand, this process was anything but simple: the two drew each 14 by 16 tile on a sheet of squared paper. The next step was to translate them into binary code, the resulting code to hexadecimal, and save everything on disk. Finally being able to start the game and check if the result was the desired one.

Arnold: "I remember working with Richard on tile editing for Ultima I through the night in the ComputerLand store. We got so tired and delirious that we were laughing hysterically saying, 'That looks like crap!' about each others' tiles. The graphics resolution and color limitations were pretty extreme, but we managed to come up with a respectable set of tiles. It was mostly Richard's work... I just served as adviser, explaining why certain colors couldn't be adjacent to certain other colors because of the way the hardware worked."

Since each box had to be hand-drawn, calculated and inserted, Richard and Arnold did not create a very large tileset, limiting themselves to only 16 tiles for the overworld, the surface world, and city maps.[43] The result of such hard work, however, was impressive and qualified Garriott's work as the first open world commercial game with tessellated graphics and Ken Arnold had played a

---

43   In 1986, the game would be reissued in an improved version, with four color tiles for each object, necessary to create the illusion of animation and movement, and arriving at more than 270 tiles just for the outside world plus a slightly lower number for the cities.

key role in this, personally devising the innovative code that allowed the game to create a detailed world, piece by piece.

Arnold: "I think I probably wrote all of the 6502 assembly portions of Ultima I, but I don't really remember. I wrote the tile graphics routines, and the hyper-jump routine. I remember 'inventing' fixed point math for the hyper-jump, not knowing it was a standard technique. The dungeon graphics remained in BASIC, and were quite slow."

Garriott: "Ken wrote the first tile graphic copying routine in assembly for me. While his later work in Ultima music is still great, it was that one subroutine that put Ultima on track!"[44]

The underground section, with the first-person view representation borrowed from Akalabeth, after having underwent some improvements. The game no longer needed the "Lucky Number", the seed for Akalabeth's pseudo-random generation, but Richard didn't want to deviate too much from the system he had designed for the dungeons. Instead of asking the player for a lucky number, he used the name of the player's character as a seed for the generation of the dungeons, ensuring that once the player had entered their name, the dungeons were predetermined according to the internal algorithm. While still written in Applesoft BASIC, the dungeon generation and display routine were enhanced, including an increased number of enemies and the ability to display longer and more complex corridors.

When the game was completed, Garriott sent it to CPCC which, at last, could begin to prepare its mass production. Expectations were high because, meanwhile, Akalabeth had come second in Softalk's top 30 ranking and the entire market for microcomputer software was warming up.

The game Garriott handed over to CPCC was, in many ways, as innovative a title as Akalabeth had been, but much better cared for than his debut work. Traveling along the surface world, Arnold's efficiently written code kicked in, speeding up the game's rendering, and therefore being able to present a vast and detailed world in a way never seen before; in which the player could explore the castle of Lord British, various dungeons and, for the first time, the cities. On the other hand, when the game moved into the dungeons the execution was very slow, even slower than Akalabeth's.

CPCC set all its forces in motion to get the game to market as quickly as possible and in June 1981, Ultima made its official debut in stores across North America. It would soon face a fearsome competitor, but the sales results were very encouraging and in line with their high expectations. Unfortunately, for Al Remmers' company, this would be its last successful title. Shortly after the publication of Ultima, CPCC would close its doors for good, however Richard Garriott's star would continue to rise in the video game industry as Ultima demonstrated that Akalabeth's success was not the result of coincidences or luck, but something more.

---

44   Garriott, Richard (2011) interview with Robert Kosarko "Bladed Edge", http:// www.hardcoregaming101.net

The difficult chronology of the dawn of CRPG

"Either the game was omitted from the list for some reason or by accident, or it didn't sell much more (maybe even less) than 1,000 copies, at least not until it was bundled with later Ultima games (which happened quite early). The legendary rarity of the original also seems rather suspicious."

Sam Derboo, Ultima, Wizardry, The Black Onyx and the origin of JRPGs

Although the history of Akalabeth's birth is quite famous, partially thanks to the abundance of details by which its creator described the circumstances that led him to selling his software commercially for the first time, some details remain unclear. Particularly, the exact sequence of events and the date on which a copy of the version produced for ComputerLand arrived in the hands of Al Remmers. Garriott has always stated that the fateful phone call which kick-started his career as a professional programmer came at the end of summer 1979. According to his version, freshly contacted by Remmers, Richard removed unsold copies from ComputerLand's shelves and went to CPCC's headquarters to sign the contract. In a few weeks, the game would be put on sale with new artwork instead of the drawing made by his mother for the home version. After signing the commercial agreement, Richard would then leave for the University of Austin where at the beginning of 1980, he would take his first steps in the SCA, meeting many of the people who would inspire him to create the characters of his later game, Ultima.

This is the best known version of Garriott's early career, but it suffers from some fairly obvious discrepancies.

Akalabeth: World of Doom, was only published in 1980 and not a few weeks after the end of the summer, as recalled by Garriott. In addition, the game sold by CPCC didn't appear in Apple II magazines until January 1981.[45] This fact implies its commercialization actually took place in the second half of 1980 and not in the first months of the same year, as per Garriott's chronology.

The first edition of the game, the one offered for sale in ComputerLand, is dated 1980 both on the floppy disk labels and on the boot screen, just like the first edition of CPCC, also dated 1980. The CPCC edition is in all aspects very similar to Garriott's self-produced one. The Castle edition differed only by the inclusion of a sheet with the artwork, as well as a small reworking of the manual that Richard had written and that his mother had accompanied with drawings.

Furthermore, CPCC was not incorporated into the State of California Register until November 21 1980,[46] while Softsel Computer Products Inc., the distributor Al Remmers relied on to sell his products, had only been incorporated a few weeks earlier, on October 1, 1980, by David S. Wagman.[47] Softsel would soon become one of the most important distributors in North America in the rapidly expanding market of microcomputer software.

The second printing of Akalabeth by CPCC came the following year, with the art work of Denis Loubet. The Demon Painting had just appeared on the 28th of May/June 1980 issue of Space Gamer, without any reference to Garriott's game. Even inside the magazine, despite the presence of a column called "Deus ex machina", dedicated to computer gaming, there were no references to the Texan programmer or his debut work.

Garriott also said he was a fan of Bill Budge and knew about the company publishing his games before being called by Remmers.[48] Bill Budge, however, began programming games in 1979, producing clones of major arcade games on his Apple II. When he showed Apple his Penny Arcade, a clone of the very popular game Pong, the managers offered Budge to publish the game along with others in The Apple Tapes, a booklet distributed with the Apple II Plus since June 1979.[49] His collabo-

---

45   Softalk, published a short review in its January 1981 issue, showing appreciation for the game but criticizing the lack of a saving system.

46   https://www.ca-registry.com/C1009918-california-pacific-computer-co-inc

47   https://www.ca-registry.com/C1026068-softsel-computer-products-inc

48   Fields, Tim (2014) Mobile & Social Game Design: Monetization Methods and Mechanics

49   curiously Bill Budge was compensated with a printer for his game

ration with Al Remmers started only a few months later, when the entrepreneur proposed to sell the games of Budge door-to-door.

All this raises a big question, shared by other researchers such as Jimmy Maher and Sam Derboo, namely: did the events that Garriott place in the summer of 1979 happen in a handful of hectic weeks, from June to September, or did they evolve over 12 months, between June '79 and end of summer '80 (the purchase of the Apple II Plus, just released in June of the same year, the experiencing Escape! by Silas Warner, the reworking of DND28 into DND28B, with the addition of a first-person view for dungeons, the employment at ComputerLand, the appreciation expressed by John Mayer and the consequent publication of Akalabeth, the intervention of Al Remmers and the signing of the contract with CPCC)?

In the second case, the fateful telephone call on which Richard was invited to visit CPCC's offices did not come at the end of the summer of 1979, a few days after the sale of the 12 self-made copies by Garriott, but most likely occurred during the summer of the following year. Garriott, in his Explore/Create memoirs, recalls that he worked at the ComputerLand store in the summer of 1979 and helped the owner sell Commodore 64, Apple II and Sol-20.[50] The author clearly mixes this up, since the Commodore 64 was sold for the first time in the summer of 1982. Another important model by Commodore, the VIC-20, was however presented to the public in June 1980, although for a limited commercial release to Japan under the name VIC-1001.

Richard, in his memoirs, precisely recalled the time plan by which CPCC reissued his game and put it on sale: "Within weeks Akalabeth was being distributed nationally. [...] When the game was published in the fall of 1980, it very quickly became successful and people began wondering about the true identity of Lord British."[51]

At this point, in a clever advertising move, Remmers and Garriott proposed a quiz in the magazine Softalk. The quiz was printed in the January 1981 issue a few months after the publication of the game in which they asked the public to guess who Lord British really was, starting with a simple first clue: "Lord British is not a resident of the Silicon Gulch". Clearly, no one was able to identify the real name of Lord British and with the next edition in February, Softalk gave the second lead: "Lord British attends the largest university in the state of friendship."

The quiz caught the attention of many and probably boosted Akalabeth's sales, prompting CPCC to reprint it again, this time changing the cover. None of the participants came close to the right answer although some surprised Garriott: "One example was unusually clever: The Aka in the title stood for the well-known phrase 'also known as', la of course is Los Angeles, and beth must be the creator's name. Therefore it was a woman named, Elizabeth who lived in Los Angeles. It was a gre-

50   Garriott, Richard (2017) Explore/Create, Chapter 3

51   Ibid.

at answer, even if completely wrong." For his ingenious yet inaccurate guess, the reader named Akabyramben Schwartz American, likely using an alias created with the same mechanics proposed for the quiz, won a consolation prize of fifty dollars.

After awarding the secondary prize, Softalk continued to publish further clues in March, without anyone being able to win the real prize: "He and his home city are closely related to present and future blastoff. He works at a store at the King's Highway near the city of the clear lake in the land of computers. ComputerLand knows him as the Son of the Skylab and if you call you'll know him too."

As far as the exact chronology of the Akalabeth publication is concerned, in light of the information gathered up to now, there are two possible reconstructions.

In the first case, Garriott recounted the succession of events correctly and only made a mistake in his recollection of the year of Remmers' phone call. As such, one of the copies produced for ComputerLand would have taken almost a year to reach the CPCC founder's desk and convince him to contact the young programmer to propose a distribution contract.

In the second case however, the events were canonically placed in the summer of 1979 and happened during the school year 1979, while the sale at Computer-Land took place at the beginning of summer 1980, moving by a good year the first limited commercial release of Akalabeth (buying the Apple II Plus, experiencing Escape!, transition from DND28 to DND28B). If this were the case, it would change little in substance, as Temple of Apshai would still hold the record of the first role-playing game for microcomputers, having been put on sale nationwide in August 1979. Meanwhile, according to the time-line proposed by Garriott, Akalabeth was exhibited exclusively on ComputerLand shelves in Houston.

Although second in the history of role-playing computer games, Akalabeth had a far greater influence than Dunjonquest, which quickly declined and disappeared a few years later with the entire series being withdrawn from the market. As the foundation of the Ultima series, while not officially part of it, Garriott's game system for Akalabeth would have greatly influenced subsequent titles, giving generations of programmers and game designers a blueprint for CRPGs. Upon arrival in the East, it popularized role-playing computer games and renewed its style and form several times, eventually landing in the online world and changing the way we play forever.

Ultima

"It was the first game I ever wrote on the Apple II. When I finished it, I went, 'Wow, that game sold 30,000 units and I never even meant to sell it. It doesn't have a story, and there's no way to win it.' I thought, 'Wow, I could do a much better game if I just started over.' And so I began the first Ultima."

Richard Garriott, Online game pioneers at work by Morgan Ramsey

"Ken actually did all the machine language programming on it so we could use tile graphics. If you think back to the days of the original Ultima, I don't think there was a game that used tile graphics at that stage. So I believe that we, principally Ken, invented tile graphics for Ultima."

Richard Garriott, The Official book of Ultima by Shay Addams

"Eventually, your character will discover the real object of the game. Accomplishing this is no small undertaking: it requires experience, imagination, and a lot of hit points."

John Williams, Softline, September 1981, review of Ultima

Ultima's story was not a sequel to Akalabeth's. Today we would say it was a reboot, as Garriott himself, realizing the substantial absence of plot in his first game, decided to start from scratch, having only a few points of contact between the first and second work.

The shadow of evil wizard Mondain obscured the lands of Sosaria, a world divided into four continents, each controlled by two kings, and threatened to destroy them with hordes of monsters. Sosaria's last hope was the Stranger, the only one capable of defeating Mondain. Strangely enough, in Akalabeth's introduction this archenemy had already been driven out by Lord British. Yet in Ultima, he was in control of deadly forces and indeed immortal, having forged a magical object of incredible power, the Gem of Immortality. To bring down Mondain and end his reign of terror and destruction, the Stranger had to find a way to go back in time and defeat him before he built the gem and was still mortal. Exploring the lands of Sosaria and performing various feats, some of which resembled Lord British's assignments in Akalabeth, the player would obtain the gems needed to operate the time machine.

Once again, the reference to D&D was clear, but this time the character creation system was no longer random. The player had to distribute 90 points on strength, toughness, agility, wisdom, intelligence and charisma, ranging from 6 to 20 for each.

The next step was to choose the race from human, elf, dwarf and hobbit (another Tolkien reference), which only applied race specific bonuses and penalties. Richard didn't deviate from the clichés of fantasy, giving strength bonuses to dwarves and agility to elves, except for the human race, which he decided had an increased intelligence by five points.

After selecting the character's sex (without any effect to the gameplay), the last step was to choose the avatar's class: warrior, cleric, magician or thief.

With Akalabeth, Richard had already tried to implement a system of classes that changed the gameplay (the warrior could use more powerful weapons and the magician had more effective access to the only magic object: the amulet), but the outcome of this attempt was modest. In Ultima, class played a slightly more important part as it mainly guaranteed an additional bonus (+10 strength for the warrior, +10 intelligence to the magician and so on) and limited the available equipment.

Stored on a 51/4" floppy disk, Ultima was able to save game data and then the player would create their own character, store it on a disk, and start the game. It was necessary to copy the second side of the original floppy, called Player Master, onto an empty disc, creating the Player Disk, before starting the game from the first floppy, called Program Disk. This favored players with two floppy drives.

Saving, present in the first prototypes of DND but lacking in Akalabeth[52]

---

52   Garriott only had a cassette player on his Apple II during the transition from DND28 to Akalabeth (or DND28B), and therefore didn't implement saving routines. He came into possession of a Disk II shortly before Akalabeth was put on sale in the ComputerLand store but realized its support would require more RAM. It would have required extensive work to free up space, so he continued to omit a saving routine. When asked by Mayer to display his game on the shelves of the store, Richard and Arnold prepared several copies of both, cassette and floppy. However, as popularity of cassettes was declining, only a few of the floppy versions were sold.

was essential for Ultima because of the game's length. Garriott claimed in a later interview technical reasons for why it was not possible to save during the descent into the dungeons.

The game would start with the usual top-down view of the world, but now bigger, with color, visually nicer tiles, and Arnold's Assembly routines with an unprecedented fluidity and detail.

It was possible to explore the world freely, but to complete the adventure it was necessary to find a castles to receive the first mission. Because of the greater variety of actions, the interface consisted now of more hotkeys.

The castles of the lords of Sosaria were open to visitors and led the player to maps with special tiles including guards, traders, trees and members of the royal court (King, Princess and Jester). With T (Transact), it was possible to trade with merchants or talk to hosts and lords. This was an interesting step forward from Akalabeth, where castles and cities had a textual representation and shops were the same everywhere.

The player could also attack the guards, or steal food (hotkey S) and equipment. Richard also included the first NPC, a jester, wandering the streets of the city, singing "Ho eyoh he hum!".

In the cities and castles of Sosaria, Garriott's most popular characters would make their debut. Iolo and Gwino (as jesters present in every court of the eight castles), inspired by David "Iolo" Watson and Kathleen "Gwenno" Jones, as well as Garriott's other alter ego, Shamino, sovereign of one of the four continents, lord of Lands of Danger and Despair.

The first mission was visiting a point of interest or, as in Akalabeth, defeating a certain monster. The first big surprise was that Akalabeth's turn-based system had been replaced by a rudimentary real-time system very similar to Temple of Apshai: if the player didn't take any action for a few seconds, the game continued and enemies made their moves, forcing the player to act. This applied only to the surface map, for the dungeons the system remained exclusively turn-based.

The mechanics for fights didn't change. 'A' dealt attacks while Dexterity affected success, Power determined the damage. Gladly, a single ready action (hotkey R) to equip weapon and armor, replaced the previous system of repeatedly asking the player which weapon they wanted to use.

Dungeons were generated at the start of the game, using the players name as a seed. Monsters appeared randomly based on the level of the dungeon. Finding the right monster to complete hunting missions was just a matter of luck and perseverance.

One big novelty was the system of spells, no longer based on the use of an object like the magic amulet of Akalabeth. Ultimately all characters could buy spells in cities and use them (mainly in dungeons), which required "readying" them first. Given the high cost, the player was encouraged to use disposable scrolls sparingly.

Spells were divided into two sets: those available to any character and those exclusive for wizards. The latter were understandably more powerful and gave new tactics: allowing a player to teleport a short distance with "Blink" (an extreme so-lution that could get the player into an even worse situation than the one he was trying to escape from), create a magical wall in front of themselves with "Create", or to destroy one with Destroy, and even to slay monsters using the spell "Kill".

For all other classes, the basic spells were very similar to those of the Akalabeth amulet, with small innovations. The player could go up or down a level in the dun-geons, create magic lightning with "Magic Missile" (a spell very familiar to D&D players), or reduce the risk of triggering traps from opening coffins and chests with the use of "Open". Akalabeth's "Bad?" spell, prone to abuse, was somehow repla-ced by "Prayer", with random but beneficial effects: e.g. removing a close enemy or adding food or HP in the overworld.

After completing missions on the first three continents, it became necessary to travel into space. Nowadays it may seem strange to mix fantasy and sci-fi, and Gar-riott made no attempt to explain it in Ultima. The cover of the little manual showed an artwork with a warrior, a dragon, a castle in the clouds and a spaceship, very similar to the Space Shuttle, made it clear the game would include sci-fi elements.

In fact, in the 70s and 80s, the mix of fantasy and sci-fi (also called science fan-tasy) was not uncommon. For example, Expedition to the Barrier Peaks (1980), an expansion module written by Gary Gygax for Dungeons & Dragons, was set in a spaceship whose crew had been exterminated. Players had to survive hordes of robots and strange creatures, probably of alien origin, as well as finding ad-vanced technology to proceed with the plot. This adventure wasn't an isolated case, but belonged to a fairly popular niche, reaching peak popularity with the Spelljammer setting, published in 1989.

The space section in Ultima was completely different from the other game parts. After docking at the space station, the player experienced a series of action sections, shooting down enemy spaceships curiously similar to the Star Wars Twin Ion En-gine (TIE) Fighter. The combat was reminiscent of Doug Neubauer's Star Raiders, released a couple of years earlier for the Atari 800. With a slight difference in con-trols: in the Atari game, the player moved the cross-hair to direct the laser focus on the enemy fighters, while Ultima used a fixed cross-hair, and therefore the enemy vehicles that had to end up in the middle of the screen. Garriott later admitted that he was greatly influenced by this primitive space combat game.

References to George Lucas' film continued with other pieces of equipment available in the advanced part of the games, such as blaster weapons and light-sabers. After this first appearance, the cinematic references in Garriott's works would increase over time. He also claimed that he had been less inspired by li-terary works and much more by films from his youth, a passion he shared with many of his later colleagues.

After destroying twenty enemy space vessels, the player could return to Sosaria and receive the last missions in the Lands of Danger and Despair. Once these were completed, all that was left to do was find the time machine. To do so, it was necessary to save a princess, freeing her from the prison. The only way to open the lock to her cell was to kill the city jester, that repeatedly claimed to have the key.

Contrary to later installments which rewarded the player's good behavior, in Ultima, killing, looting and theft were not only possible strategies to reach the final goal, but were essential. Without any kind of narrative explanation, the player had to kill the jester in cold blood to retrieve the cell key. Once the princess was freed, the player was then able to reach the time machine and go back a thousand years to challenge Mondain in a boss fight.

The battle with the evil wizard took place in a completely empty city map, showing only the player, Mondain and a small dot indicating the Gem of Immortality. Although the journey through time was intended to arrive before the Gem was built, at the beginning of the fight the Gem was already in existence and its magical power active, giving Mondain the ability to regenerate shortly after being killed.

To complete their mission, the player had to fight Mondain long enough to get close to the gem and interact with it, breaking it and permanently depriving his archenemy of the regeneration ability. After killing him again, the player was transported by Lord British, who informed him of the final victory and, as with Akalabeth, asked him to inform California Pacific Computer Company, 1623 fifth street, suite B, Davis (CA) 95616 about his feat.

As such, in 1981 Ultima was highly out-of-the-ordinary and many of its features later became genre standards. Its vast worlds using tessellated game maps and freedom of exploration impressed the public and inspired programmers.

Conversely, his choice to include such a variety of themes without a clear vision in Ultima resulted in serious problems that showed his naivety, but was still a stepping stone in Richard's progress towards creating a fun game with a rich and stimulating world. His main goal was to entertain the player and make the most out of the resources available on the Apple II. Garriott: "If you look a the Ultima I to III, they really were pulling from all the things I thought were cool in life [...] There were lightsabers and blasters and landspeeders and such in the first few Ultimas from, of course, 'Star Wars'. There were tons of influences from 'Lord of the Rings'. [...] The basic was an amalgamation of all the things I found inspirational around me, during those times."[53]

In this young industry where many games were one-person projects, games like Temple of Apshai advertised having being tested by seven people — a remarkably small amount compared to modern game testing and hence, hitting the market with numerous bugs and prone to crashing. Richard would also resort to his friends and members of the SCA for testing, but the resulting bugs were similar: for example, in dungeons the resistance of the player's armor wasn't taken into account in

---

53   Drachenväter: Die Interviews by Konrad Lischka & Tom Hillenbrand

damage calculations, making it easy for those more experienced to abuse or mani-
pulate many of the game's mechanics by traveling between points of interest then
receiving repeated weapon upgrades and wisdom bonuses.

Other features such as experience, made little sense as unlike in D&D this feature
did not upgrade one's character or grant them special skills, but increased the number of monsters in the overworld.

What mattered were the character statistics, which rose upon the completion of
quests or were granted by Lord British. The only innovation about life points was
the possibility to buy them from the lords of the castles but once exhausted, the
player's character was immediately regenerated with 99 HP and 99 points of food,
but lost all experience, money and equipment.

Ultima was published by CPCC in June 1981. The first version contained a 51/4"
floppy disk, a manual written by Garriott, Remmers, and Tom Luhrs, as well as
a small four-page reference guide. This time the cover artwork, a medieval knight in front of a metal dragon, was designed by Denis Loubet: "This was the first
actual commission I ever got from Richard Garriott, and he offered it to me while
I was working at Steve Jackson Games. At the same time, Richard asked me to do
the start-up screen for Ultima I as well. I did it on a Apple II graphics tablet that
was so crudly constructed that the pen would fall apart, and the line you were
drawing would constantly be interrupted by power spikes from the cobbled-to-
gether electronics. That was the first computer graphics I ever did."[54]

In the years to come the game was republished several times, often with significant changes. In the first reissue of Ultima in 1983 by Sierra On-Line for Atari's 8-bit
line of computers, Loubet's cover art was replaced with a new design depicting a
castle with similar lines to the art work of the CPCC version reference guide. In the
meantime, Ultima II had been released, which made Ultima part of a series. Therefore the edition for Atari was published under the name Ultima I The Original.

After his time with Sierra-On Line ended, Richard had to wait until 1986 to be
able to republish Ultima. The game was published after a significant improvement
to the graphics, first for Apple II then several months later for Commodore 64 and
IBM PC. The latter version in particular supported the new EGA video cards, and
was able to represent 16 colors rather than 4. All 1986 editions were published
under Origin Systems with the name Ultima I: The first Age of Darkness, its box
contained a paper map of the four continents of Sosaria, a bag with five coins (one
gold, three silver and one copper), a reference manual and the book The First Age
of Darkness, written by Garriott and illustrated by Loubet.

---

54   Curiously, Richard's choice to use Loubet's artwork for the second reissue of
Akalabeth introduced the artist to Rammers, who began to commission him for CPCC
game covers. Before making the Ultima cover, in 1980 Loubet designed the Apple-oids
cover for Remmers.

In the industry, illustrations and higher quality materials were gradually becoming more common and Richard, more than many other programmer, was ready to use this to his advantage. But he needed luck.

Luck, however, was about to turn its back on him.

Difficult choices

"The original 1981 edition of Wizardry is one of the most important, influential, and yet relatively-unknown computer RPGs ever released."

Benj Edwards, 10 Classic Computer RPGs, PC Magazine, 2012

"California Pacific was getting into financial trouble internally. This caused them to delay paying me my royalties, this was only for a short period of time at first, then they just stopped paying."

Richard Garriott, interview for The Wizard Journals, Summer 1984

Once everything was ready, Ultima was distributed throughout the country. For this occasion, Garriott wrote an article illustrating the innovation brought on by his decision to show the dungeons via a first-person perspective. This short article was published in issue 39 of Steve Jackson's magazine Space Gamer. In May 1981, Ultima was greeted with great enthusiasm both by players and specialized publications that were emerging at the beginning of the 80s. Within a few months, sales reached considerable figures, but in September, Ultima had to square off against a formidable competitor: Wizardry: Proving Grounds of the Mad Overlord.

Andrew C. Greenberg's and Robert Woodhead's Wizardry was the result of a long process starting in 1978, when Greenberg wrote it in BASIC. As with Garriott's Akalabeth, it was extremely slow and when Woodhead saw the game in June 1980, he set to work bringing Greenberg's code to UCSD Pascal. The two turned to the founder of Sir-Tech Software Inc., Norman Sirotek, for the publication of their game and managed to present a first version in November the same year. But without a 48k standalone Pascal runtime from Apple, it would require buying a Language System from Apple, priced at $495, to play it. The few months delay until Apple delivered (and many months afterwards) were used well to polish the game. Norman's father, experienced businessman Frederick Sirotek, advised his son to pay particular attention to the outer presentation of the promising game, focusing on professional packaging and a comprehensive manual; suitable even for those less experienced with computers. Following this advice, Sir-Tech enlisted a skilled draftsman, Will McLean, well known to role-players for his brilliant illustrations in the Dragon magazine and the Dungeon Master Manual.

Wizardry was very different from Ultima in many ways: The first feature that stood out was its party of six adventurers, which the player had to create at the beginning of the game by juggling classes, races, and alignments from AD&D. The goals of the game were to explore dungeons, gain experience, and advance one's characters, all while finding weapons, magic items, and trying to survive hordes of enemies, as each dungeon level increased in difficulty.

A large part of the screen was occupied by the user interface which listed party members while the top right dialogue box explained what was going on to the player. There was also a 3D display of the dungeon, in Akalabeth/Escape! style. Encounters with monsters were random and not displayed via the first-person view and were therefore unavoidable; differing from Garriott's classic game design.

Although in some ways more complex due to the high number of classes, levels, skill combinations and the party system, the combat scheme took place in a less interactive and engaging form, instead relying upon tactical immersion. Party members occupying the top positions on the list were in direct contact with the enemy, while those placed in positions 4 to 6 were closer to the rear, and limited to performing a small number of skills or support actions.

Overall, Wizardry was a fun and innovative game,[55] a dungeon crawler CRPG that focused on exploring one's surroundings and fighting monsters. While resembling Akalabeth and Ultima in terms of having a small part of the screen dedicated to the 3D visualization of the dungeons, Wizardry was equipped with a completely different method of gameplay: there was no overworld but it possessed a sophisticated party system that Garriott's games were lacking.

Greenberg and Woodhead's game won over the public and media with a presentation superior to the competition, along with intriguing gameplay. Starting in the first weeks with an unexpectedly high sales performance, by mid-1982 Wizardry

---

55   The combination of a party system, small first-person view and the party list were heavily inspired by games programmed for the PLATO, and were now brought to the microcomputer audience. Temple of Apshai was mainly inspired by dnd, while Wizardry was very similar, in gameplay and interface, to Oubliette, a game available for PLATO since 1977 and in turn inspired by Moria of 1975. Even Escape!, the inspirational title of Akalabeth's first-person view, was most likely influenced by Moria.

sold 24,000 copies, winning the best-selling CRPG to date[56] title and beating Ultima by 4,000 copies, even thought Ultima had a head start of a few months.

Together with Akalabeth and Ultima, Wizardry had a strong influence on the gaming industry, much more than Dunjonquest. Many players (who later became programmers) decided to take over Greenberg and Woodhead's famous system and improve upon it. The success of the two CRPGs was a clear sign that the market was hungry for these kind of products and an increasing number of software houses began developing similar games or real clones, giving rise to two subgenres that would compete for over a decade. The unique duel between Ultima and Wizardry would not last long: despite Ultima's success and the production of other software like Brainteaser Boulevard (the first video game by Chuck Bueche, one of Richard's old companions in D&D), at the beginning of 1982 CPCC stopped paying royalties.

The reasons for CPCC's failure have never been clarified. Garriott dramatically recounted his first encounter with Remmers and how he was a spectator of a drug deal in a hotel room in Explore/Create. According to him, the closure of California Pacific Computer Company was closely linked to the drug addiction of its founder. To much surprise, when royalties for Ultima began to arrive late CPCC's offices had already been long deserted.

In truth, CPCC did not close down immediately. Records report that Remmers' last year of business was 1984, with a final administrative document submitted on May 22, 1985. In an interview[57] taking place after the aftermath of Ultima II's launch, Garriott still claimed to earn about $1,000 a month in royalties from his first game with the company. Garriott's abandonment of CPCC was not only a consequence of CPCC's economic difficulties, but also the most logical choice as he evaluated other opportunities. CPCC was a minor publisher that, apart from the connections made by Remmers in California, was without a national network and had to rely on Softsel. It probably wasn't able to provide Garriott with the resources necessary to support his professional growth, especially given the projects he was starting to consider. At the same time, Bill Budge also decided to leave CPCC and signed a contract with Electronic Arts. The loss of Remmers' main two programming stars put a heavy burden on the balance sheets of his company, and CPCC folded within two years.

With a rift between Garriott and Remmers, copies of Ultima already on the shelves were not replaced and soon sold out. This was also a catalyst for losing the clash with Wizardry, which would continue to remain in the ranking of best-selling games for over three years until 1985, reaching the astonishing figure

---

56   With the exclusion of Apshai, which placed first in the charts with 30,000 copies sold in the three years since its release. Its very high number of sales was also due to selling subsequent adventures as modules which required the basic game.

57   National Enquirer, 1983

of 50,000 copies sold on various platforms.

Faced with CPCC's crisis, Richard's first reaction was to confide in his brother Robert, who was studying economics at MIT. The two soon realized that CPCC's conditions were such that it would be very difficult to pursue any outstanding royalties. A backup plan was therefore required.

Richard also had other things to think about.

In addition to losing his publisher, he experienced problems performing at school. He had spent too much time engrossed in SCA's activities, friends and programming — this was simply a natural result. Richard also began further reflecting on the idea of becoming a full-time developer and abandoning his studies. Ultima's success confirmed that he had more talent than luck and that perhaps, video games weren't a temporary craze like Hula Hoops. Finally convinced that video games were more futuristic than fad, as soon as he completed his second game, he immediately set to work on a sequel. However, with Remmers' company out of the picture, he was left without a publisher or source of income.

With two successful titles on his resume, it wouldn't be a problem finding a company interested in publishing it. However, Richard had very high expectations, not only from an economic perspective (CPCC had paid high percentages), but particularly from a production standpoint. In competing with Wizardry, he experienced for himself how much of a difference professional packaging makes, and understood that to be successful it was not enough to create a new game, but a different approach to the overall product was necessary.

Wizardry's well-prepared and printed packaging with its professional manual, detailed and embellished with Will McLean's remarkable drawings was no new phenomenon. An increasing number of publications could boast ever higher production value; with large illustrated cardboard boxes instead of Ziploc bags and professionally written manuals replacing typewritten and photocopied sheets. This higher quality increased production costs, but the public unreservedly rewarded them with good sales.

One company whose name is inseparably linked to this trend, is Infocom.

Their story started in MIT's computer rooms, where another fundamental title was being played profusely. Colossal Cave Adventure, the first example of a text adventure, written by Will Crowther; a programmer who loved visiting caves and D&D, mainly to entertain his daughters. Colossal Cave Adventure allowed the player to interact with the program using elementary constructs very similar to natural language. The game accepted phrases of two words as commands, such as "Go east", "Look up" and "Get food". Like Star Trek, Colossal Cave Adventure passed from hand to hand, undergoing changes and expansions and influencing students, teachers and programmers, becoming the progenitor of a new genre of games.

Inspired by Crowther's creation, four MIT students decided to make a similar but more sophisticated game. Their game, initially called Dungeon, understood more complex sentences, including articles, numbers and more. Too big to fit into the limited memory available on early 80s microcomputers, the text adventure was divided into three parts, publishing the first one in 1980 under the name of Zork.

Thanks to their excellent writing, Zork was a huge success and the small company would grow quickly; going on to create more games. Specializing in text adventures, Infocom became the champion of this market and by December 1983, all ten games produced so far were in Softsel's top 40. With Zork in the leading position and three other Infocom games in the top ten, the four partners were ready to be even more daring. Having chosen the path of self-publication from the beginning, the founders of Infocom had total freedom and did not hesitate to do what other publishers wouldn't.

The software house created more and more ambitious games, investing in the quality of its products and accompanying them with a growing amount of inserts. Other early developers had already begun creating support materials alongside their installation instructions to supply the player with supplementary text and images that would otherwise not fit into the tiny memory of computers at the time. But Infocom was aiming much higher.

Infocom's mystery adventure Deadline (March 1982) came with a folder labeled "Police", containing a notepad for the inspector (the player), a small plastic bag with three small white pills (in the game found next to the victim's body), a transcript of some suspects interrogations, the coroner's report, a letter from the victim's lawyer, a police memorandum, a laboratory report on the analysis of the cup of tea drunk by the victim and a photo of the crime scene.

Soon Infocom's extras became their trademark, also known as "feelies" in reference to the movies in Aldous Huxley's novel Brave New World (cinematographic works that could be seen, listened to and felt at the same time). Skillfully designed to enrich the player's experience of the game, it also acted as an effective anti-piracy system by continually asking the player to refer to the feelies in order to solve a puzzle, answer a question correctly or perform an action.

Given the difficulty level of some games, many users had begun to contact the software house directly for help to overcome the more challenging obstacles. The boom in popularity of Infocom's adventures caused a flood of calls and letters; thus prompting their management team to create a dedicated paid telephone helpline, which was followed by further publishing manuals containing hints and even complete guides. They were called InvisiClues[58] and were among the first clue books of its kind to become extremely popular in the 80s and 90s, before the Internet took over as the prime source of information for desperate players. Garriott would

---

58   The name was a reference to printing the text with invisible ink, requiring a special highlighter included with the book to read them. It discouraged photocopying as well.

soon provide Ultima players with dedicated solution books as well.[59]

For his next title, Richard wanted to do something similar to Infocom's packaging. A first step to immersing the player was taken when Remmers advised him to use his pseudonym Lord British. The choice was purely based on marketing, but it had created an unexpected yet interesting consequence: the player found themselves to be buying a game written by the ruler of its world, the programmer himself, who entrusted them with the mission of saving the world of Sosaria.

Garriott wanted to continue pushing the boundaries of creativity, however this was something that not all publishers were willing to do. Despite his track record, many backed down when he presented his requests, namely the freedom to create material to be included in the packaging. The founders of Infocom had gambled with their own money and won, but few publishers were ready to follow this path and spend more than the competition; turned off by the risk of their profit margins narrowing.

Founded only a year earlier by Trip Hawkins, Electronic Arts was interested in Garriott as they had been on the hunt for well-known brands to buy and publish. A newcomer to the market but with an innovative business plan and solid financial support from some of the most skilled venture capitalists in history (including Don Valentine, a key person in the birth and success of Atari and then Apple). Richard didn't have a real brand yet, since Ultima wasn't a sequel to Akalabeth, but Hawkins would have gladly recruited Garriott in his team as he was very focused on prominent personalities, as he was trying to stand out from the politics of managers like Atari's CEO, Ray Kassar, who considered programmers as simple workers.

Years later Hawkins would recall his failed attempt at recruiting Richard to his first core of superstar programmers for the "We See Farther" campaign, which included Bill Budge: "I initially targeted Lord British, and we met in 1982. He was tied up with a really bad distributor and wanted to do it himself. He had the brand power and guts to do it".[60] The time was not yet ripe, but sooner or later Hawkins would somehow bring Garriott aboard his battleship.

Leaving out all publishers who didn't want to deal with a risky commercial operation like Richard's, only one software house remained in the race: On-Line Systems, founded a few years earlier by the Williams couple.

---

59   This series of books would be called Ultima Companion Clue Books. Starting in 1983 with Ultima III: Exodus, players in trouble could find help in these manuals, sometimes written in a cryptic way and therefore not always easy to read or understand

60   Hawkins, Trip (2012) Trip Hawkins on 30 Years of Electronic Arts (Edge.com)

Sierra On-Line

"From the beginning, I recognized that Sierra was in a different industry than most. […] We were selling creativity."

Ken Williams, interview by Philip Jong, 2006

"They allowed me to program Ultima II the way I wanted. They even included in the contract that they would let me put a cloth map in with the game along with the documentation."

Richard Garriott, interview for The Wizard Journals, Summer 1984

"I thought that this was just something to do for a little bit. In fact, a couple of years later when I was making the decision to drop out of college, which I sort of had to do because I was failing classes, my family was like 'Well, of course, you should go pursue that. There's no college degree for that! But surely this will end. And when it does you can go back to school, finish your degree and go get a real job."

Richard Garriott, interview by Tom Caswell for Gamezone, 2016

Roberta and Ken Williams got married very young, at the ages of 18 and 19 respectively. They had met by chance during a double date. After only two evenings, Ken realized that he was more interested in the girl his friend was dating rather than the one he was with. Immediately showing some of the qualities that would distinguish him in the following years — determination first of all — Ken cut to the chase, called Roberta and asked her out: within a year the two were married. When Roberta became pregnant, Ken was a university student with little income, and decided to make a radical change to his existence.

It was the early 1970s and the market for mainframes and the sale of time-sharing services were among the most lively and profitable businesses. Ken saw the possibility of finding a good job and decided to attend a 9 month course in programming. It paid off, he managed to advance and achieve some economic stability. Meanwhile, the family had expanded with the arrival of D.J. (1973).

Unfortunately, Ken's income was never enough and this led him to look for ways to earn extra money, mainly via collaborations and consulting. Roberta's life was far from perfect as well. Relegated to the home, the young mother felt bored as a housewife.

However, something suddenly brightened up her gray existence for a few weeks: for work reasons, Ken had installed a terminal connected to a mainframe at home and showed Roberta the video game Colossal Cave Adventure, an inspiration for the creators of Zork and many other developers in the 70s and 80s. The game didn't impress Ken, who found it boring, not appreciating the logic of the puzzles. On the contrary, Roberta had developed a deep interest, and sometimes forgot to do housework or missed out on caring for her children (a second child, Chris, was born in 1979) until she had solved all the game's puzzles. Colossal Cave Adventure put stress on the family during the time which she was completely absorbed in her new hobby. Once she had finished the game, life returned to normal.

With the release of the Trinity computers a momentous change was set in motion that would soon transform Ken's life. In 1977 more and more professionals and entrepreneurs were ready to buy one to free themselves from the costs of renting teletypewriters and time-sharing services that giants like GE charged dearly for. A big challenge was the lack of software, forcing most microcomputer enthusiasts to learn BASIC and write programs for their needs. This shifted in 1979 with the release of VisiCalc, the first spreadsheet, a software tool so useful and desired that it would become one of the first killer applications; making the sales of Apple II skyrocket.

Ken understood that the emerging new market was an incredible opportunity to get rich by having the right combination of ideas, products, determination, and skill. Ken was keen on success and as for the right idea, he decided it would be the programming language Fortran. Aware that programmers like Richard Garriott or Bill Budge, could realistically pick either a limited BASIC or the challenging and laborious Assembly language to create their own software on the Apple II, he was convinced that a Fortran compiler on the Apple II would enable programmers to work with a powerful and efficient yet not too complex language. Microsoft had become the reference point for BASIC interpreters on microcomputers, and managed to impose their main product on a good part of the market. Ken strongly believed that Fortran had an even higher potential.

With Ken bringing home a TSR-80 from the office, Roberta soon discovered more games like the one that had made her lose so many nights of sleep. This time, it was the video games written by Scott Adams, a pioneer of the text adventure genre, which Roberta found irresistible.

Having played many of the games available on the market at the time, Roberta considered creating her own. She explained the project to her husband, who was still working on his Fortran endeavor. He expressed interest, but pointed out that it would take something revolutionary to break through in the market. Roberta already had something in mind.

She pondered for a long time about how much nicer it would be to draw scenes other games were describing in words only. Ken agreed and they started working on it. The Apple II had a new expensive accessory at $199 which would make creating drawings a lot easier. The VersaWriter was the precursor to today's graphics tablets, being able to record shapes drawn by the user. It wasn't particularly precise and the arm mechanism the user had to move was difficult to master, but Roberta used it with enthusiasm to draw the scenes she had in mind while writing her first computer adventure.

With Mistery House (1980), the couple created the genre of graphic adventures and started their own entrepreneurial adventure. The titles written by Roberta became an unexpected success and On-Line Systems, the company founded by Ken in 1975[61] as a consulting practice, became a video game studio.

In just one year, their company hired about twenty people and by 1982, they had moved their headquarters and the small community of dedicated developers to a custom-made chalet. Roberta's games, without exception, yielded huge profits and the company seemed set to become one of the most important players in the industry. Even IBM, the giant from Armonk N.Y., offered the Williams an agreement to bring Roberta's brilliant adventures onto their new PCjr platform.

Bold and innovative, at On-Line Systems (soon renamed Sierra On-Line), Richard's requests seemed reasonable. After spending nearly a million dollars building a chalet for a hundred employees, the Williams did not feel discouraged by Garriott's stringent condition to include a fabric map with his new game. Even the slowness with which Richard had completed his first games, a sore point that discouraged more than one publisher, did not intimidate the Williams: having employed a large number of programmers and having several games under development, they could afford to give Garriott the time needed to work. They were not worried about cash flow as their accounts were kept in the green by the high sales of Roberta's works.

So Richard signed a contract with Ken Williams: by April 1982, he would deliver the full game and On-Line Systems would publish it in a professional and rich package, just as the programmer wanted. The agreement also included an option for the Williams to go and recover the rights for Akalabeth and Ultima directly from CPCC and proceed with a re-release. In the case of Ultima, this would guarantee good earnings, since the title was still in its first year of release.

As soon as the latest title for CPCC was finished, Richard immediately set to

---

61   Ramsay, Morgan (2012) Gamers at Work: Stories Behind the Games People Play, Chapter 11

work on a sequel to Ultima. To improve upon the first installment, Garriott's only option was to learn Assembly language before starting with the programming. To achieve faster and better results, he needed a good mentor and decided to turn to an old acquaintance at CPCC.

In the previous year, Tom Luhrs had distinguished himself by programming Apple-oids, a game very similar to Atari's Asteroids, but with apples instead of asteroids. Entirely written in Assembly, Apple-oids was the classic example of how the video game industry was sometimes still run in an amateur way: companies often ended up copying each other openly, with little respect for the work of others. Soon everything would change and Atari, along with many other companies, would start resorting to the courts.

Luhrs had already helped Richard write Ultima's manual and now did his best helping Garriott to master the new language in an intensive programming course that lasted almost a month, during the summer of '81. He made sure Garriott could finally set aside BASIC for the better, enabling him to directly access the hardware of the Apple II and use it as efficiently as possible.

Using a different programming language, Richard had no choice but to rework his game again. As he had done many times with his university project DND and then with Ultima, Richard rewrote his entire program to create an even better game.

The return to school, however, was another source of trouble for Richard. Having to split his time between work and study, his school performance subsequently began to suffer as a consequence. Richard was already thinking about leaving university for good. The biggest obstacle was his father Owen, who would hardly accept a drop-out. Regretfully, Richard continued trying to combine work life with the high expectations of his parents but it was clear that the situation would continue to deteriorate.

Richard learned the tricks of the trade from Tom Luhrs and over time improved his skills by collaborating with fellow programmers at Sierra On-Line and, also thanks to practice while writing Ultima II, slowly turning into an Assembly expert. In '81, he had to attend an Assembly course and thought he could get the highest mark while putting in little effort: after all, he was a professional programmer with two commercial successes under his belt.

What Richard couldn't foresee was that the Assembly course would not be held on the Apple II, his favorite platform, but on a much more powerful computer: Commodore's SuperPET 9000.

The SuperPET was a machine designed for education, the result of a curious collaboration between Commodore and the University of Waterloo. It was expensive and powerful, equipped with two CPUs (a MOS 6502 and a Motorola 6809) and much more ram than Trinity's microcomputers. In comparison to Apple II's 6502, the 6809 had powerful additional instructions. Thanks to his experience, Richard was able to complete assignments using only the 6502. When the teacher began to evaluate his homework negatively, Richard was unable to cope with the disappointment. His programs were working and he didn't feel the need to study the additional Motorola 6809 instructions. Hoping to dissuade Richard from completing tasks unconventionally, the teacher increasingly marked each assignment with a lower grade. Stubbornly, Richard did not deviate from the path he had taken and when he finally received an F, he decided that he had had enough and was ready to leave university.

His father Owen wasn't ready for his son's sudden change of mind. Richard's family had a higher-than-average education level. His father had been a respected university lecturer and famous astronaut, his mother was an artist, and both his older brothers were studying. In particular, Robert had just obtained a master's degree at MIT and was determined to pursue further academia while gaining experience at major companies such as Texas Instruments. Richard's dropping out after only obtaining a high school diploma was not a viable option for his parents.

Richard did not immediately face his father but first confided in his older brother. Evaluating the situation in a practical way, Robert gladly accepted his younger brother's aspirations: thanks to his master's degree in economics, Robert was perhaps the most suitable person to understand that a career in the software industry could guarantee Richard a bright future. Even his mother Helen, who had helped Richard so much since his first venture, designing the cover of the version of Akalabeth sold to ComputerLand, testing the next games and giving advice, and was receptive to Richard's aspirations. Being an artist herself, and Richard being the most imaginative and creative of her children, she had no difficulty understanding his reasoning.

She formed a family alliance to support Richard in the face of his biggest obstacle: convincing Owen that university was not the best choice for his son.

It's not hard to imagine Owen's reaction to the unexpected news. Despite the support of a large part of the family, Richard's father didn't budge easily. According to his understanding, it was not only an unexpected turning point in Richard's life, but a defeat that would divert him from the right path. For Owen video games were just a fad; an expensive pastime with no future, and Richard's choice to pursue their development would only lead him to regret the time and opportunities lost once they had gone out of fashion.

In times past when Richard had entered his father's studio or the principal's office to propose a compromise, he always came out with a good deal. This time, it was Richard's turn to accept an uncomfortable agreement: he would move to Hudson University, and could only continue to write games if he was successful studying part-time. Otherwise he would have to give up game design and return to full-time study. On the bright side, he would have time to program again.

After all, returning home had its advantages as it allowed Richard to meet old D&D friends and get help in testing games. Ken Arnold also returned to the team and helped with programming.

Curiously, Richard's passion for computer science and game creation had brought many of his D&D buddies closer to the world of game design. Keith Zabala-oui, Richard's neighbor who helped design the title screen for Akalabeth, had started programming and was ready to help him do more than just test the new title. Chuck Bueche, one of his classmates recruited for the first D&D campaign after returning from his stay at Oklahoma University, was also interested in programming and published Brainteaser Boulevard[62] through CPCC, thanks to a contact provided by his friend. Richard's passion was contagious and his personality had a strong influence on all those around him.

Finally returning home and partly freed from the cumbersome burden of university, Richard began to think about how to organize his new game and slowly a plot took shape based on the map from a movie he had seen the year before, Time Bandits.

An English fantasy comedy directed by Terry Gilliam, starring former members of Monty Python with guest stars such as Sean Connery.[63] Richard decided to take inspiration from this film and went so far as to watch it several times in the cinema, in order to copy the map as the base of the story, with the help of some friends.

Garriott: "Since I wanted to have time travel in Ultima II, when Time Bandits first came out, before it was on video, I actually went night after night to the dollar theater with pad and pencil to draw a copy of their map, to see if it had any logic to it. It sort of did, but not really. After I did all this it came out on video, so it was a total waste of time."[64]

Time Bandits stars a group of robbers using portals to travel through time and to distant places, enriching themselves in the process. In order to use the map from the film, Richard needed a plot that made sense and, if possible, had a link to the first Ultima.

---

62   Brainteaser Boulevard (1982), a game clearly inspired by Frogger, the Konami arcade game released in 1981. Instead of a frog however, the player has to lead a scout in the work of helping elderly ladies cross a busy street.

63   The Scottish actor, whose presence was desired by the production team, but considered extremely unlikely because of his fame, participated with enthusiasm, being a long time fan of Monty Python.

64   Ultima IX: Ascension - Prima's Official Strategy Guide (1999)

Ultima II: The Revenge of the Enchantress

"For Ultima II Richard said 'Well I should learn 6502 assembly language like Ken and make a better game'. And he did. His first assembly language program happened to be a big hit game you know unlike most people's first one."

Dr. Cat, interview with Matt Barton, Matt Chat, 2017

"Ultima II is unique and its storyline is original. That's why i like it."

David Langendoen, review of Ultima II, K-Power Magazine, 1984

The foreigner from another world had restored peace to the lands of Sosaria, but the truce did not last long. Once Mondain was killed, the stranger had returned to his world, unaware of the sorcerer's young apprentice and lover: Minax. She swore revenge on those who had deprived her of her companion and mentor.

Her blood-thirst was not satisfied with spreading death and destruction in the form of wild beasts and ferocious monsters. Then she discovered that the hero who put an end to the immortal existence of Mondain was no inhabitant of Sosaria. Following the trail, she reached the world from which the Stranger came, Earth, and began her diabolical plan. Sowing hatred and resentment since ancient times, in 2111, Minax managed to unleash a nuclear war that devastated the planet, breaking the continents into fragments and reducing humanity to ashes. Only a handful of survivors remained thanks to space-time portals, and founded Pirates Harbour; the only city to exist after the devastation.

Once again, the fate of an entire world was in the hands of the foreigner. Summoned by Lord British, the player's mission was to visit Earth at various times via time portals to find the objects needed to stop Minax's plan. Having obtained the necessary tools to defeat the sorceress, the player had to penetrate Castle Shadowguard, the enemy's headquarters, and face her in a showdown. After defeating the sorceress, the evil influence on humanity's fate immediately ended; retroactively changing the course of history and avoiding the thermonuclear war.

As in the two previous games, Ultima II's plot was mostly told by the manual. Over the course of the game, there were few references to the story and Lord British was little more than an NPC equipped with a certain degree of invulnerability and the special power to heal, provided the player had at least 50 gold coins.

It made little sense to return to the future and be thanked by Lord British for this accomplishment because of the time paradox that should have made everyone forget about the foreigner and the evil deeds of Minax. The issue was not ignored by the manual: "And if — no, when — you succeed, you will return to the present as it might have and should have been. Those in this small group can guarantee from their very souls that they will never forget your great deed. But you should be aware that by the very nature of your success, that future generations prospering in the sunlit glory of the universe as you have made, are apt to forget. Your satisfaction must be self-sufficient."

Nevertheless, the plot was very sketchy and in its outlines, similar to that of Ultima. Represented by a short introduction in the manual and few references in the game as Richard was mainly looking for a possibility to use the map inspired by Time Bandits. When he was a DM, he focused on creating challenges for his players, confronting them with complex tasks and battles. The plots of his adventures, by his own admission, had never been strong. As a game developer, Richard was still a DM for whom the plot and character development were not a priority, for now.

Despite the long development time, Ultima II was not much different from its predecessor. Except for small aesthetic changes to improve the interface, it was very similar to Ultima. E.g. character creation was similar in terms of the interface and the choices possible for sex, race or class. A first clue that the game engine of Ultima II was just a slight enhancement.

The adventure started in 1423 B.C. on Earth, with a stylized representation taking some freedoms for the sake of gameplay: e.g. starting in North America, the player could easily enter Asia over a land bridge. Simply exploring or using the fabric map for orientation, the player could access all the portals and move through different epochs on Earth. the control system with hotkeys remained unchanged and the tileset was very similar to that of Ultima, with the exception of new monsters in the overworld.

The first big novelty one experienced was the cities: unlike Ultima, where the cities were shown on a single screen, in Ultima II they were much larger and more detailed. To overcome the limits of the rudimentary graphics allowed by the game engine, Richard created tiles with letters to write on the walls of the cities as directions for the players. This way e.g. the inn at Port Bonifice in the Land of 1990 indicated the business was called Ronall Mc Donall, a clear reference to a fast food chain.

Popular culture and real life references were numerous: from the video game industry (Andrew Greenberg and Robert Woodhead were depicted in their magic shop called, of course, Wizardry) to movies (Commander Decker of Star Trek: The Motion Picture), but the main plot was made up of protagonists from Garriott's life; the family and friends who supported him during the creation of the game. For example, the player would meet characters inspired by Richard's parents as well as Mayer, the owner of the ComputerLand store. In Ultima, there were only Iolo, Gwino and Richard's two alter egos, Lord British and Shamino. With The Revenge of the Enchantress This would become a trademark of Garriott's games — inserting many characters from his life and creating a virtual world full of inside-jokes strongly inspired by his personal experiences.

Cities became more than simple trading hubs and were now inhabited by characters with names and dialogues. It had become a necessity for the player to explore their surroundings and talk to people (besides guards and traders) to gather information. Richard had gone from representing cities with a simple text screen for buying and selling equipment and food, to drawing landscapes and populating them with guards and characters with a name and a trade, modeling a world.

Visiting the dungeons, the technological evolution was quite obvious as they were now handcrafted rather than randomly generated. The new engine, written in fast assembly language, allowed for a much more fluid experience and monsters in color. However, due to time constrains and more attention payed to the development of the overworld's numerous maps, the dungeons fell short on player expectations and had a limited bestiary.

The dungeons contained even more hidden jokes. Players drawing maps would recognize hidden graffiti such as "Lord Brit", "Ultima II" or "Zab" (the initials of Keith Zabalaoui, for the first time credited as a programmer). In cities Richard aligned tiles of bushes, plants and road pavements in the shape of one of the four ghosts from Namco's Pac-Man and even of ET in New Jester, a city inhabited exclusively by noisy jesters.

Combat and spells remained substantially unchanged, as did the system of obtaining HP when exiting a dungeons or by/through purchasing. Lacking the plethora of lords from the first installment, unintentionally the figure of Lord British had turned into that of a collector, ready to ask for money at every visit and provide life points in return albeit very sparingly.

Completed as quickly as possible in order meet Ken's deadline, upon release Ultima II was an incomplete and buggy game; some of which were quite serious. One bug was called "roll over" and occurred when a player exceeded the limit of life points (9999) or attributes (99), after buying them from Lord British. In such cases, the counter would automatically reset to 0, resulting in the instant death of the main character. Lacking time to solve the issue, Richard hastily implemented a band-aid solution by decreasing the amount of HP Lord British awarded the player.

To fix Ultima II, Garriott would need more time which Ken Williams was unwilling to provide. Consequently, the game was published with many maps that were either almost empty or completely deserted. Richard's original design included a space section with the possibility of visiting other planets of the solar system. Besides the empty planets, the dungeons were also superfluous, containing no objects relevant to the quest.

Despite numerous flaws, the game received good ratings from magazines. Softalk reviewed it, believing that "the interplanetary saga with a creative programming flair far beyond the scope of most fantasy or adventure games", although the only required interplanetary journey was to Planet X and most of the other planets were empty maps.

Continuing the tradition, the game was put on sale in the summer: on August 24th 1982, the long-awaited sequel to what was about to become a saga, appeared on the shelves of computer stores and video games, accompanied by a remarkable advertising campaign.

This cover, for once, did not bear the signature of Loubet because Ken Williams had instead entrusted Sierra On-Line's reference artist with the main art work: Paul Stinson. At the time, Stinson worked in New York and contact was made exclusively by either letter or telephone to his agent. Stinson: "I had no direct conversations with Richard Garriott regarding the game nor did I play it. I was provided an overview of the game and a basic direction Sierra was looking for. Of course I was given creative freedom."

Even without having played Ultima II, just with the supplied information, Stinson was able to grasp the essence of Garriott's game: the result was a cover depicting a traveler about to enter a portal and being threatened by a dragon. The illustration continued on the back of the box with a representation of a castle with steep lines, clinging to a rock spire and reachable only through a steep winding zigzag path. This second part of the artwork was very similar to the one designed by Laura Phillips for CPCC's Ultima manual, and which Sierra later reused for the port of Ultima on Atari 400/800 and for Mt. Drash. Only years later, with Richard Garriott's consent, did Loubet receive the satisfaction of drawing the cover of Ultima II as it could have been.[65]

---

65   https://www.patreon.com/posts/1858658

In addition to the fabric map that had prompted Richard to choose Sierra On-Line as publisher and that represented the network of space-time links between the portals, the package included a 16-page manual explaining the user interface, some indications on the gameplay, information on the setting, and a bestiary of the monsters. In addition, a paper galactic map with the coordinates (Xeno, Yako, Zabo) needed to travel with the spaceship, a postcard to register the product, and 5 1/4" floppy disks.

This was a big step forward compared to the CPCC's edition, which was sold for only 5 dollars less than that of Sierra On-Line. In the future Garriott would focus even more on this aspect, increasing the retail price of his games several times.

This reflected immediately in the sales numbers, being much better than what his previous titles achieved. Ultima II had to compete with another sequel: Wizardry II: The Knight of Diamonds, the second act of the history making game series of Greenberg and Woodhead. However, this time the two did not have as much time to develop it and the result was not well received by all. The riskiest choice was to follow in the footsteps of Temple of Apshai and make a game that could not be played without the first installment.

However, both games continued with unprecedented sales numbers, riding what would later be called the boom in the Golden Age of computer role-playing games. In truth, the growth was not driven uniquely by RPGs but the entire video game industry.

Storm clouds would soon start to form for Richard…

Escape from Mt. Drash to Origin Systems Inc.

"Contrary to rumors, Garriott was fully aware of the game and consented to the use of the Ultima name to help out Zabalaoui, whose game would not otherwise have been published by Sierra."

Giant Bomb overview of Escape from Mt. Drash

"Technically everybody is freelance, including myself. Chuck (Charles Bueshe[sic]) and I actually work in the office, so we call ourselves resident freelancers. We're the only two resident freelancers, but we do have three outside freelancers who do both translations and some original work. Also Andy Greenburg, author of Wizardry(tm), is working for us. He is currently working on a new game called, 'Ogre'. That should be ready in the next couple of months."

Richard Garriott, interview by Peter Ellison, ROM Magazine
Vol. 1 Issue 6, June 1984

"When Richard, his father Owen, his brother Robert, and his friend Chuck Bueche decided to start a company, I was invited to join by investing $5,000 for a 5% stake in the company. Being a starving student, I declined. Big mistake. That's why I'm still working :)"

Kenneth Arnold

The Williams company not only gave the young programmer the necessary supports to carry out his project: Ken and Roberta also welcomed him into their home in California. Here, together with other guests of the Williams, Richard found shelter and could concentrate on making giant strides in the programming of Ultima II. Yet his stay at Sierra On-Line's headquarters did not leave him with a good impression. He would explain years later that many of the same problems he had experienced at CPCC were also present at Sierra On-Line and that it was hard to forgive himself for stumbling twice into the same error.

In 1982 Sierra On-Line was already a rapidly expanding colossus in the computer game market; many investors wanted to buy it. Their staff was constantly increasing and the lifestyle in the chalet was, to say the least, very informal. Similar to Atari under Bushnell's leadership, parties were not uncommon and often young programmers, suddenly independent and with a relatively well paid and satisfactory job, had no problem indulging in alcohol consumption. Richard later recounted that there were also drugs on the Williams campus: "A high-ranking employee with close ties to the principals of the company was dealing pot on the side, some of it to coworkers."[66]

Sadly, the relationship between Ken and Richard soon began to deteriorate. The first point of contention was the Spiradisk system implementation (writing data on floppies along a spiral rather than in the usual concentric circles) to protect Ultima II from the spread of illicit copies. Its inventor, Mark Duchaineau, was a brilliant hacker but according to Ken, loved to be the prima donna of the company.

Garriott, who had exchanged pirated games in the dawn of his computer life, was against the use of Spiradisk because it increased the already long loading times and was unreliable. Duchaineau, as Sierra On-Line's technician in charge of the anti-copy protection, and participating in profits of any game using his copy protection, insisted on using it, effectively blocking the publication of the game.

Only under great pressure, including from Chuck Bueche, Duchaineau suddenly realized that he was blocking a fellow programmer's software to promote his own, and eventually gave in, implementing the anti-copy system without further ado. However, Garriott was disturbed by the incident. Once Ken found out about Duchaineau's conduct, he went on to replace him as soon as possible.[67]

Struggling again to fit into new environments, Richard interrupted his stay at Sierra and returned home. It had been profitable, but Richard would remember it in negative terms, showing his uncompromising personality. The idyll with the Williams was about to end.

When Ultima II was published and the hoped-for success was evident, Ken considered possible strategies to exploit the popularity of the brand. Signing the contract Richard had given Sierra On-Line much more authority over the series, than just the right of republishing the first episode of the series.

Meanwhile, the market had radically changed with the appearance of new microcomputers like the Commodore VIC-20. Entering the market in the second half of 1981 at an incredibly low price of $299.95, the VIC-20 had impressive graphics

---

66   Garriott, Richard (2017) Explore/Create, Chapter 3

67   Levy, Steven (2010) Hackers: Heroes of the Computer Revolution, Chapter 19: Applefest

and sound capabilities. The only weakness, its 5Kb of RAM (expandable with add-ons), was negated by the widespread use of cartridge games. Tramiel had finally what he wanted: a cheap product for everyone that managed to conquer the market selling almost 800,000 pieces in 1982 alone, overtaking the Apple II in a single year.

In mid-1982, Ken Williams faced the fragmenting market with the attitude of new opportunities and decided to use the popularity of the Garriott series. Having just bought back the rights from CPCC to release Ultima, Williams decided to take it to Atari's 8-bit platform (also known as Atari 400/800) under the name Ultima I The Original.

At the same time, Keith Zabalaoui showed Williams his first work, a game in which the player had to find his way out of a maze, collecting gems and defeating monsters, programmed for the VIC-20. It wasn't a particularly brilliant game, but still attractive to Sierra as the company had not yet produced anything for this platform.

There are several possible explanations why Ken Williams said yes to Zabalaoui. Maybe trying to please Richard, in anticipation of the games that Garriott would produce in the future and the money to be made. But it could have been simply chaos caused by the wild growth of Sierra, that made Ken throw an inferior product on the market for the promising VIC-20. Unbeknown to all, the North American video game industry was in a crazy race to an invisible chasm.

However, Sierra's CEO did not completely believe in Zabalaoui's product and decided that it needed a good push with a marketing trick. Riding the current success of Ultima Williams bet on tying the game to Garriott's series.

In the first Ultima, one of the points of interest represented on the maps, included in the version republished by Sierra, was Mount Drash on the continent ruled by Lord British, located south of its castle. Williams decided the maze game could be set in the basement of Mt. Drash, linking it to the fame of Ultima.

In terms of gameplay, Ken did not expect any changes. The game was completed and Zabalaoui had to adapt the title, add a credit to Lord British and the copyright of Sierra on the home screen. Apart from that, there was no real connection between his maze game and the RPG series.

But the VIC-20 would not have the deserved future, even after being the champion in 1982. Jack Tramiel unleashed his offensive to all microcomputer manufacturers in 1983 with unprecedented price cuts of his new jewel, the Commodore 64, putting all other products on the market in serious trouble. The VIC-20 suffered a severe blow as well, as its price was now almost equal to that of its much more powerful younger sibling, with less to offer for the price: its meteoric rise was nearing its end.

Appreciating their long friendship and Zabalaoui's help on his previous projects, Garriott agreed that the game should be published under the brand name of Ultima. It's hard to imagine nowadays, such a casual use of a brand. In the pioneering early 1980s, however, Richard didn't have any major problems and generously agreed to this use of his IP. After overcoming the legal obstacle, Williams realized he had a less promising game with a high-flying name produced for a platform in rapid decline. But he had to honor the contract and, also to not offend Richard, he decided to go ahead anyway, but made sure to give the product a limited release.

Ultima: Escape from Mount Drash was published in mid-1983, and although produced in small numbers, sold even less, was advertised only in a couple of newspapers and finally hastily withdrawn from the market. Its sudden disappearance made the game a legend similar to that of the E.T. cartridges buried in the desert. For a long time fans and collectors failed to solve the enigma of its existence and it would be twenty years before a badly worn copy of Mt. Drash emerged from a pile of rubbish in British Columbia.

This mess reduced Richard's faith in the Williams even more. Soon after Ken decided to bring Ultima II onto a new platform, the IBM PC which Garriott considered cumbersome, expensive and underpowered, and therefore uninteresting for video games. Richard was also displeased with the contract terms for this port, but he decided it was still better having his game on another platform. However, Garriott realized that he had had enough and it was time to end the collaboration with Sierra. Unfortunately, he understood too late that with the contract he had signed away creative control over his games to Ken Williams. It would take several years to regain the rights and republish his first three works. In the meantime they would remain in Sierra's hands.

Ken Williams also had his concerns. On one hand he was beginning to be annoyed by the undisciplined behavior of programmers like Duchaineau. His company had grown to become a giant in the video game industry and management wanted to bring organization into the ranks of programmers, turning them into orderly and disciplined employees. On the other hand, the economic state of his company began to deteriorate rapidly because of the sudden and severe crisis that had affected the entire North American video game industry. The firmness with which he faced Garriott and the low royalties imposed for the Ultima II IBM PC port were a direct consequence of Williams' change of course towards his staff and a way to cope with increasing losses of other Sierra On-Line productions.

There was more to it. On the occasion of Sierra's fifteenth anniversary, Ken and Roberta Williams wrote in a short article in Sierra's InterAction magazine dedicated to Ultima with the artwork of Escape from Mt. Drash, covering their version of the story: "Back in the days of Ultima I and II, these games were not the 3/4 overhead view graphics extravaganzas they are today. Instead they were more like 'board game-like' still pieces on a map that scrolled around on screen. They were quite popular (and players seemed to love them), but Ken never really understood the real attraction. For this reason, he probably didn't treat Garriot[sic] as well as he did some other authors, and Garriot[sic] eventually decided to start a company of his own."[68]

---

68   InterAction Magazine - Vol. VII Number 1 - Fall 1994 (1994)(Sierra On-Line) pp. 44

Garriott's version was much simpler: "THEY QUIT PAYING THE ROYA[L] TIES I WAS DUE! My first publisher California Pacific quit paying me because the owner was a major drug user and squandered the money they owed me. Sierra also just up and stopped paying, as they had financial troubles as well. In both cases I brought in my brother Robert to try and collect… never could… so we went into business ourselves, and started Origin!"[69]

When the experience with Sierra was over, Richard needed to start working on his new game, continuing the success of Ultima II. The Sword of Damocles, represented by the agreement with his father, looked more risky as he had no publisher. After two negative experiences, Garriott didn't feel ready to try his luck with a third publisher. Again he turned to his brother Robert for advice.

Robert studied the situation for a long time and concluded that by proceeding with a well-targeted business plan, Richard could attempt self-publication and create his own company. To ensure success, Richard had to churn out a new title within a year, and it had to perform as well as his first three games. If he was too late, or if the game turned out to be a failure, the company would not survive and Richard, to the satisfaction of his father, would return to study.

Listening to the detailed explanations of his son Robert, Owen Garriott agreed that the project sounded reasonable. For him the fad of video games should have passed already, but still continued. Owen said he was in favor of the project and indeed participated in the founding of the company, financing it in part. The largest share belonged to Richard who also had the most money to invest, thanks to his first three games.

The twenty-two-year-old had gone from creating software as an assignment in school, to producing games and now running a video game company with his brother. Richard accepted the challenge and responsibility. If the company would fail, it would go down with most of his savings.

Origin Systems Inc. was founded on March 4, 1983 by the brothers Richard and Robert, their father Owen Garriott and their old friend Chuck Bueche, with an initial investment of $70,000. The name was borrowed from the Origins Game Fair, a yearly exhibition of the table and role-playing games industry since 1975, showcasing the most important news on the market. In a great moment of creativity, Robert chose Origin's motto: "We create worlds". Richard was ecstatic about it. He couldn't have said it better. The company's temporary logo was improvised by Softalk magazine's graphic designers and, although periodically revised, it was never completely abandoned.

Despite its high sounding name, Origin Systems Inc. (OSI) started with a much less impressive headquarter: a small and simple building behind the Garriott residence. The garage his mother had escaped to from Richard's D&D addicted friends

69   Garriott, Richard (2011) interview with Robert Kosarko "Bladed Edge", http://www.hardcoregaming101.net

invading the house. Once again, she had to move her tools to make room for her son.

Having finally the opportunity to work in his own way, Richard was not discouraged by the modest means available: his friend Steve Jackson, for example, had started in a barn. Even technologically, his Apple II plus was outdated. In 1983 the IIe revision came out and the market was crowded with new computers, dominated at that time by the Commodore 64. True to his first microcomputer, Richard continued to develop for Apple II, reserving the right to have some of his collaborators do ports to other platforms.

It was practical thinking as well: Having invested so much time to get proficient with the Apple II and time being a luxury that the newborn OSI could not afford, switching to another platform as main system would have been a costly if not devastating decision. Richard could proceed faster on the Apple II, starting with a repeatedly reworked and optimized code, and then delegate the versions for other platforms. Especially the 6502 based platforms did not require recreating the code.

Richard started with Ultima II's code and tried to remedy previous mistakes. He had given too much attention to improve the game engine resulting in a game with serious design flaws: the dungeons were skip-able, players found many exploits in the hastily created mechanics and overall, the game had been plagued by serious bugs. Knowing that the new installment had to be a success or the company would fail, Richard went on adapting in the code what he was the least convinced of, like the management of life points and statistics.

Meanwhile, Robert had the difficult task of putting order into the company and making it work with the few resources available. His biggest problem was, recently married, he had moved to another state with his wife and had to commute, often taking the plane. His frequent absences did not help his marriage and gave rise to tensions with which, sooner or later, he would have to deal.

Richard and his games were central for the company's fortune, but Garriott wasn't the only one at work. Chuck Bueche was busy with an action game called Caverns of Callisto, of course for the Apple II. Also, Richard had brought with him a couple of trusted people, when leaving Sierra: Jeff Hillhouse, who moved into a cot in the loft of the garage, i.e. the headquarters of OSI, and Mary Fenton who had taken care of customer care at Sierra. In addition, Richard had called together his old friends and people he had previously relied on. So it was that Ken Arnold and Keith Zabalaoui, while not joining the company's staff, helped Garriott.

Steve Jackson decided to give his friends formation a media coverage, writing a short extract in issue 63 of Space Gamer: "Richard Garriott, aka Lord British, who has been designing computer games for several years, has formed a new software company with five other designers. Origins Systems Inc. will publish arcade and role-playing software and eventually will expand into business and educational software markets. The first releases will include Exodus, third in the Ultima series of computer role-playing adventures. Garriott and partners Chuck Bueche, Keith Zabalaoui, Ken Arnold, and John Kennedy, are seeking freelance programmers for software game design."

It's unclear who had the idea to add the last sentence or who decided to publish an entire ad announcing that Origin Systems Inc. was looking for new staff, but the message was replicated in Softalk in May 1983, with a challenging full-page color ad and the company's logo:[70] "Origin Systems presents a new dimension. Software without equal. The ultimate in design, execution, and value. Taking your machine where you want to go. We invite you to join us. 19202 Back Bay Court, Houston, Texas 77058, (713) 333-4716"

Garriott: "This (was) the actual first advertisement for Origin Systems, before we even had a logo! Softalk magazine made it for us, to announce our existence. Address was our parents home in Houston, Texas."

Shortly after these announcements were published, a certain David Shapiro, a.k.a. Dr. Cat,[71] showed up at Richard's garage with high expectations: "There was an issue that had a full page advertisement, taken out by Origin, that said 'Our new game company exists and we're going to be making Ultima and other cool games and here we are'. There was no product for sale yet, they were just announcing the company. They mentioned at the bottom they were looking for programmers, game designers, artists, writers, etc. (I forget the exact list), which was a little surprising to me at the time, since games were made pretty much entirely by programmers at that time."

Dr. Cat called and spoke to Richard's brother. The two agreed to meet, so he took a plane and Robert went to pick him up at the airport. It was August 1983 and Hurricane Alicia had hit Texas hard, killing more than twenty people and also devastating the town of Austin: "I arrived right after a hurricane had hit the area, so most businesses had their signs blown down, and it was trickier to find things until those got replaced."

The arrival of Dr. Cat was a surprise for Richard, who had not been informed by his brother about the previous phone call. Unfortunately for the candidate, despite the advertisements and newspaper articles, the company was not yet ready to hire other collaborators. Although Dr. Cat's preparation and great skills did not escape Richard, Robert informed his brother that the company was unable to hire him and would not be able to do so for a long time to come. However, this fact, was not

---

70   OSI's first advertising logo consisted of a compass on a sky-blue background, superimposed on the letter O of Origin, written with a font reminiscent of the LCD displays of calculators

71   Although his legal name is David Shapiro, he has long since affixed his nickname to all of his work, and even to his driving license. Dr. Cat: "The name Dr. Cat comes from my first two online handles, from when I got my first modem in 1980. I used the names of two favorite characters, Dr. Who (Tom Baker rules!) and Samurai Cat. One day I shoved them together to make a name that was uniquely my own."

explained as clearly to Dr. Cat who continued to stay, first as a guest of the Garriotts and then in a hotel, waiting for a response to his candidacy: "I waited for Origin to tell me what to do, and they waited for me to just start doing something. And then I ran out of money and got my mom to help me pay for a plane ticket back to Indiana. As he was driving me back to the airport Robert said to me 'I tried to hint to you on the phone that we weren't ready for you yet.' And I thought silently to myself, this is business, not like teenagers dating or something. Isn't the correct approach 'tell' rather than 'hint'?"

Under pressure for success and a hard time limit, Richard worked at a fast pace and by August 23, 1983, a few months after the creation of OSI, Ultima III: Exodus was ready. The first order would have been enough on its own to repay the investment and the time spent. The problem was that, as a software house and publisher, OSI had to do everything by itself and the staff consisted only of a handful of programmers, two all-rounder employees and Robert.

The programmers had to suspend their work and start printing, packing the boxes and copying the 5 1/4" floppies. In each box they placed a copy of The Book of Play, The Ancient Liturgy of Truth, the cleric's guide containing also information about the setting of the game in the form of an ancient prophecy and The Book of Amber Runes, containing the magician's arcane spells. Completing it with a cloth map of the world of Sosaria and the advertising for Secrets of Sosaria, the clue book.

It was a very rich package, with many pamphlets of more than ten pages each, in addition to the fabric map. Free from creative constraints, Richard applied the lesson from Wizardry, caring about the package content, and from Infocom, offering clue books.[72] That's what other publishers, apart from Sierra On-Line, were not willing to do.

Now he had to find out if it was worth it.

---

72   The first book of Ultima's solutions, Secret of Sosaria, was written by Robert Garriott himself under the pseudonym of Lord Robert, master of scribes, and was sold for $12.95. It contained 48 pages of information and suggestions provided not in a very direct form, but through the words of scribes and other characters from the world of Ultima. Curiously simple, the manual was equipped with maps drawn with alphanumeric characters and the only artwork present were graphic decorations around the text and corners. The editing was done by Mary Fenton, accredited as Scribe Fenton.

Ultima III: Exodus

"I was caught up in the rapid expansion of my skills… Ultima I in BASIC, Ultima II in assembly, Ultima III in far better assembly… I knew I could get much more out of the little machine, with each fresh restart."

Richard Garriott, interview with Robert Kosarko "Bladed Edge", 2011

"The title, Exodus, is a nice irony, considering that Lord British aka Richard Garriott left Sierra to found his own company, Origin, during the game's development."

Bogdan Ion Purcaru, Games vs. Hardware.
The History of PC video games: The 80's

Ultima II proved to be very similar to its predecessor with the exception of the engine written entirely in Assembly, which released additional resources used for a bigger game world. The experiment was successful in the sense that the players could finally enjoy a fast game, a feature that was painfully missed, particularly in the dungeons.

Switching from random to hand-crafted maps raised the player's expectations of the game world. All of these elements were carefully contrived by a designer as the map had to be consistent and without flaws. "We create worlds", said Origin's motto, and now Richard was living up to it.

After the events described in Ultima and Ultima II: The Revenge of the Enchantress, evil seemed defeated, unfortunately before perishing, Mondain and Minax had generated their own offspring, just as evil and even more powerful. Exodus was terrorizing Sosaria with his hordes of bloodthirsty and destructive monsters from his fortress on Fire Island. Once again, the Stranger from another world was called upon to defeat the new enemy.

As before, Richard chose the name "Exodus" for the new opponent purely out of fascination; and without knowing the real meaning of the word.

Loubet's artwork (which initially should have been done by Richard's mother) on the box presented Exodus as similar to a demon or diabolical being. This choice would create a series of headaches for Richard's company with accusations of satanism and corruption of young gamers, all of which were inconsistent with the true nature of the game's arch-enemy. Exodus was neither human nor demonic, but something very similar to an intelligent super computer with its own will.

To defeat Exodus, the player first had to understand its weak points, exploring the cities of Sosaria and collecting information from its inhabitants. Once this was done, the Stranger could leave for the actual mission, which was to recover three tools that were indispensable for the final fight: four marks found in the lowest and most dangerous levels of the dungeons, exotic arms, which were on two islands, and four arcane objects known as cards, placed in the sanctuaries of the continent of Ambrosia (although the correct translation would rather be Perforated Cards, very similar to the early computer storage systems Richard had worked with in school, and which would therefore qualify Exodus as a vintage computer).

Equipped with these objects, the Stranger was ready to travel to Fire Island, fighting Exodus' hordes of creatures, surviving continuous explosions in the fortress and, finally, facing Exodus in a showdown. The last challenge was to insert the punch cards in the correct order, as previously indicated by the Time Lord. Failure to do so led to player's death and the end of the adventure.

Garriott had finally created a well-balanced system in which the four main activities of the game (exploration, visiting cities to talk to the NPCs, descending into the dungeons and combat) finally came together. None of the Exodus maps were as empty as some of the planets of Ultima II and the dungeons, negligible in the previous adventure, were again indispensable in order to defeat the ultimate enemy.

The result was a better designed and much more interesting and complex game than the previous title. Where Ultima II was "more of the same", Exodus was a clear step forward, while not departing much from the established game model — the engine was basically the same, although very enhanced and retouched.

One of the biggest innovations was the introduction of the party system.

Its predecessors were role-playing games in which the player could only control a single character, while other popular titles of the period (the Wizardry series or Dungeon for PLATO) were focused on managing a group of adventurers.

XP until now only influenced the amount of spawning monsters and classes had no influence beside changing stats, except for Ultima II with its spell systems for magicians and clerics.

With Ultima III Garriott completed the greatest transformation to date, implementing an XP and leveling system more similar to that of D&D and a party system controlling a group of four heroes. Life points started at 100 and were raised by 100 on every level (gaining one every 1000 XP) up to a maximum of

2550. Lord British's donations were also linked to level increases and therefore required the player to adventure and collect XP.

The HP limit avoided the problem of deadly roll over and the new feature system, which tied the maximum value achievable to the character's race, solved the problem of statistics roll over. Statistics were reduced from 6 to 4 with Strength and Dexterity affecting the outcome of fights and Intelligence and Wisdom used for spells and magic points (MPs) .

Players could compose their party freely by choosing from 4 classes, two of them spell casters (magicians and clerics).

In addition, Richard implemented another level of hero customization called Professions. This added further limits and character specializations, since each profession affected a character's equipment, ability to steal or disarm traps, and available magic points. The division of spells between wizards and clerics, moreover, was completed with a distinct set of spells.

Although a big step closer to games like Wizardry, for Exodus Richard maintained many features known from earlier Ultimas. In particular, the need for food and the different representations of overworld maps and dungeons, the latter enhanced by using solid color planes instead of wireframe graphics.

The combat system was completely revolutionized, having to take into account a party. On the surface map and in dungeons the party moved like a single character, switching to a special combat screen when meeting enemies (in the dungeon the prior visible enemies were replaced with random encounters similar to the Wizardry system). The combat screen was a tactical view showing each party member and enemy, using a turn-based system. With each turn, players chose whether their character would attack, cast a spell or move a square.

The Wizardry series had the party system from the first installment on, but in combat mode the party was simply split into a front line (for melee fighters) and a rearguard (support characters with range weapons or magic skills). These concepts were copied by many other games in the following years.

On the contrary, in Ultima III, the player had to take into account a further element: tactical movement on a small map and trying to maintain a defensive front line that would prevent enemies from breaking through and attacking the more vulnerable members of a party.

Garriott's system was innovative, but not flawless. Enemies were guided by a simple algorithm and ended up moving in a straight line to the nearest player character and were therefore were easy targets for long range weapons. To counterbalance the lack of a sophisticated AI, Garriott decided to give the monsters the ability to attack diagonally, which is impossible for player-led party members.

In Exodus, compared to previous games with parties like Wizardry, the player did not choose the actions of their characters in advance as these were executed simultaneously along with those of the enemies. Instead, the player picked the action for a character and saw the outcome immediately.

Another flaw in Richard's combat system was that battles took longer; causing repercussions on the pace of play. More complex clashes benefited from the turn-based system, but the numerous random encounters with weak enemies were cumbersome. The same could be said of character creation at the beginning: the player had to first create all four members of the party, save them, select them from the group of heroes with whom he or she intended to play, before finally starting the game.

In the clashes, experience was attributed only to the character who executed the final deadly blow. Supporting heroes, such as clerics or thieves, had to be used offensively (at least launching the fatal attack) in order to gain experience points.

In fact, via the professions the game system of Exodus favored hybrid characters that were able to use powerful weapons and armor, as well as cast some spells. In Ultima II death led to resurrection at the starting point near Lord British's castle. In Exodus the death of all party members ended the game, while single characters could be resurrected.

As Lord British no longer demanded gifts from the player, it was advisable to create a party maximizing the number of characters capable of healing and, in the advanced stages of the game, to perform the resurrection spell Dag Mentar.

Ultima III: Exodus became an unexpected success: the first 100,000 copies printed in August 1983 were followed by more orders. The ranking of the retailer Softline saw Exodus in third place on Apple's platform in 1984, but the overall result was even more encouraging since OSI published Exodus at the same time for the Atari 800, Commodore 64 and IBM PC.

Given Richard's passion and the choice to develop on the Apple II, the most accurate version was certainly the one for Cupertino's computers. To make Exodus even more enjoyable, he decided to equip his new game with sound effects and music.

The Apple II was only stocked with an internal loudspeaker operated by a clicker. Just as Silas Warner had managed to get such a poorly equipped system to produce speech, many other programmers soon managed the complex task of producing music. Ultima II had also used the basic Apple II speaker to create simple sound effects, but OSI had a bigger surprise for Exodus.

Since his early youth, Wozniak stood out for his hacker personality. The anecdotes about his Blue Box, a device built and marketed together with Jobs and used to confuse telecommunications companies' switchboards to make free phone calls, explain his attitude to electronics as tools for a tinkerer. His Apple II was created as an open and expandable machine, able to benefit from technology that in 1977 was not yet available in the form of expansion cards.[73]

For example, the Language card was an expansion that allowed Apple II owners to program in Pascal and also increased RAM by a further 16K. In

---

73   All this would change later, when Jobs' position would prevail over Wozniak's open hacker attitude.

1980, Microsoft produced its first hardware component: the Microsoft Z-80 SoftCard. Equipped with a Zilog Z-80 chip, it enabled Wozniak's microcomputer to run the CP/M operating system, at the time the most popular OS, while MS-DOS was yet to be released a year later.

One of the most interesting expansion boards was the Sweet Micro Systems Mockingboard. It gave the Apple II good sound capabilities but was slightly inferior to the excellent SID of the Commodore 64. Depending on the version, the Mockingboard was equipped with one or two General Instruments AY-3-8910 chips, with which it could generate up to six audio channels, and a chip dedicated to the reproduction of the human voice. A big strength was that the audio chips could work independently without the Apple II CPU reserving too many resources to control them.

Introduced in 1981, it was not yet widespread in 1983. Kenneth Arnold came across one of these just before Richard started programming Exodus and proposed using it to give the new Garriott game a musical feature that previous installments lacked — as well as almost all Apple II games.

Arnold: "When I approached Richard with the idea of adding a Soundtrack to Ultima III, he was excited. I described how different phases of the game could have different tunes to set the mood, adding that some tunes could be special effects to indicate specific achievements. He loved the idea. I told him there was a lot of Renaissance music available that would fit his game, and that it was royalty-free. But he said, 'Oh, no. I want an original score!' And so began my mini-career as a game music composer."

Kenneth had always been a music lover as well as a computer enthusiast: "At age 14 I was frequenting the local music stores to play with the music synthesizers. I played the Minimoog, ARP Oddysey, and ARP 2600 synths until the shopkeepers threw me out. At 15 I had raised enough money flipping hamburgers to purchase my own synthesizer in kit form… an Aries."

Using the Mockingboard to make music on the Apple II was no easy task. There were several technical obstacles to overcome, the first of which was the fact that when Wozniak designed his most famous microcomputer, he had not imagined the usefulness of a hardware clock for timer interrupts. This would be a show-stopper for preemptive multitasking[74] and a big issue to play music synchronized. In addition, there was no free space left in the memory of the Apple II to load the data needed for the music.

Arnold had to find solutions to all of these problems. For the memory, he used the Language Card and a trick that allowed him to exploit an additional 4K that normally remained unused. As for the timing of the notes, James VanArtsdalen came to his rescue, the friend with whom he had prepared the demonstration for the Computer Lovers' Club and who now worked with Origin.

---

74   That is, interrupt a process, move it from the CPU and start to carry out a second one without cooperation from the first process

The Mockingboard had a timer that could be used to interrupt the CPU, if properly programmed. The problem was that it ended up corrupting the Disk Operating System.[75] VanArtsdalen was able to find a way to modify the DOS and prevent it from crashing, allowing the Mockingboard to interrupt the CPU and play the notes at the right time.

Arnold: "We still had the problem of inter-process communication… a way for the game to signal the music system what tune to play. I came up with a simple and foolproof method. When the game wanted to switch the tune, it simply wrote a song selection value (0 to 15, with 0 meaning silent) to a specific location in memory. The music system polled the song value during the ISR. If it had changed, the music system stopped the current song, started the new song, and reported the new selection in another location which the game could poll. This proved to be a good and stable solution."

After Arnold finally solved all the complex issues with interrupts, lack of a clock, lack of memory and even fighting with the OS, there was still the issue of creating the actual music. Not having any expertise in the field, Garriott gave Arnold carte blanche, but he wanted an original soundtrack. Arnold: "In Ultima III I chose the British National Anthem as Lord British's theme, and it always appeared in a minor key when he was absent or imprisoned. It was fairly easy to come up with themes for Ultima III, because I could write anything. But for Ultima's IV and V I had to remain truthful to the original series. There were a number of tunes I wrote which Richard rejected, but he became more cooperative as deadlines approached =). (Actually, it was Robert who often said 'Good enough!' Richard and I could have polished forever.)".

The result were seven compositions (Wanderer, Towne, Castle, Dungeon, Combat, Shopping and Exodus' Castle - The Isle of Fire) that were loaded and played in a contextual way to the game situation: Wanderer in the introduction and exploration of the overworld, Towne and Castle when the action moved to the cities or castle of Lord British, Combat during the battles and so on.

Arnold: "I often dedicated them to friends and relatives. Lady Nan refers to my wife (at the time), and Jo refers to my daughter Joanna. I chose duple meter for walking around music (left-right-left-right), triple meter for courtly tunes (ala Minuets), hextuple meter for at least one of the battle tunes (jarring effect), etc."

Despite the low impact on the public — there were very few users in possession

---

75   The technical problem was definitely not trivial and came from the Apple II being designed to use cheap magnetic tape drives. Only later did Wozniak create the Disk II and write a special Disk Operating System for it. Arnold: "When Apple started selling floppy disk drives, it provided a Disk Operating System (DOS). It seems the developers of the DOS were unaware that the Interrupt Service Routine (ISR) in the ROM would store data in certain areas of memory whenever an interrupt request was made. DOS variables were located in the same area, causing catastrophic results when interrupts occurred."

of an Apple II with the expensive Language Card and the Mockingboard installed simultaneously — it would be repeated in all subsequent games with an increasingly expanding soundtrack. In 1983 it was quite common that a video game had accompanying music, for microcomputers like the Commodore 64, which being equipped with the powerful SID chip. But Ken Arnold had gone further, creating a high quality soundtrack adapting to the game situation, solemn in the presence of Lord British, more animated in a combat.

Ultima III: Exodus was released simultaneously for three different platforms, in addition to the Apple II. As Sierra On-Line had done with Ultima II, OSI immediately marketed a version for the Atari 800, a very popular platform in North America. Since the basic Atari 800 was equipped with quite advanced sound capabilities, the soundtrack was included without the need for expansions and the game reproduced faithfully, thanks to the fact that the computer was based on the MOS 6502.

The Commodore 64 version could rely on the SID and came with the complete soundtrack. Again, due to the fact that the Commodore 64 was based on the MOS 6510, the evolution of the 6502, the porting was done by Chuck Bueche without modifications, except for the black and white dungeons.

Much less ambitious was the IBM PC port. In 1983 Garriott was right to consider IBM's new machine as uninteresting for games. Released just two years ago, the IBM PC was equipped with an internal speaker only slightly more advanced compared to the 6 years old Apple II. Early games used it for sound effects and music, but Arnold's complex soundtrack was beyond the speaker's limited capabilities. More capable sound devices (PCjr, Tandy) would be available in 1984 and dedicated PC sound cards wouldn't come on the market until 1987.

Despite its young age, the IBM PC was unimpressive in the graphics department as it was created to serve as a business machine. The CGA (Color Graphics Adapter) graphics system, the standard created in 1981 at the launch of the PC only supported resolutions of 320×200 with 4 colors from a palette of 16 or, in high resolution mode, 640×200 monochrome. This would change the following year with the introduction of the EGA standard but in 1983, the IBM PC was still unattractive for video games.

Consequently, the PC version offered simple graphics and no soundtrack but had a high number of bugs, some of which were very serious. Additionally the IBM PC (or its clones) would over time get faster CPUs and many games would run too fast and become unplayable.

The Age of Enlightenment

THROUGH THE MOONGATE

1983

"Atari was stuck with enormous inventories of worthless game cartridges. With no hope of selling them, Atari dumped millions of cartridges in a landfill in the New Mexico desert. When reports came out that people had discovered the landfill, Atari sent steamrollers to crush the cartridges, then poured cement over the rubble. By the end of 1983, Atari had racked up $536 million in losses. Warner Communications sold the company the following year."

Kent L. Steven, The Ultimate History of Video Games

Leaving Sierra On-Line, with his third consecutive success Richard could easily have found a publisher. His fame and the strength of the Ultima brand would have allowed him to dictate his conditions or even find a company willing to give him carte blanche. Garriott decided that he would no longer put himself in the hands of those who, according to him, were incompetent actors in an industry they did not understand. People like Al Remmers or Ken Williams with their corporate and entrepreneurial logic would no longer have his trust.

Richard, however, was willing to entrust his brother Robert with his savings and career. The beginning of 1983 seemed the right time to create a video game company as the market was still growing every year.

There had been slow downs. After the initial boom caused by Pong, the market declined in 1977, once saturated with clones of the arcade game. This changed immediately with the release of Space Invaders the following year and hysteria reached unprecedented levels. According to a well-known urban legend, in Japan 100-yen coins became rare because they were commonly used in the coin-ops ("coin operated machines"). Even if it was just a rumor, it was a good indication of the spreading arcade fever. Many famous arcade games continued to feed into this craze: Asteroids and Galaxian in 1979, Missile Command and Pac-Man in 1980, Donkey Kong in 1981 and Ms. Pac-Man in 1982...

The video game trend continued in North American, Japanese and European homes in the form of the second generation of consoles using cartridges, that were therefore capable of running various games unlike the first generation. On the wave of Atari's success, many American and Japanese companies tried to get their share of the video game market. Coleco (Connecticut Leather Company), for example, started its activity in the '30s with leather goods, then moved on to pinball machines. They entered the video game industry in 1976 with their Pong clone, the Coleco Telstar, and followed it with the ColecoVision in 1982, which used cartridges. On the other side of the Pacific Ocean, the first activity of NAMCO (Nakamura Manufacturing Company) had been a coin-operated merry-go-round for children, while Nintendo was producing playing cards and tried other activities, such as taxis, with little success, before landing in the world of toys and finally gaining traction in the gaming market with an arcade smash hit (Donkey Kong) and portable consoles (Game & Watch).

Until 1982, the video game market seemed like a new, unexplored and wild enterprise, offering rewards to anyone who entered it. Atari was literally born out of nothing and didn't need much capital to become a global giant, while many other companies found success simply by copying the competition.

The hysteria surrounding video games turned into a euphoria; with many sharing the belief that the market was able to absorb any product, regardless of quality. Profit was only limited by how many games or consoles a company would be able to produce and market.

Atari's founder, Nolan Bushnell, had led his company in a disorderly way, making amateur mistakes when, for example, he transformed a great success like Gran Trak 10 (1974), one of the first racing arcades, into a financial disaster because of a trivial accounting error: he sold the cabinets for 100 dollars less than the cost of production. But Bushnell, who had literally created the video game market from scratch, demonstrated extraordinary levels of intuition and creativity, along with an understanding of what the public wanted.

After selling Atari to entertainment giant Warner, Bushnell was replaced by Ray Kassar, an established and capable manager, who turned Bushnell's company into a finely-honed machine. What Kassar lacked however, was Bushnell's intuition and ability to understand the market. Having made his career in a textile company, Kassar considered games as a product like all others and programmers as workers, and lacked a critical understanding of the role creativity played in designing successful games.

Atari, like many other American companies such as Mattel, Coleco and Milton Bradley, got carried away by unfounded optimism. Kassar's skills and experience were not very helpful when at the end of 1982, the bubble was ready to burst and the resulting crash in 1983 would take many victims; annihilating many of the main competitors within the North American video game industry.

During the months Richard and Robert were planning the foundations of Origin Systems Inc., unbeknownst to either, the first signs of the crisis were manifesting. Video game stores were literally flooded with products and the market was getting saturated. In 1982 alone, five home consoles had been released: the Atari 5200, the Coleco Gemini (a 5200 clone), Emerson's Arcadia 2001, the ColecoVision and the Vectrex.

When the market was no longer able to absorb such large volumes, retailers encountering difficulty due to a high amount of unsold products, began asking for more lenient return policies. Some companies absorbed the costs and spiraled downwards into crisis while others refused to accept returns. Consequently, retailers began cutting prices to empty the shelves.

To make matters worse, Jack Tramiel had started a price war in order to crush the competition and conquer the microcomputer market. Holding an unrivaled product, the Commodore 64, he made repeated cuts in the price of his microcomputer which threw his old rival, Texas Instruments, out of the market and also put many other manufacturers in serious trouble. Incidentally, Tramiel also left his first commercial success behind, the VIC-20, on the eve of Zabalaoui's launch of Ultima: Escape from Mt. Drash.

William Shatner, otherwise known as Star Trek Commander Kirk, asked the audience in one of Commodore's most aggressive advertisements "Why buy a video game when you can have a computer?". As the price gap between the Commodore 64 and the consoles narrowed down, many consumers took Tramiel's bait and opted for the Commodore 64 that in addition to having quality games in unprecedented quantity, could also be used for other purposes.

Towards the middle of 1983, the signs of the coming crisis were clear and when the disappointing earnings of Atari was shared with investors, the industry bubble had finally burst. Atari's shares collapsed within a few months and the company had to be restructured several times with painful cuts. After the crisis, Atari would never regain the leading role and acclaim it once had. Coleco, Mattel and Milton Bradley paid a higher price and left the market definitively, selling everything to cut their losses. The era of American dominance over the console market came to an end.

Commodore suffered a collapse of their shares as well. The price cuts had won the battle, but reduced profits weakened Tramiel's position as CEO. Even software companies such as Activision faced serious difficulties when a large part of their market evaporated; despite having earned a reputation for excellent, innovative and well-programmed games.

Even Ken Williams had fallen for the craze and listened to the advice of his investors, he had recruited a large group of programmers and started as many projects as possible, not all of which had the quality of those of his wife. The overheated market of 1982 had dazzled him and convinced him to invest into growth.

Cartridges were widespread in the early 1980s because it was more impervious to piracy than software distributed on magnetic tape or floppy disks. On the other hand, cartridges were a big investment and unsold inventory was a big loss for any software house. Ken, always attentive to the problem of piracy that drove him to adopt Spiradisk for Sierra On-Line games, chose to produce software on cartridges, but he had to make very substantial orders. Contributing to their demise were wrong choices, such as betting on Texas Instruments' microcomputer on the eve of the price war sparked by Tramiel. The Commodore 64 triumphed over the TI 99/4A, forcing Texas Instruments out of the market before financial losses overwhelmed it and Ken found himself with an inventory full of cartridges and audio cassettes for machines no longer on the market or in crisis, such as the VIC-20.

As sales began to slow down, Sierra On-Line had to lay off a good part of their staff, relying only on Roberta's games as their hope to survive the crisis. Salvation came in the form of the contract signed with IBM, which took shape in a new masterpiece by Roberta Williams: King's Quest for PCjr.

Companies that focused mainly on microcomputers did a little better that year, such as Automated Simulations, which repositioned themselves with a new name: Epyx. In 1983, under the new leadership of Michael V. Katz (former vice president of marketing for Coleco Industries and future president of SEGA of America during the first year since the launch of SEGA Genesis), Epyx shifted its focus from role-playing and strategy games to action games, becoming one of the most popular companies in North America with games like Summer Games, Mission Impossible, California Games and Barbarian, as well as a less famous game, but one that we'll hear about later, G.I. Joe: A Real American Hero.

Unaware of the risk, OSI was founded in March 1983, at the dawn of the looming crash. Based mainly on his Ultima series, Richard needed time to grow and expanding the business with more games. The target platforms were microcomputers, based on the teams capabilities and it was a better fit for CRPGs than consoles, which commonly offered a variety of action games and arcade ports. There were very few titles on consoles somehow related to the genre of role-playing games with notable exceptions, such as Warren Robinett's Adventure for Atari 2600 (1980), a hybrid of adventure, maze and dungeon crawling.

This platform choice saved Garriott from the worst consequences of 1983, but still left a bad feeling that the craze around computer games was finally over. The North American industry had been decimated and many retailers were strongly determined to avoid meddling in consoles and cartridges again.

This was the environment Garriott had to survive with his new company after Ultima III's great success, knowing that for the near future the fate of the company would be resting on his shoulders.

Changes

"I had already done three hack-and-slash kind of games and quite frankly, I was bored with that. I wanted to do something with more lasting meaning to it."

Richard Garriott, interview with J.C. Herz, Joystick Nation (1997)

"So I'd see these letters that called the game a satanic perverter of America's youth. Suddenly I realized how much people were reading into these really simple games that I'd never intended to have within them."

Richard Garriott, interview with Computer Games Online, 1999

"Speaking of Ultimas, Lord British was concerned enough about the criticism which the fantasy role-playing genre receives to invest thought on what the game itself does to the players. He did not want to be guilty of designing a game which implied that violence was the answer to all or even many of life's problems. That is why he, along with Roe Adams, developed the eight virtues to be measured in Ultima IV."

Wyatt Lee, A foreshadowing of fantasy jewels in a duel arcane:
Ultima V and Wizardry IV, Computer Gaming World, 1987

With the publication and marketing of the first game, Origin's small team could momentarily catch their breath. Preparation of the 100,000 copies of Ultima III had put a strain on its programmers and employees, while its newest preoccupation was to respond to customers who turned to OSI for technical support, help solving the game, replacing defective floppies and reporting their triumph over Exodus; as requested at the end of the game by Lord British himself.

Unhappy that he had never received feedback from CPCC and Sierra On-Line, Richard had decided to include an invitation to contact him in OSI's offices: "CONGRATULATIONS! THOU HAST COMPLEATED EXODUS: ULTIMA 3 IN XXXX MOVES REPORT THY FEAT!" To players who did report this feat, Garriott sent a special certificate signed by Lord British.

Many users also felt the need to contact Origin to recount their experience and give advice or positive feedback about the game, a great pleasure for Richard. To a lesser extent, Richard did not derive pleasure in reading letters from some players bragging about having found a way to kill Lord British. Garriott had not been too concerned with protecting his virtual alter ego in the first two installments, giving him extremely high characteristics and many life points. This didn't stop particularly determined players from maximizing the stats of their characters and taking on the challenge of killing the ruler of Sosaria. In Ultima III, Garriott did everything to make his alter ego invulnerable. Unfortunately for him, some users discovered that Lord British was unaffected by weapons but not by naval cannons. Entering combat with him and luring him out of the castle, until within reach of the naval weapons and then perish rather ingloriously, taken by cannon. For me as an Italian an amusing parallel to 'Giovanni dalle Bande Nere'[76] (or Lodovico de Medici), a famous Italian condottiero (mercenary military leader) in the early 16th century, who fought against 12,000 infantrymen with his 400 knights. They were so heavily armored, virtually 'invulnerable' to arquebuses (the state-of-the-art firearm of its time), that a clever ploy was needed: The enemy lured his troops into an ambush and fired at them with falconets (small 2" cannons), mortally injuring Giovanni.

With Lord British's first documented death at the hands of a player, Richard had to reckon with the fact that once the player was given a certain amount of freedom of action, the game had escaped beyond his control. The problem would arise again in the future with even more frustrating consequences for the game designer.

Meanwhile Chuck Bueche's Caverns of Callisto achieved modest sales and made it evident that the entire financial success of the company still depended on Richard. Garriott estimated he had no more than two years to produce another chapter that had to sell at least as well as Ultima III. This lack of profits also limited OSI's potential to grow.

Not that Richard had to cope with big sacrifices: with his Mitsubishi sports car, Garriott was doing much better than his old acquaintances in Austin. In one of his numerous visits to SJG headquarters, the re-purposed barn, Richard met for the first time a young man named Warren Spector, recently hired as editor of Space Gamer magazine. Spector: "I looked out the window of my office and saw a black Mitsubishi pull into the gravel driveway at Steve Jackson Games in a cloud of dust. My first thought was, 'Wow, none of us can afford a fancy car like that!' Then I remem-

---

76   His unit was called the 'Black Band' (Banda Nera) after adding black stripes to their insignia showing sorrow for his deceased uncle, Pope Leo X, whom he served at the time

ber Richard walking in the office in his full all-black regalia, bling and braid. And I do remember thinking Richard personified what I thought success looked like."

The separation of Robert Garriott from his wife took a toll on the marriage. Therefore in the second half of 1983, trying to convince Richard to move the company to New England, Robert proposed a deal to his brother: move OSI to Massachusetts for three years, the time needed for his wife Mary to get a promotion and with it, the possibility to move back to Austin with the whole group.

Every time Richard had moved away from Austin, he struggled getting used to new environments, but this time was different. Richard could take his most trusted friends with him. Robert, after all, could no longer ask his wife to be patient while he spent three weeks a month in Austin, thousands of miles away.

When the decision was finally made, it was November.

Each one of the seven OSI staff members drove a vehicle. With five cars and a pair of rented moving trucks to transport the bulkiest material, the caravan set off. No one had considered that the New England winter would be harsher than the one in Texas. Soon the roads turned into icy, snowy avenues and rear-wheel-drive cars such as Richard's Mitsubishi, proved unsuitable for the extreme weather conditions.

Nevertheless, the company arrived at its destination and took its place in a large two-story house beside a forest. Compared to their 'garage' in Austin, the new OSI headquarters was a respectable step forward and Richard decided to celebrate by spending $10,000 on new electronic equipment, stereos and televisions. Being far from home and parents while running a small but promising company with his brother Robert, Richard wanted to give everyone an encouraging signal. Unfortunately, before the group could unpack, a band of thieves broke into the house and took everything of value. Richard filed a complaint, received a refund from the insurance company, and replaced what was stolen. Ironically, the thieves decided to give it another try and cleaned out the place again.

In fact, the problems had just begun.

It was at this point that the feedback on Exodus arrived and Richard learned about the controversy his game had ignited. Some interpreted Loubet's art work as a demonic image and certain associations, already fighting since a long time against D&D, had expanded their list of targets to include Garriott's latest creation.

Taking into account the personal experiences of players and the controversy, in addition to the killing of his alter ego Lord British, Richard began to rethink how to evolve the game. Until then, the game mechanics not only allowed players to save the world by acting like bandits and psychopathic killers, but made crime the most convenient way to finish the game. Garriott wasn't the best Dungeon Master in the company, but he understood something was profoundly wrong with a role-playing game where the goal was to save the world from evil by committing malicious acts against the same population that the player was aiming to save.

Garriott admits "The early Ultimas and all of my competitors have what I call standard fantasy role-playing scenario number one, where you're the great hero, and your job is to kill the big bad guy, and what you end up doing is you travel around the world pillaging and plundering, beg-borrow-and-stealing, and doing everything you can until you build up enough magic and power to assault this supposed bad guy, who never did anything to anybody in the game, and you wipe him out and you win. And I thought, there's not much meaning to that."[77]

Richard was starting to change his mind about how to design his games, when a chance encounter changed the history of computer role-playing games forever.

When Roe Adams III obtained his Bachelor's degree in Applied Mathematics from Brown University in Providence, he had no idea how much life would take him away from what he had studied. Worldly, and possessing excellent writing, inventiveness, creativity and intuition, Adams was an experienced board game player, especially at D&D. His favorite character, born on paper in a role-playing session, was Hawkwind. He was also fascinated by Japan and anime, as well as Skara Brae, a Neolithic village brought to light a hundred years earlier by a violent storm.

Passionate about video games, Adams began a career as writer and journalist in 1981 for Softalk, and authored analysis of the nascent video game industry, as well as reviews, comments, and reporting on market trends. He wasn't a prolific writer, but his articles were very interesting and sometimes showed extraordinary insight, like in the September/October 1985 issue of Computer Gaming World, he dedicated his column to the boom in computer role-playing games in Japan and how the local industry had been influenced by Wizardry and Ultima.

Being an avid text adventurer, he didn't skip the ones written by Roberta Williams and played them with determination. During Christmas of 1982, Sierra On-Line had published Time Zone, an adventure so big that it was advertised as "twelve times" greater than Wizard and the Princess. Despite the very high price ($99, $243 today), Roe Adams III bought it and after playing it day and night for a week, defeated Ramadu and named Williams' work as one of the most beautiful games ever. Despite this, the sales were actually quite disappointing.

His continuous contacts with software companies led Adams in 1983 to start a career in the video game industry; OSI itself was the first company to enlist him to write Exodus' Book of Play. The following year, Adams started a collaboration with Greenberg and Woodhead for the Wizardry manual, which sold well thanks to the continuous expansions for the game. This collaboration would prove to be particularly important and fruitful, both for the evolution of the series of Wizar-

---

77   Herz, J.C. (1997) Joystick Nation

dry[78] (the fourth scenario The Return of Werdna saw a radical change in design) and for the distribution of anime in the United States (Adams and Woodhead ended up founding AnimEigo).[79]

The move of OSI and Garriott to New Hampshire made cooperation with Adams much easier. Adams must have liked the experience a lot because he was actively involved in the development of a new Ultima, but not only through writing the documentation. At the same time he began working on other collaborations, including a CRPG for Interplay Productions that a programmer named Michael Cranford was developing mainly by himself, titled Tales of the Unknown: Volume I.

The proximity not only enabled Adams to actively participate in the creation of Ultima IV, but allowed Richard to introduce him to the SCA. The writer took part with increasing momentum in the activities of the Society, to the point of obtaining recognition as a Grand Master of Arc in the registers of the Kingdom of the East on December 1st, 1987. Given his interest in writing, archery, and history, Adams did use the opportunity to lend his pen to the SCA. In addition to becoming Chronicler of the Kingdom of the East 1986 to 1987 (together with Nan Neillillian of Skara Brae), he personally edited volume 37 of the series The Compleat Anachronist, dedicated to the long bow and published in 1988.

Together with Roe Adams III, Garriott developed the idea of a game system that would secretly take into account the player's actions in a way very similar to how he had done when he was a DM, evaluating them and possibly penalizing those who

---

78   Woodhead: "I met Roe Adams when he was a reviewer for Softalk, IIRC magazine. He handled all the design, and the basic idea for the game was his. We did multiple endings and a 3D maze that was kind of cute from a programming perspective. Since you start as the evil wizard at the bottom level, Wizardry players sent in disks with their characters to act as enemies. We received hundreds of disks, which resulted in some players having the experience of killing their own parties after the product shipped. I'd say we used 40-50 complete parties from players." Interview with Jared Petty, http://www.hardcoregaming101.net

79   "[…] one day in 1988 in Ithaca, NY. Robert Woodhead and Roe Adams were at the time allegedly working on a computer game (Wizardry IV, the Return of Werdna[…]). One afternoon, while taking a break from pretending to program, Robert was playing with a new toy, a 'Colorspace II' video board that let him superimpose Macintosh graphics on video. Roe, taking a break from pretending to design the game, wandered by and saw this. Roe was a huge anime fan, and he inquired as to whether it would be possible to use this hardware to subtitle some of these weird videos he loved. […] Robert thought about it for a moment, and said 'sure, it'd be easy' [5]. Roe then suggested that we could make copies of the videos and send them around to other anime clubs so they could see them [6]. Robert thought about this for a moment, and then replied, 'I have a better idea — I'm always going to Japan on business, why don't I go get some licenses and we'll try and sell the videos?' Five minutes later, after both Robert and Roe had finished laughing their asses off about this really stupid idea that could not possibly ever make any money, AnimEigo [7] was born […]", https://www.animeigo.com/about/secret-history-animeigo/

deviated too much from their morale with dramatic changes in alignment.

Later, Garriott revealed that the idea behind this system had come from watching a television documentary of the Avatars in Hindu mythology. Realizing that the sixteen virtues of Hinduism were far too many for a video game, Garriott tried to simplify the model. Perhaps at the suggestion of Adams, who was certainly the most literate of the two,[80] the ethical model of the new game ended up being directly influenced by The Wizard of Oz, using the three principles of Truth, Love and Courage. The combinations thereof, made up the eight virtues in his new system of values: Honesty (from Truth), Compassion (from Love), Value (from Courage), Justice (from Truth and Love), Honor (from Truth and Courage), Sacrifice (from Love and Courage), Spirituality (from Truth, Love and Courage), Humility (from the absence of the three values of Truth, Love and Courage).

The resulting system was not without its flaws. The graphic representation (very similar to the Star of David) was unable to explain how the absence of the three principles could give rise to the virtue of Humility. The system was original and using virtues, a complete novelty for CRPGs — this was just what Garriott needed to generate a new hit.

The implementation, as you will see, would be very complex.

Curiously, the mechanics of virtues were born before the story in which they were supposed to be used. Richard felt that the first three episodes of his series only repeated the pattern of gaining experience until the player could beat the ultimate enemy, i.e. the story was only a pretext. Garriott and Adams decided to break with the past and start from scratch.

The decision was made that the destruction of Exodus in part 3 had triggered a planetary cataclysm, upsetting the world of Sosaria, reshaping it with the destruction of cities and the cancellation of entire continents. The new world finally changed its name to Britannia and was once again ruled by Lord British. The big novelty: this time the world was not in danger or on the brink of an abyss, ready to be annihilated by an enemy. Britannia was a flourishing land, in the middle of its renaissance, just like Camelot before the knights of the Round Table dispersed in search of the Holy Grail. The eight major cities were each the capital of one of the eight virtues, each holding a companion to the player character's party, this time no longer named the Stranger but Avatar,[81] in his own search for the Virtues.

---

80   "Richard Garriott might have displayed Joycean ambition and intricacy, but he admittedly lacked literary skills: 'I can't spell, have no grammar techniques, and have read less than twenty-five books in my life.' " Levy, Steven (2010) Hackers: Heroes of the Computer Revolution, Chapter 19: Applefest

81   The choice of the name Avatar was particularly apt, inextricably linked to the series of Ultima. Later on, thanks to a lucky circumstance, it would take a further step becoming mainstream. The representation of the virtual alter ego of the player, or of the Internet user.

Having conceived the game system and created an intriguing background, Richard was only at the beginning of a long journey that would lead him to the completion of the new chapter of his saga.

Origin Systems Inc. thrives

"The games industry was quite small in those days and we all did a lot of computer shows. I suspect our first meeting [Dave with Richard Garriott] was at one of the Applefests or the SF Computer show. My area of expertise in those days was Adventure and FRP games, so we had a lot in common and a love of the same genres."

Dave Albert

"Then I played Ultima and loved it. I'd never played anything like it. I really didn't have experience with RPGs, so it blew me away with the sheer adventure of it."

Chuck Dougherty, interview with Chester Bolingbroke, The CRPG Addict, 2015

"The fantasy begins with Origin Systems... and never ends."

Origin Systems Inc., 1987 Catalog

Far from home, demoralized by the two thefts, and having to put aside programming and design to deal with production, packaging and customer support, Richard began to feel depressed. Even contact with the locals felt difficult, due to the different accent. The solution was the same as on Oklahoma campus, in Austin and in the Sierra On-Line chalet: Richard needed creative activity to break the routine and find back his strength to get to work. This time, however, the opportunity came on its own, on Halloween.

With help from a couple of programmers, he began to transform the two-story house into a haunted house in his free time. It was the first time he had tried it and he liked the experiment so much that it lifted him up and gave him the needed boost to start programming again, leaving him convinced to try it again later with more time and means at his disposal.

The neighbors were invited to enter the house in groups to check out the special effects and tricks that Garriott and his colleagues had devised. It's unknown what they thought of experience, but in the following months, the dismantled and abandoned material in the garden caused misunderstandings between the new Texans and the neighborhood.

Garriott had a new problem to solve: Origin System Inc. needed to grow. The proceeds from Exodus made it possible to hire some skilled programmers which would help Richard develop the next Ultima and as well put new games in the pipeline. Ultima IV would not be ready for a couple of years and Origin could not survive for so long without publishing something else. The Garriott brothers knew well that they were taking a gamble by focusing on the next chapter of Richard's saga.

Commercial games grew in production quality and complexity, particularly CRPGs, which often overburdened the lone programmer. Before then, Richard had personally taken care of a good part of the code, delegating only a few sections to his friends and collaborators, and was not ready to take on the role of leading a team of programmers rather than doing it all himself. Some studios were transitioning to a more collaborative development model, where teams of specialists worked on several projects in their field of expertise.

One of the first hires was Dave Albert of Penguin Software, a company well known for the Transylvania graphic adventure he programmed together with Antonio Antiochia and Mark Pelczarski. Albert was not only a programmer but also possessed considerable managerial and creative skills; the Garriott brothers tried long and hard to get him on board. Albert: "I joined Origin in September of 1984. I had previously worked at Penguin Software and felt a need to move on in my career. Robert & Richard Garriott had made a standing offer some months before, so I called them and accepted the position of VP Development & Marketing. Origin had 5 employees at the time I joined".

Despite the high-profile title, Albert would be freshman number five in the budding Origin Systems Inc.. One of his first assignments was to look for new products and developers. At Penguin Software, he had worked with Greg Paul Malone when the latter wrote Minit Man, "a Choplifter[82] style game". Back then, the two had discussed another project, a martial arts game. Malone decided to propose his idea to Origin and Albert was immediately in charge of its production, named Moebius: The Orb of Celestial Harmony.

Production didn't go smoothly: during development, the programmer changed his mind regarding the art style, setting the project back several months. Fortunately, Origin was able to resolve this big problem quickly. Albert: "Greg was a very talented and headstrong developer and the game took some time to complete. He was finally persuaded to revert to the original style of art against a black background and then the project got back on track and was completed."

Albert wrote the documentation and gave a hand with the storyline, mythology

---

82   A horizontal scrolling action game, developed in 1982 by Dan Gorlin and published by Brøderbund for Apple II

and some game mechanics. Once Moebius was finished, Origin Systems had their first collaboration with Electronic Arts. Their agreement allowed Origin to take advantage of the considerable commercial channels of Hawkins' company.

Already on the way to becoming a giant in the industry, EA gave Origin access to Toys "R" Us, one of North America's largest retailers. This was an incredible increase in visibility for any producer. Nintendo would conceive a clever strategy the following year to be able to place their Nintendo Entertainment System at Toys "R" Us. In partnership with Worlds of Wonder, a toy company founded by former employees of Atari (left out of work after the crisis of 1983), which had just produced a lovely talking teddy bear named Teddy Ruxpin. It became the best-selling toy of 1985 and to get the stuffed animal, Toys "R" Us was, in a way, forced to display the initially less desirable NES as well. Within just one year, the situation reversed: while the bear had diminished in popularity, the NES had become one of the most wanted products, pushing Worlds of Wonder to now seek Nintendo's support to stay in touch with Toys "R" Us but they would not be successful.

This was not the first time a toy was used as leverage against retailers to sell a computer. In 1983, Coleco tried breaking into the microcomputer market with their Coleco Adam (compatible with the 1982 ColecoVision console). Poor design decisions led to an unreliable system[83] with a bad reputation and low sales, which caused dismal returns and unhappy retailers. Out of sheer luck, the same year Coleco also released something that all children wanted for Christmas 1983: "Cabbage Patch Kids" dolls. They compelled the retailers to continue selling their ill-fated Adams Computer if they wanted their share of the Cabbage Patch Kids craze. As soon as the latter faded, the days for the Adam were numbered and Coleco never recovered.[84] Moebius had been developed for the Apple II, but the Commodore 64 had largely surpassed its installation base. Only Exodus had experienced a conversion for the Commodore 64, carried out by Chuck Bueche, who was busy programming a strategy game called Ogre, supported, at least initially, by Greenberg. Therefore, Robert and Richard decided to outsource the conversion to an external company that had only done a sports game for the Apple II called Computer Baseball. Dr. Cat: "Origin had contracted a company called Softmates to program a Commodore 64 version of Moebius. But they were behind schedule and not showing proof that they were even partly finishing anything, and they were worried that Softmates wouldn't deliver a shippable product in time for Christmas."

Coincidentally, Dr. Cat had also worked for Penguin Software when Dave Albert was still its vice president. Knowing the programmer's skill and familiarity with

---

83   The few working machines had issues like erasing removable media on startup. A sticker was added on later Adams, warning the user not to turn on the machine while a tape was in the drive.

84   Matt Chat 372 with David Wesley

Commodore's platform, Albert suggested that Dr. Cat should also be commissioned to convert Moebius: "Dr. Cat and I had worked on a handful of projects prior to this when I was at Penguin and I had a good deal of respect for his talents and confidence in his work ethic and ability to complete the project in the allotted time."

Dr. Cat: "Dave told Richard and Robert something like 'Let me contract Dr. Cat to start a C64 version from scratch, with three months to finish it. He can do that. If Softmates finished, well, we just spend a few thousand dollars on an insurance policy. But if Softmates fails and Dr. Cat completes it, we'll have made a very sound investment that will make a big difference. And you can offer him a full-time job if you like his work.' "

Softmates was unable to deliver a quality product on time but Dr. Cat made up for it, achieving a very good conversion. Seeing that the stakes were very high, he invested a lot of hard work: "I delivered a high quality complete working version in three months, complete with integration of the open source Sizzle[85] fastloader to speed up disk loads 5 times. Moebius was the first Origin game that did so much disk loading[86] that it wouldn't be playable on the Commodore 64 without a fastloader — but hardly the last, we used Sizzle in every C64 release after that."

After the mishap of 1983 when Dr. Cat showed up at Origin's Texas office, this time he had earned himself the job. His role consisted essentially of porting to the C64, while the games were still first developed for the Apple II.

Looking for new titles to support the company, Richard turned to an old friendship: Steve Jackson. The founder of SJG had already considered expanding his business in the field of computers. Observing the fortune Richard had flaunted without any problems, Jackson had ordered the purchase of an Apple II. However, it remained unused for a long time and later turned on only to store the company's data and for word processing. No one knew how to program it, and Jackson had too many commitments to personally create video games.

One of SJG's first successes was Car Wars (1980), set in a dystopian future where right of way "belonged to the vehicle with the biggest cannon", as stated in the tag line of the package. On one of his visits to Austin, Garriott was asked to create a video game adaption. He hoped this would give OSI the relieve it needed, gladly accepting and assigning it to Chuck Bueche. Chuck received help for the Commodore port from Steven Meuse, another programmer from Penguin Software.

The result was Autoduel (1985), a real-time action game with RPG elements,

---

85   The source code was made publicly available in Run and Loadstar magazines starting in 1986.

86   The C64 allowed users to reuse their VIC-20 floppy drives, which were slow due to a last-minute solution for a hardware defect. Not a big issue for the VIC-20 with just 5Kb RAM, but the C64 had 64kB to fill and did it even slower in order to be compatible with those drives. The story is told in great detail by Brian Bagnall in Commodore, a Company on the Edge, Chapter 28

that OSI published for the usual platforms, Apple II, Commodore 64, Atari 400/800 and IBM PC, as well as a newly released machine, called Amiga. Overall, it sold about 100,000 copies, achieving great success.

Next, the game designer proposed that Garriott create a computer adaption of one of his best creations so far: Ogre. A special science fiction game with an asymmetric gameplay: two players challenged each other in a deadly fight where one side controlled a combat vehicle (a giant super-armed tank protected by heavy armor, named Ogre), while the other had to stop the opponent by relying on a large number of much less powerful units and defenses.

Origin now used feelies consistently, and in Ogre, included an identity card that classified the bearer as a member of the command staff, the 6502nd infantry Division, the 2033rd armored Division, the 8088th Ordinance & Service Tech Division or the AI Programming Division, among other things. The card was sensitive to radiation and would change color when exposed to gamma rays, or, at least, so it was written in the instructions.

The electronic version of Ogre was programmed by Steven Meuse, this time with the support of Chuck Bueche and Dallas Snell, a new entry at OSI. The latter, had until then several experiences in video game programming; mainly as a freelancer. He had been the chief programmer of the graphic adventure The Quest by Penguin Software (1983), their best-selling title, created in the wake of the success of Roberta Williams from Sierra On-Line. Snell was a good programmer and already had several commercial successes to his credit, yet Ogre would be his penultimate feat as a developer, after which he would become a key player at OSI, first as a producer and later rising to the highest levels of the company.

The development of Ogre was particularly demanding for the artificial intelligence capable of handling the turn-based game's complex system of rules. Ogre could be played by a single player against the computer, or by two users via the hot-seat system, i.e. changing computer controls. To give players a challenge, Albert put a good part of the available programmers to work.

OSI was still small but very dynamic. Equipped with a handful of core technicians, the company had a secret weapon: its offices were home to a number of independent developers and programmers. By providing infrastructure, office space, and logistical support, Origin functioned as a sort of start-up incubator; as we would call it today. In 1986, there were two unofficially employed programmers working independently on their own projects and at the same time, contributing to Origin's other titles: Stuart Marks and Paul Neurath.

Snell, Marks and Neurath implemented Ogre's AI, Garriott and Bueche helped the programmer with suggestions, changes and an in-depth play-testing that also involved Jeff Hillhouse and Jackson himself. It was a great effort that made an impression upon Albert's memory: "My particular favorite endeavor of that era was the work done by all of the devs on AI for the Steve Jackson game

OGRE. After weeks of work it was demonstrated that there was a slight imbalance in the game design that favored one side of the game (super-tank versus 'conventional' forces)". As a consequence Jackson also slightly retouched some of the features of Ogre MkV in the next edition.

Placing itself in an even smaller niche than Autoduel, Ogre was not as successful as hoped and sold just about 10,000 copies.

Origin continued to be a small independent software house in an industry where smaller players in the market ended up gravitating around entertainment giants or were steadily attracted and sooner or later absorbed by them.

Despite its modest size, OSI's influence on the market was proportionally very strong. The success of Garriott's role-playing games set an example and made other players in the software industry feel that the CRPG genre should be exploited.

One of the first results of this growing influence came in 1984, with the publication of Questron by Strategic Simulations Inc. (SSI). Programmed by Charles Dougherty and Gerald Wieczore, Questron was very similar to the first installment of Ultima. A role-playing game in which the hero had to defeat an evil ruler named Montor by exploring a world shown with a bird's eye view and tile graphics, as well as delve into dungeons that were shown via a first-person view. Sounds familiar?

The two programmers, looking for a publisher, even forwarded it to Sierra On-Line during Richard's brief stay in the Williams' chalet. Perhaps because of the great resemblance to Ultima, Ken Williams refused the offer and next they tried their luck with Brøderbund. The similarity, Dougherty assured, was partly due to the obvious inspiration by Ultima, but fate also had a hand in it. Chuck Dougherty: "The outside terrain originally was very similar to Ultima, the menu system and overall screen layout was quite similar. But the other thing that happened was that somewhere around the time I was finishing Questron, Ultima II was published. Bear in mind I'd never seen Ultima II prior to sending Questron off to publishers, but when it was released I realized that Questron was far more similar to Ultima II then it had ever been to Ultima. This was horrifying, and the changes/advancements I'd made to not be too similar to Ultima were often quite similar to what turned out to be natural advancements between Ultima and Ultima II."[87]

The brothers Doug and Gary Carlston founded Brøderbund to publish Galactic Empire (1980), a game Doug had written for TRS-80 the year before. They experienced four years of continuous success, before becoming the tenth largest company in the market for microcomputer software in 1984, according to InfoWorld magazine. Started as a family business, Brøderbund took its name from the Boer word Broederbond, which means "band of brothers", but soon Doug and Gary felt the need to change some letters to avoid the uncomfortable association with the homonymous South African secret society.

---

87   Questron: More from the Creator by Chester Bolingbroke (CRPG Addict)

The Carlston brothers decided that Questron deserved a chance. Their business was going very well and a series of successes had made them a small giant, among them an action game called Raid on Bungeling Bay, the first experiment of a then unknown Will Wright.

Now came a cold shower for the two Dougherty brothers. Chuck Dougherty: "What Brøderbund told me was they were at some trade show showing a preview of Questron and Richard Garriott saw it. Apparently he was upset — and knowing what I know now I don't blame him. This was of great concern to Brøderbund, and they were no longer sure they were going to publish."[88]

The Doughertys tried to make changes that made Questron different from Ultima II. Unfortunately, when the game was ready again, Brøderbund was no longer interested and the two had no choice but to look for a new publisher, trying their luck with SSI. This publisher was created to sell small strategy games written in BASIC for the TRS-80. Soon it had given up this platform and, on the advice of Trip Hawkins, had started publishing for the Apple II. Thanks to the success, SSI had expanded from strategy and war games to role-playing games.

Questron would be the third CRPG in 1984 for SSI but, once again, when Garriott learned about the plan, he proceeded the same way as with Brøderbund. SSI's management did not immediately give in and for the first time Richard threatened to protect his interests in court. In fact, the two companies managed to solve the dispute with an extra-judicial agreement, which guaranteed Garriott to appear in the accreditations of Questron as creator of "structure and style of play", licensed from Origin against payment of a percentage.[89] Nevertheless, the fact that first Brøderbund and then SSI had recognized Garriott's work in this game was a clear indication that the style of play created by Richard had become influential. The market, until then populated by actors not hesitating to copy other software, was about to mature.[90]

Having won his first legal battle, Garriott was about to prepare for the release of his fourth Ultima. He didn't know, however, that on the other side of the ocean, many other programmers would soon get to work inspired by his games. The video game industry was about to change again much faster than Richard expected, and the boom in Japanese role-playing games would be the least of his worries.

---

88   Ibid.

89   https://web.archive.org/web/20070601183414/http://vorlon.case.edu/ zwb2/ Ultima/1984-06-14.txt

90   Also in 1984, Brøderbund published The Print Shop, a software for printing covers and product packs, innovative also because it included an extensive clip-arts library. The following year, Unison World published Printmaster, a software very similar to The Print Shop, and Brøderbund immediately mobilized its lawyers. The resulting legal action established criterias (later radically reduced) for the application of copyright on software based on look and feel

Ultima IV: Quest of the Avatar

"In a sense, the game grew up with its audience."

Herz J.C., Joystick Nation (1997)

"All the information is available; you just have to dig it out. So expect to spending quite some time with this epic… it's a major undertaking!"

Scorpia, review of Ultima IV, Computer Gaming World, January/February 1986

Before the release of Exodus Garriott had already started working on his next Ultima, which would be a revolution for CRPGs. The game engine for it would change so much over the course of its two year development that it carried little resemblance to Exodus, despite the clear legacy.

During development, Richard took several opportunities to explain some of the revolutionary innovations he intended to include in his new game. In an interview published shortly after the release of Exodus, he revealed that he was already working on the sequel and that players would have to contend with a path to progress in sixteen virtues (twice as many as in the final product).

In the meantime, reading player feedback, Richard realized the extent of how much his work had been sifted through, and some particularly engaged players found meanings and messages that Richard never inserted intentionally. Others, such as religious extremists, went so far as to call him a satanic corrupter of the American youth due to Loubet's cover art. Taking the feedback seriously he incorporated changes: The setting would be more coherent, removing the sci-fi elements and expanding upon discreet cameos from his friends and collaborators (often with their SCA name) as a tribute for their support.

Until then, Richard had written games mainly to test his ability as a programmer. The writing of each game focused on reworking the code and adding features that made it more streamlined and efficient. Just because there was space on the floppy disk, he added the space battle in Ultima, imagining that everyone likes to shoot down TIE fighters, between a rescue of the princess and the final clash with Mondain.

After Ultima III, something changed: Richard asked himself for the first time what he would really want to include in his work. Fresh from his experience with the zealots who had branded him as a Satanist, he decided to free his work from any religious references to avoid further controversy. The initially conceived sixteen virtues were replaced by a new model created specifically for the game. Richard introduced a new world which reflected some continuity with the previous episodes, that had in the meantime, gathered a certain number of fans.

Afters Exodus' defeat Sosaria experienced an era of cultural, economic and civil blossoming. The people gathered under the wise and enlightened guidance of Lord British to form a new kingdom: Britannia. They were following the eight virtues, but needed spiritual guidance, somebody would serve as an example by becoming the Avatar of the Virtues. Once again, the stranger from another world was called by Lord British: this time the task was not to save the world from a fearsome enemy, but to pursue the eight virtues and transcend to the state of Avatar. To crown the feat, the player would descend into the Great Stygian Abyss (a clear reference to Dante Alighieri's Divine Comedy, which Richard read during the programming of Ultima IV to draw inspiration for the player's final journey) in search of the Codex of Ultimate Wisdom.

Prior to the release, Garriott announced in an interview that to finish the game, the player had to embody a paradigm shift; adapting to the revolution devised with Roe Adams III. For the first time in a CRPG, the purpose of an adventure was not to defeat an enemy, but to accomplish an abstract undertaking such as that of embodying the eight virtues.

In retrospect, it is evident why the two-year period preceding the publication of Ultima IV was so difficult and challenging.

Richard suffered from anxiety and gastritis because of the enormous pressure. Creating a new way of playing was not just a challenge in programming skills , but a big and dangerous bet: Would the public appreciate it? Would the players understand the novelty?

For an audience that was used to an interface which had changed very little over the course of four years, the first moments of the game were certainly disorienting. No character creation, no statistics, instead players were greeted by a full-fledged introduction.

Richard used a style similar to the narrative method of Roberta Williams' graphic adventures: An almost full screen of memorable art, underlined with the first sentences of his new game:

"The day is warm, yet there is a cooling breeze. The latest in a series of personal crises seems insurmountable. You are being pulled apart in all directions. Yet this afternoon walk in the countryside slowly brings relaxation to your harried mind. The soil and stain of modern high-tech living begins to wash off in layers. That willow tree near the stream looks comfortable and inviting. The buzz of dragonflies and the whisper of the willow's swaying branches bring a deep peace. Searching inward for tranquility and happiness, you close your eyes. A high-pitched cascading sound like crystal wind chimes impinges on your floating awareness. As you open your eyes, you see a shimmering blueness rise from the ground. The sound seems to be emanating from this glowing portal."

So began the player's journey into the world of Britannia. Then followed a dialogue with a fortune-teller (a trope Garriott would reuse later), based on hypothetical situations that imposed moral choices, clarifying which of the eight virtues was most important to the player and determining their starting profession.

Each question was a choice between two virtues: "Entrusted to deliver an uncounted purse of gold, thou dost meet a poor beggar. Dost thou: A) deliver the gold knowing the Trust in thee was well-placed; or B) show Compassion, giving the Beggar a coin, knowing it won't be missed?"

These few rounds of questions to eliminate all but the one virtue the player cared most about was already part of the adventure. Then the player was reminded that Ultima IV was a journey that required much more than the usual skills needed to complete a video game of the mid-80s: determination, patience, stubbornness and scrupulous application of the system trial and error were not enough. It was necessary for the player to identify and live the virtues for the ultimate goal, namely to transcend to Avatarhood. CRPGs had grown up, from merely adopting some rules, mechanics and the fantasy setting AD&D to embracing role-playing in the most complete sense of the word.

The in-game experience resembled Ultima III with one big innovation: Fog of war. Trees, walls and closed doors hampered the view and prevented the player from knowing what was around the corner or beyond the nearest row of trees.

The game began without a party, similar to earlier Ultimas. The simple single words dialogue system, where NPCs answered with new clues when the right keyword was typed in, wasn't extended, but played now a much bigger role. Instead of advancing levels by killing monsters, the game revolved about collecting clues on virtues. Some of the NPC would also accept offers to "join" the player as companions, forming a party of up to 8.

The system of tiles didn't change much beside the evolution in graphics and adding tiles specific to the dungeon during tactical combat.

The game engine was reworked to accommodate a party twice the size than in the previous game. Unbeknownst to the user, the biggest differences in Ultima IV were completely invisible: Garriott's engine kept track of player's actions or more specifically their behavior. Usually accustomed to stealing from merchants, killing jesters to save princesses (and getting gold); this time dubious activities would not lead to success. The player had to make a paradigm shift and identify with their role. The end no longer justified the means and if the foreigner wanted to become an Avatar, the player had to act accordingly.

Regarding talking to NPCs, one could run into beggars and donate to them, thus taking a small step to obtain the virtue of Compassion or by defeating an evil enemy, achieve a progress in the virtue of Valor. Each action had an consequence, invisible but nonetheless important and the final success was the sum of all these small steps taken during the game.

For every virtue, Richard implemented a system that based on the player's actions or choices, would either advance or hinder their progress. In addition, every virtue had a representative city and sanctuary, along with an NPC that embodied it perfectly. Additionally, each virtue had a corresponding dungeon and Moongate; a portal leading to each city. Moongates were remnants of the map from Time Bandits.

Some of these systems were quite intuitive: In addition to giving experience through the same mechanics as in Ultima III, fights gave Valor to the player character, provided that the opponent was evil. Others were less immediate to understand: it was possible, for example, to buy reagents from a blind seller and pay less than necessary, taking advantage of the dealer's disability. In this case however, the character lost points in Justice, while being honest gave a small progress towards obtaining this virtue. This hidden change was one of the many systems implemented by Garriott to force the user, accustomed to steal and kill for convenience and to arrive first at the final fight, to change the way of play and reflect on their actions.

Before it became common in CRPGs to face moral dilemmas and deal with the consequences of actions, it would take many years during which the novelty introduced by Richard would remain a curious and unusual anomaly. Yet, the mark had been made and games like Mass Effect, in which the player was often called to a field choice between the virtuous way (Paragon) or the ruthless way (Renegade), are clearly heirs to the system introduced for the first time by Ultima IV in 1985.

Unfortunately, the result was not without its flaws. Firstly, the fact that these mechanics were unknown to the player meant they were unaware if any wrong decisions had been made. For example, it was possible to lose Compassion points for letting evil creatures escape in a fight, in Spirituality for reciting the wrong mantra at a shrine, or in Humility for speaking proudly to an NPC. For Richard, all these actions could only have negative consequences, but the simple dialogue system sometimes lead to penalizing the player for accidentally selecting an interaction.

In his Computer Gaming World interview, given shortly after August 1985, Garriott explained that at Origin he had only tested and completed Ultima IV before it shipped. It was published with a series of very serious bugs, capable of ruining the gaming experience or making it much more difficult to complete. Some fundamental dialogues for example were linked to incorrectly written keywords ("re-asearch" instead of "research"). The total lack of play testing deprived Garriott of any feedback, and some serious flaws affected the enjoyment of the final game. I.e. several of the keywords in conversations were anything but intuitive, unfortunately also some of the indispensable ones. Nonetheless, Ultima IV was immediately triumphantly welcomed by critics. Computer Gaming World, which had given so much space to the author before the release of his last game, reviewed Quest of the Avatar judging it "an incredible game", predicting that it would become a classic. Equally positive was the evaluation in Dragon magazine, writing the following year about Ultima IV calling it "the most impressive and complex adventure to date".

On September 16, 1985, the versions for Apple II and Commodore 64 were released, while the Atari 800 port would arrive only the following year. The PC version would not come out before 1987, as the platform did not use the MOS 6502 and required a whole re-implementation. This strong focus on the meanwhile 10 year old CPU would have serious consequences in the near future.

Again the Apple II enjoyed a soundtrack written by Ken Arnold, a composition of nine tracks, some inspired or taken from Exodus. Designed for users with a Mockingboard, his music was also brought on to the Commodore 64, but not on the Atari 800 and PC, despite the latter enjoying the first sound cards. On the other hand, the graphics were superior thanks to the new EGA video cards recently available.

Other design errors were easier to circumvent: Shamino (Garriott's other alter ego), together with three other NPCs surrounded the Ankh of Spirituality, symbol of the virtue of Spirituality, preventing the player from approaching and interacting with it. The player could talk to Shamino and convince him to join the party, thus making space to approach the Ankh, but only if the main character was not a ranger. In this case Shamino could not be recruited and the player's only option was to attack one of the four NPCs, with the serious consequences on Value, Honor and Compassion.

Despite all these issues, the public again rewarded OSI with sales of over 300,000 units, giving them the coveted breath of fresh air needed to keep the accounting in order until the completion of the inevitable sequel.

The game was sold in a material-rich packaging. The box, with a cover by Loubet, was accompanied by the usual fabric map depicting the world of Britannia (which will remain substantially unchanged in the following chapters), the book The History of Britannia, containing information on the game environment and professions, a bestiary of the monsters present and a concluding note written by Lord British himself, the book The Book of Mystic Wisdom describing 26 spells with their reagents and a metal pendant in the shape of an ankh, identical to that given to the Foreigner during his search for virtues.

Richard Garriott was very satisfied with his work. It proved a CRPG could be deeper and more personal than similar games like Wizardry, and the audience responded enthusiastically, although the attempt the implementation was rudimentary and not always working.

Even Dave Arneson, co-creator of D&D, Garriott's first inspiration for creating games, would have given Ultima IV the credit for having tried to go beyond the known horizon of skills, life points, characteristics, fighting and experience accumulation.[91] Arneson, however, had also correctly observed that Garriott's experiment had remained an isolated case, an extravagance of the world of video games that would take many years before having a successor.

Ultima IV's main competitor was not another sequel of a known behemoth in the world of CRPGs but an unexpected newcomer, destined to become the head of a new dynasty.

Released just ten days before Quest of the Avatar (September 3, 1985) by Electronic Arts on behalf of Interplay, Tales of the Unknown: Volume I was intended to be the first chapter of a saga. The title being slightly clunky, and the box design blending it in with the background, emphasized the slicker subtitle The Bard's Tale. The creator Michael Cranford about the title: "This particular class simply stood out the most during development, because of the unique nature of the class and the musical aspect of the game, and we had a consultant who named the game after the bard class. I didn't name the game. So the bard became central because people at Interplay and EA loved it."[92] Who was this consultant proposing to use the subtitle as title for the sequels? The name will be familiar: "[the music] also inspired the revised name of the game. (I did not come up with the name, it was a third party consultant, Roe [R.] Adams [III])"[93]

Cranford had conceived, designed and programmed almost everything, receiving support from Lawrence Holland (who would later make a career at LucasArts Entertainment Company directing major titles such as X-Wing and TIE Fighter) for the music, Brian Fargo (founder of Interplay and guiding projects such as Wasteland, Star Trek: 25th Anniversary and Fallout) would design some levels and Rebecca Ann Heineman (at the time Bill Heineman, known later for porting id titles to the 3DO, such as Wolfenstein and Doom) wrote some data compression procedures. In addition to these, also Roe Adams III had given a hand in design (earning him an accreditation for "additional design"). Adams was at the same time involved in Ultima, Wizardry and Bard's Tale, something that allowed him to insert his beloved Skara Brae in two of those titles and his favorite alter ego, Hawkwind of Skara Brae, in all three.

Strongly inspired by Wizardry, in Bard's Tale the player created and managed a party of six heroes saving the town of Skara Brae, whose inhabitants mysteriously

91   Arneson, David L., Computer Gaming World (May 1988)

92   Interview with Michael Cranford, https://rpgcodex.net/content.php?id=9163

93   Interview with Michael Cranford, https://www.lemon64.com/forum/viewtopic.php?t=40586&sid=7e84ac3f2d7b35003f342a6ccaee8c14

disappeared at the hands of the evil wizard Mangar. Also the similar user interface and the turn-based combat system followed the common style of Wizardry.

Bard's Tale immediately distinguished itself with the beautiful art in the perspective view: Enemies were well designed by David Lowery and even equipped with a rudimentary animation. A complex system of 85 spells, the presence of numerous well-designed puzzles and the character of the Bard, the class that gave its name to the episode, were refreshing and well received. The bard, a character class designed to support the companions with 'buff' and 'de-buff' spells, would become an often copied trope in later CRPGs and the game series' signature class would even carry over to the title.

Overall less innovative than Ultima IV, it had a much greater commercial success, selling 400,000 copies in total on numerous platforms, from Apple II, then to PC and the Commodore 64 to the ZX Spectrum. Part of the success also came from the choice of the Wizardry creators not to sell their title on the Commodore 64 until 1987 and on the very interesting feature to import player parties from Ultima and Wizardry.

The star of Bard's Tale was not destined to last, however. The second chapter, published only a year later, in 1986, was less successful both commercially and critically. Differences between Cranford and Fargo led to the removal of the first from Interplay and the third chapter (1988) saw the light without him, achieving less and less compelling reviews and sales. The fourth chapter, in development at EA, had to undergo a sudden change of IP when collaboration between Interplay and EA broke down. It would take 30 years for Bard's Tale IV to materialize in 2018, this time developed by inXile Entertainment, the company founded by Fargo after leaving Interplay.

Although imperfect and defeated in terms of sales, Ultima IV represented one of proudest moments in Garriott's career. The following successful years would see many other acclaimed projects, but from a creative and innovative point of view, it would take another dozen years for Richard to be able to imagine an equally new and revolutionary game changing the market forever.

Return home

"I showed up just in time to pick sides in a war between two giants"

John Miles

"The weather was a little nicer in Austin. The American girls seemed to like the English accent, which wasn't bad, and there was definitely a lot… everything seemed like it was cheaper and there was more of it, especially back then. […] So I came over and was like, 'Ah, you know, this is pretty cool.' I met and hooked up with Origin when it was just starting in Austin and the rest, I guess, is history. I just basically never went back."

Chris Roberts, The forgotten interview with Chris Roberts, by Paul Dean

John Miles, a young geek with an inordinate passion for hardware,[94] was an admirer of the Ultima series and Zork. When he started programming on his Apple II, he began working on a product that was supposed to be the synthesis of his two favorite video games: combining a role-playing game with a parser as powerful as the one that made Infocom famous.

By the end of summer 1985, his game was in an advanced state of development. Ultima IV had been released and Miles, along with his dorm mates, lost many hours of sleep and skipped many university classes to finish Garriott's game. Despite the break, soon the prototype reached a playable stage and John considered leaving university to look for a job thanks to his experiment. Miles: "Once I had a demo working, I started cold calling all of the companies whose games I was into, looking for a publisher. Infocom was high on that list but Origin Systems came first."

With great determination, Miles called Origin and the receptionist passed him on to Chuck Bueche who, in turn, transferred the call to Dave Albert. Unbeknownst to him, the timing of his call was perfect: Richard had just given up on programming the next Ultima alone and his staff was looking for Apple II experts to support him.

Albert wasn't very enthusiastic about Miles' project, "a bit too derivative for publication". But the candidate's talent was obvious and there could be room for him in Origin. Miles: "Dave explained that while they weren't currently in the market for a Zork parser, they had finally convinced Richard to start hiring additional programmers for Ultima V, and would be interested in checking out my demo".

Without wasting time, John headed straight to New Hampshire, but this time the timing couldn't be more unfortunate as tensions between Richard and his brother Robert were beginning to reach a breaking point. OSI had overcome obstacles and faced perils like the market crisis in its founding year, and still managed to do better than just survive. It had several successes and was able to recruit excellent staff, becoming a powerhouse in the CRPG sector, and to a lesser extent getting a foothold in other genres.

Success slowly took its toll on both due to high stress and the continuous risks. The strong bond between Richard and Robert had suffered from the inevitable tensions. His older brother, who had a strong university background, had taken aim at setting up OSI as an efficient and productive organization, while Richard took care of the creative aspects and planning. Soon however, Richard's way of working created organizational problems for Robert. The younger brother adapted a habit of showing up for work in the middle of the day or after lunch and staying in the office late. This was soon imitated by other staff members, creating some embarrassment for Robert, who, on the contrary, was trying implement well-defined work hours that were the same for everyone.

When the two clashed, Richard had to capitulate and adapt, understanding that his conduct had to be an example to all the others. Nonetheless, the subject came up again and again, especially when Richard, in search of inspiration or in an attempt to experiment with something new, put aside programming for a few hours — or an entire afternoon — opting instead to have casual, non-work related conversations with colleagues. According to Robert, Richard's main job had to be programming and the company, which could not afford any delays in the release of the next Ultima. Every hour lost could spell the difference between Origin's survival or exit from the market. On the contrary, Richard felt the need to stimulate his creativity and experiment with new ideas, believing that the design process of a game was different from other work activities, especially rules and schedules.

Richard also never really felt comfortable about the move to New England, and therefore never managed to settle down. His neighbors did not accept him and when misunderstandings occurred, Robert often took their side over his. The cold climate also played a depressing role on the morale of most programmers, who were used to the heat of Texas.

The unresolved accumulated tensions were in danger of exploding due to minor or even irrelevant issues, such as a quarreling about the ownership of a pencil which almost led Richard and Robert to a physical confrontation.[95] The two brothers Garriott ended up resorting to their parents Owen and Helen as mediators.

Other conflicts were not just about the duo in charge of Origin. The move to New England was planned as a temporary measure, waiting for Roberts wife Mary to receive the promotion that would allow her to move with the company. The deadline passed and several members of the original nucleus, including Richard, began to express a certain impatience about the return to Texas.

Robert had no intention of accepting another separation that a few years earlier had almost ruined his marriage. Knowing that OSI had expanded hiring local staff into administrative and operational roles, Robert proposed to submit the question of a transfer to the entire staff.

The original core of OSI, mainly Texan programmers, had by now become a minority and a vote would clearly favor the newcomers' party. Richard had enough of New England. Since the move his life had changed radically and the experience pushed him into what he would later call the "black period", both from a moral point of view and because he had begun to dress in black, reflecting his own mood through the leather jackets and clothing that he frequently wore.

The fracture between the two brothers had become unbearable, but the worst was yet to come and would be totally unexpected...

Chuck Bueche was very worried about the postponed return to Texas and Robert's trick proposal to let staff vote on it — even though it was dominated by local New Hampshire hires — fed his unhappiness even more, prompting Chuck to doubt his professional prospects at Origin.

In his early youth, Chuck had spent many hours playing D&D with Richard and later, they would become roommates when he was attending Austin University in 1981. Chuck would soon leave school to follow his friend's brilliant career with the foundation of OSI.

His career as a game developer started with clones of successful titles. The arcade shooter Caverns of Callisto was his first genuine game but it was a limi-

95   Garriott, Richard (2017) Explore/Create, Chapter 5

ted success. Also due to the low diffusion of Origin titles other than Ultima, it went quite unnoticed. Subsequent projects taken from Steve Jackson's works bore good results but aimed at a niche audience that could not give them the explosive success and popularity of Ultima.

Having collaborated with Garriott on several Ultimas, Chuck set to work on his own sci-fi RPG called 2400 A.D. Released in 1987, Bueche's role-playing game was panned by critics. Computer Gaming World criticized game's graphics, pointing to design and development flaws including lack of intensity, puzzles and challenges.[96]

The work on the sequel 2500 A.D. was started, including a planned C64 port. For this, Origin had commissioned a promising programmer: John Romero. A few months earlier at a fair, Romero appeared at Origin's stand and loaded one of his games on an Apple II, which was running a demo copy of Ultima. His game was using high resolution mode, the most complex and therefore, least used. This impressed the stand manager who after repeated solicitations from Romero, put him in touch with Origin's HR department.

The experience with Moebius was still fresh and Origin continued to carry out conversions internally. With an initial salary of $22,000 a year, more than he had previously made working in fast food and for a temporary employment agency, Romero was assigned to the new division created to make the ports: "But when I started working on the port, I immediately ran into a wall. I said, 'I need to move this code over to the Commodore. Where's the cable, guys?" They went, 'What? There's no cable. We don't port stuff here; you're the first guy to port stuff."[97]

Romero's stay at Origin would last only eight months. When sales of 2400 A.D. on Apple II and PC began to look disappointing, development of the sequel came to a sudden halt. Romero's work was blocked as well and he left OSI shortly thereafter to create Inside-Out Software and later id Software, the company that would later launch the first-person shooter boom with Wolfenstein and Doom in the 90s. The more grave and unexpected consequence of the project's halt was that Bueche had had enough. He decided to return to Texas and continue with his studies.

Bueche's departure was a painful experience for Richard, growing his urge to go back to Texas, with or without his brother's consent. Robert soon realized that blocking the move could cause the company's dissolution. It was in this unfortunate moment that Miles arrived at OSI. John: "Richard was not willing to spend another winter in what he considered a frozen hellhole where people were rude and talked funny and couldn't cook up a decent fajita to save their lives."

Miles' first assignment was to help with updating Ultima. Origin had just bought back the rights from Sierra On-Line to republish Richard's second game. The CRPG audience had meanwhile grown at an incredible rate and Ultima had beco-

---

96   Scorpia, Computer Gaming World (February 1988)

97   Ramsay, Morgan (2015) Online Game Pioneers at Work, Chapter 10

me an extremely popular series. A re-release would tap into a potential revenue stream with new fans. The Garriott brothers decided to increase their return on investment by assigning a team — led by Dave Albert, with John Fachini as chief programmer and a team of four programmers, including Richard, Steven Meuse, Dallas Snell and Dr. Cat — to update and improve the game for the re-release.

Being assigned to work on an IBM PC, Dr. Cat decided to adapt his clothing to a satirical spin on the formal business attire of IBM employees. Albert: "My favorite Dr. Cat moment was when he was given a IBM PC conversion to work on. He showed up the next day in a three-piece suit, saying that if was going to work on an IBM PC he had to dress properly. (Fortunately he did not hold to this regimen for more than a day.)"

In the mid-1980s, organization and planning was not one of Origin's strengths, so the newcomer Miles wasn't given many instructions on how to work. The young man, at his first experience, wanted to show his skills and put a lot of effort and creativity into his work. When he was hastily hired, the improved version of Ultima I was practically ready and Miles had no choice but to do "just the title screen and one or two other cleanup tasks that I don't really recall".

On the contrary, Dr. Cat was impressed with the demonstration: "John Miles was hired while the project was already underway, and he moved from his home in Antlers, Oklahoma. He loaded some clothes and his Apple computer into his car and started driving from Oklahoma to New Hampshire. Every night he would stop and check into a hotel room, set up his Apple there, and work on an animated title screen for the game. He hadn't been given any detailed instructions on how it should look, he thought up his own ideas for it. When he arrived in New Hampshire, he brought a floppy disk into the office, told us he had made it entirely while on the road."

Miles uploaded his program and showed everyone what he had planned. The scene is told by Shay Addams: "His boot-up sequence for the Apple rewrite of Ultima I consisted of a series of animated scenes that looped endlessly until the player started the game. Miles sketched a medieval landscape where a castle rose from the forest beside a pastoral lake; a bird would fly past and perch in a tree, and the word Ultima would descend while a hand gripping a sword rose slowly from the lake."[98]

With clear Arthurian references, Miles' intro seemed very classical. Imagining that the game would be left running in computer stores and booths, playing the animation in an endless loop, Miles hid a couple of little secrets. Every four cycles was followed by a small variation: a knight in armor entered the screen from the left, passed behind the castle and headed towards the lake.

Addams: "It was just a little joke that made him laugh when he pictured someone watching it in a store, noticing the knight and telling a friend to watch for it — and then wondering what happened when it failed to appear."

98   Addams, Shay (1990) The Official Book of Ultima, Chapter 7

The knight wasn't the only surprise of the introduction. After three appearances on horseback, he was replaced by a Lamborghini that entered the castle fast, the door then closing behind the car. Not satisfied, Miles had also decided to give the user the opportunity to trigger the animations after discovering the right combination of keys, even simultaneously which resulted in a race between rider and sports car.

The introduction was very enjoyable. Dr. Cat: "His animated title sequence was used pretty much as-is for the game."

Soon after the game with the new graphics was republished under the name Ultima I: The First Age of Darkness and the team was dissolved. Richard then returned to Texas, where he created a small detached section of Origin's labs and set to work on Ultima V along with Snell and Meuse. Miles was given the opportunity to decide what to do: "Robert offered me the choice of staying in New Hampshire and working on ports to Atari, Commodore, Mac, and IBM/Tandy, or following his brother down to Austin to lend a hand on Ultima V."

The choice was not easy at all and Miles, feeling the pressure, went for the most diplomatic solution possible: "Being the new guy, wanting to score loyalty points with upper management and apparently suffering from an undiagnosed brain condition, I actually agreed to stay."

It was only a momentary lapse because "That very night, I spun out my Camaro in a snowstorm and wrecked it on the way home from the office. It wasn't even Thanksgiving yet, for Chrissakes! What kind of hellhole was this, anyway? This was a huge mistake! I didn't belong here! So I gave Robert my regrets and cast my lot with the rebels. He was understanding enough."

Richard's breakup had immediate negative consequences. The rebel faction he was about to take with him to Texas was the result of Dave Albert's long and patient recruitment work as VP Development & Marketing. The separation of Origin's staff into two parts threatened to harm his work. Dave: "Richard hated living in New England and strongly wanted to return to Texas. The initial discussions had him moving back there and building a small development office there."

Soon the situation changed radically. What was supposed to be just Richard's move took the form of a real schism that left Albert disappointed: "That evolved into him actively recruiting staff from the existing group in New England... I was prohibited from trying to dissuade them from leaving and was quite frustrated at seeing a couple of years of team-building being destroyed because Richard didn't like New England."

Already partially disillusioned by the management of the small family company, "with decisions being made for personal rather than business reasons", Albert realized it was time for him to look further. Having already received offers from Electronic Arts and Brøderbund for some time, Albert discussed his professional future with Doug Carlston and Trip Hawkins, after which he decided for EA.

The experience with OSI was very important for Dave Albert's career follow-up:

"It was a wonderful experience full of learning and growth". When he joined EA, Albert became the producer of Joe Ybarra's RPG development team. With this role he collaborated not only on important CRPGs like Wasteland (1988), a sci-fi title set in a post-apocalyptic future and developed by the Interplay team led by Brian Fargo, the sequel Fountain of Dreams (1990) and the third chapter of The Bard's Tale series (1988), but also on Centurion: Defender of Rome (1990), a hybrid of strategy, tactics, adventure and action, heir to the famous Defender of the Crown (1986) and influential in the creation and success of the games in the Total War series by The Creative Assembly.

When Miles joined the team in Texas, work had already begun. Snell had worked on the initial titles and Meuse was working on the procedure that scheduled NPC's daily tasks. The space initially available at the new Austin site was very modest, enough for about fifteen workstations in several offices along a corridor. Most of Origin's staff remained in New England and only a handful of programmers had followed him to Texas, including Miles and Snell. Richard started looking for new employees.

Among the first hires there were Mark Hamner and Toshi Morita, Miles recalls: "They focused on the first-person dungeon elements of the game and various other tasks such as maintaining and updating Steve's pathfinder".

For the first time, most of the programming escaped from Garriott's complete control and ended up in with Miles: "I did the combat / magic / inventory systems and took over the core subroutine library and most of the 'business logic' behind the gameflow".

On this occasion Miles managed to recover only a small part of the code of his game programmed in the university dormitory: "None of the tech that went into my prototype game was used at Origin except for the Huffman compression code used to store the text, which did make it into Ultima V. It came in handy when we ran out of room for conversation text."[99]

Now that developer studios grew beyond the one or two programmers taking care of everything, Origin was also maturing. Yet, something of the old organization still remained: like many of his colleagues, Miles also took care of the documentation and even the clue books that should have been sold together with Ultima V to help less determined users to finish the game and Origin to earn a few dollars more. Miles: "I also wrote a fair bit of collateral material for Ultima V, from the scroll that recounts the party's descent into the Underworld and loss of Lord British to the (famously unhelpful) hint book."

One of the funniest moments in the development of Ultima V happened shortly after a lunch break. Dr. Cat: "One day the team is out at lunch, and came back and saw all the graphics on the game screen were upside-down. John Miles called the whole team into his office and said 'Hey everybody look, I ran into a weird bug.

99   Escape from Belsaena, Interactive Fiction Database, http://ifdb.tads.org/viewga-me?id=00cm1r4ysim2hkcc

Instead of just crashing the game it made this funny visual effect happen!' Ken tried to keep a straight face and not laugh as long as he good while everybody looked at it and talked about it. Finally he confessed. He had hidden some code in the music driver that would watch and see if you ever went half an hour without touching any key on the keyboard. If you did, it would flip everything upside-down. The team was so amused they kept that code in the game as an Easter egg, where if you yell 'flipflop' it turns the screen upside-down."

Arnold: "It was done specifically to fool Richard, and it worked. John Miles, the other victim, figured it out quickly."

The move to Austin separated them but didn't help with the incompatibility between Richard's creative visions and Robert's pragmatic motivations. The tension still created friction and misunderstandings between the two Garriott brothers. One of the most lively clashes of that time period occurred when Robert asked Richard to remove a room where the party came across some monsters that looked like normal children, on the recommendation of an Ultima V testing officer. Chained and locked in cells, they could be released using a lever or left to their own fate. In case the player, moved by Compassion, decided to free the children, it turned out they were shape-shifters and would immediately attack, giving the player the option to fight or escape.

The tester found the scenario intolerable from a moral point of view, talked to Robert who, fearing that the game would feed the anger of associations like the one that had branded Exodus as satanic, agreed to remove it. Richard explained the situation and was satisfied with the tester's reaction. It confirmed that the event had proven effective, designed to put the player in front of a moral choice. When Richard stone-walled, the conflict escalated to the parents who, in unison, supported their eldest son. Despite everything, Richard remained stubborn and the prison with the shape-shifting "children" stayed intact, without the much feared negative consequences.

While Richard and his staff were working on Ultima V, Denis Loubet was informed of OSI's transfer from New England to Texas. The artist still worked for SJG and until then had only done contract work for most of the Ultima titles, was contacted directly by Garriott. Loubet: "I was afraid to go full on into comic books because it's lot of work for not much pay. And i was not fast. But as i was contemplating that, i got a call and Richard said 'I moved the Origin offices to Austin, you wanna come work for me?' And i t[h]ought about that for about a quarter of second and then 'Yes absolutely!' "[100]

He joined the team when Ultima V was already at an advanced stage of development and drew some of the tiles with which the engine drew the game world. The engine was modified by Miles and still derived from the routines written by Ken-

---

100   Loubet, Denis (2017) Denis Loubet Interview (Origin Systems Illustrator) by BBPCGC VidCast

neth Arnold for Ultima. Loubet's hiring gave OSI not only a very skilled graphic designer, but proved to be a double stroke of luck: The artist was working with a young programmer named Chris Roberts.

Born on May 27, 1968 in Redwood City, California, Roberts had spent several years of his youth in England in Manchester. In the mid-1980s, little more than a teenager, he began programming video games in BASIC on Acorn Computers' BBC Micro, a much beloved platform in the UK but fairly unknown elsewhere.

Based on the usual MOS 6502, the BBC Micro was especially interesting because of its BASIC loaded in the ROM, one of the most powerful and versatile ever. Compared to Microsoft's BASIC, the most popular dialect, the BBC Micro's one had made the evolution from "spaghetti code" to a structured and procedural language.[101] It was also equipped with high resolution graphics, four audio channels, pointers and support for variable names with more than two characters. Beside being an excellent teaching tool it was a good platform for video games, as proven by David Braben with the first installment of his legendary Elite (1984).

Roberts' first game was Wizadore, an extremely difficult[102] platform game, in which the player had to retrieve three pieces of a sword and defeat a dragon. For release, Roberts' first choice was a small but promising British publisher called Ultimate Play the Game (UPG), founded a few years earlier by Tim and Chris Stamper.

UPG (later renamed Rare, churning out blockbusters like Donkey Kong Country) was focused on the much more promising market for Commodore 64 and Spectrum ZX and declined to publish Roberts' BBC micro game. The computer's higher price meant that it had a smaller share of the gaming market.

Imagine Software, recently founded by Mark Butler and David Lawson, was looking for some games to publish until the in-house software developed was ready. The contact between Roberts and Imagine was successfully established by Martin Galway, who at the time, was already working at Ocean Software in Manchester. Thanks to this, Roberts had his first game published at the tender age of sixteen.

Wizadore became a great success for the BBC Micro and launched his early career. Just a year later in 1986, Roberts released his second work, Strykers Run, another horizontal scrolling platform game. He was helped by Galway, who composed the music and created the sound effects. Galway, in fact, had meanwhile established himself as one of the most creative and skilled audio specialists and was well known for his memorable Rambo II soundtrack on the Commodore 64.

Meanwhile, Roberts' father had accepted a job offer at the University of Texas and despite his son's initial resistance, had arranged for his family to move back to the United States. However, collaboration with Galway was far from over.

---

101   GOTOs were replaced with much more readable IF...THEN...ELSE, REPEAT... UNTIL statements, but available for compatibility

102   so difficult that it was marketed with a monthly prize for completing it.

Arriving in Austin, Roberts learned about the North American market. The British BBC micro and Spectrum were virtually unknown in Texas and Roberts replaced his favorite platform with the more popular Commodore 64. To make the big leap he needed help and seeing a poster hanging in a board games store, asked about the artist — who happened to be Denis Loubet.

Thanks to being connected by the trader, the two creatives were able to meet. Understanding the potential of Roberts' project, the artist decided to collaborate with him but a few months later, moved to Texas after having been hired by OSI. What could have been the end to Roberts' project, which would later be known under the name of Times of Lore, actually became serendipity when Loubet mentioned it to Garriott.

Garriott and Roberts met, with the latter very impressed by Roberts' ability to conceive and explain his projects down to the last detail, and suggested that Roberts join Origin's Texan branch. The twenty year old accepted and immediately joined the Ultima V team. While helping out with the sequel, Roberts continued to devote time to Times of Lore, while being encouraged by Snell, Garriott and Loubet, who sensed the potential.

None of the three foresaw how instrumental the young programmer would be in the continuation of the Ultima series and the fate of Origin.

Ultima V: Warriors of Destiny

"You can stand outside Lord British's castle and watch the day go by. In the evening you'll see a new set of guards come out, and the current guards go to bed. Alternately one guard will go eat at the pub, and the other will do so when he returns."

Richard Garriott, interview in Questbusters The Adventurer's Newsletter, June 1987

"Ultima IV demonstrated the need for virtue and goodness; Ultima V shows what happens when that goodness is taken too far and becomes oppressive evil. Bottom line: Not to be missed!"

Scorpia, Ultima V review in Computer Gaming World, May 1988, n. 47

In the long journey from Akalabeth to Ultima IV, Richard had slowly matured from an imaginative and adventurous boy to a skillful and innovative game designer. From unusual mixes of science fiction and fantasy, combining elements that young nerds like him would surely enjoy, his attention had shifted to the player's experience and the moral dilemmas they would have to face in order to complete the adventure. With Ultima IV, Garriott had revolutionized the CRPG genre itself and a new world had opened up, but there was still one last step to be taken: What remained missing from his series was a complex and non-trivial plot, that was integrated into the gaming experience.

Even in Ultima IV the game world was static and while the story proceeded, the player's choices did not impact the world. NPCs were either enemies to be defeated or stand-ins, sources of information through the complicated — and not very successful — dialogue system.

For Ultima V, however, Garriott had other and more ambitious ideas.

After the events of Ultima IV, the world of Britannia continued to enjoy a period of peace and prosperity, enlightened by the virtues embodied by the Avatar. With the dungeons sealed by the Great Council and the population now prosperous and happy, everything seemed to be going well until a mysterious and vast underground world, the Underworld, was discovered. Intrigued, Lord British decided to make an expedition and explore it, but the group led by the wise ruler of Britannia ended up in the hands of an unknown and powerful force.

With Lord British missing, the land was left without leadership and it was up to Lord Blackthorn to take over the administration of the kingdom on an interim basis. Influenced by three ghostly figures, the Shadowlords, Blackthorn quickly fell victim to moral corruption and began to impose a tyrannical and ruthless regime upon the citizens of Britannia, outlawing the heroes who had been the Avatar's fellow adventurers.

This time the player was called back by his old companions Iolo and Shamino, rather than by Lord British, to take on the role of the Avatar once more and save the kingdom of from oblivion. The player must first recover four powerful artifacts possessed by the King (Crown, Scepter, Amulet and Sandalwood Box), defeat the Shadowlords and, finally, descend into the Underworld and save Lord British. Over the course of the adventure the player would reach the discouraging conclusion that the Shadowlords were nothing more than the incarnated antitheses of the three Principles (False instead of Truth, Cowardice instead of Courage and Hate instead of Love).

Generated from three splinters of Mondain's Immortality Gem, destroyed by the Stranger in Ultima, the Shadowlords had long been imprisoned in the Underworld but once freed by adventurers, they began to take over Lord Blackthorn's mind. The latter became blinded by their evil influence and began to impose the Virtues with a cruel and intransigent system of laws, transforming them into strict precepts such as: "You will have to give half of your earnings in charity works, or you will have nothing" for the virtue of the Sacrifice, "If you lose your honor, you will end your life" for that of the Honour or "You will confess your crime and suffer the just penalty, or you will be put to death" for Justice.

For the player, the first surprise was to discover that their previous actions had tragic consequences: the destruction of the Gem of Immortality created the Shadowlords. The second surprise was that Lord Blackthorn was not moved by his own wickedness, but by very good intentions perverted by brutal and dictatorial methods. At the end of the game, freed from the Shadowlords' influence and faced with the consequences of his own interim rule, Blackthorn would accept the sentence handed down to him by Lord British by entering a Moongate; never to return (except in the last episode of the saga).

Ultima IV, with its Virtues, was a good versus evil dynamic. In Ultima V everything was different: as the good deeds and intentions had turned into a code of draconian laws and a ruthless and cruel reign, the player was sometimes faced with very complex choices.

In addition to the shape-shifting children's room, during the exploration of Blackthorn's Castle, if in possession of a badge named Black Badge to move freely, the party could use the password of Oppression. This was a sort of secret society of special agents that the ruler used as a violent arm to impose his dominion. Without the Black Badge, the guards imprisoned the party and the action moved to the torture chambers where Blackthorn imposed a very hard choice on the Avatar: handing over the mantra of a virtue to him or seeing one of his companions (usually Iolo) perish cut in half by a pendulum, in other words, betray the cause or sacrifice a friend.

Unfortunately, any choice made by the player led to the same result: their companion was cut in half and permanently eliminated from the game (deleted the character from the rescue disk). This diminished the drama of the choice because whether the player decided to give in to blackmail or not, the captured companion was still executed; which pushed the player to reload rather than living with the consequences of their choice.

The Shadowlords' influence had an immediate impact on the behavior of NPCs: Cowardice made the inhabitants of the cities escape at the sight of the Avatar, Falsehood made them thieves and with Hate they became aggressive.

Overland and dungeon views were more polished, the dialogue system slightly improved and more spells were available. With emphasis on the story, the technical side of the game changed little except for a great innovation: Garriott's intense attention to detail while recreating Britannia. The interaction with the game world took a leap forward when Richard spent resources to allow players taking torches from walls, sit at tables or use the tools found in rooms and laboratories. One of the most interesting was the telescope that allowed players to observe the eight planets of the world of Britannia, as well as the two moons, and then to discover that their position and orientation changed over time. Richard, already an amateur astronomer at the time, took the luxury to implement an astronomical system on the limited Apple II. The result was that players with lots of patience to observe the sky of Britannia would see the conjunction of the eight planets (each representing one of the Virtues) taking place punctually every five and a half years.

Time in Ultima V was not only fundamental for the movement of the stars. Actions of non-player characters were scheduled, allowing the player to follow the townspeople and discover their habits and more. This choice required more effort and led to less NPCs (189 in comparison to Ultima IV's 309) in the game, but each character had more things to say and information to share, not only through dialogues but also through the observation of daily activity.

Origin would grow to the point of being equipped with a QA department but that came after Ultima V. The only testing of the game was done at the end of the production cycle and manifested as a competition between the two program-mers who had worked the most on it. Garriott and Miles had made a bet on who could complete a playthrough the fastest.

Miles focused on upgrading his character and using a magic object, an axe, to take on any challenge and get to the end of the game as quickly as possible. Gar-riott focused on creating a party, powering it up and facing the strongest enemies. John: "The magic axe was overpowered to the point of unbalancing the game. It was basically a long-range boomerang that did as much damage as a good sword. So it was possible to gain a lot of gold in a hurry once you had it, and plow through the game with little resistance. […] The important thing was getting the magic axe ASAP. Since the other party members wouldn't have had the benefit of the axe, I certainly wouldn't have been in a hurry to recruit them."

Richard's strategy did not work as well. Miles, beating him on time and re-trieving the magic axe before anything else, managed to take the lead and finish the game first: "I beat Richard by immediately setting out for one of the towns on the western isles — I think it was Skara Brae, but it might have been Jhe-lom — as soon as possible after the game started. I vaguely remember using the magic carpet from LB's castle to get there."

Published for Apple II in March 1988, Ultima V came with a generous load of documentation and gadgets: the extensive Book of Lore containing game infor-mation on spells, bestiary and equipment, the usual fabric map of Britannia, the Journal of Lord British's Journey to the Underworld, ie the diary of Lord Briti-sh's inauspicious expedition to the Underworld and a medallion, the Codex Coin, with the diagram of the Virtues.

Curiously, the Codex Coin also appeared depicted in the introduction, described as the magic object Iolo and Shamino used to transport the player to Britannia and, immediately after, to drive away the Shadowlords (an action no longer repeatable during the game). Since Lord British was missing, the supplied Codex Coin was a tangible link between the game and reality.

Developed on Apple II, Ultima V once again used the Mockingboard for music and sound effects. Users with newer and more powerful sound cards, such as Ap-plied Engineering's Phasor and Passport Designs' MIDI interface, could further enjoy the 14 tracks composed by Ken Arnold and the song Stones written by Iolo and Gwenno, aka David R. Watson and Kathleen Jones.

Watson: "My late wife, Gwenno wrote the words (mostly) and I composed the tune. We had just come home from our honeymoon in Britain, and I was fitting new strings to my lute. The tuning process led to the first bars of the tune: Gwen-no, who was very fond of Stonehenge immediately started work on the poem. We had the whole thing worked out in less than an hour. Later Richard needed music for one of his games, and we offered Stones and a couple of others as a simple handshake deal. Later when EA bought Origin, and Gwenno was ill with Cancer,

EA formalized the use of Stones with an actual legal permission, with a formal contract and nice check. We really needed that infusion of cash at the time."

Arnold: "For Ultima V, Richard wanted to include a tune by a friend colleague in the Society for Creative Anachronism (SCA) named Iolo Fitzowen. We went to his house and recorded him singing and playing Lute. I tried to be as faithful as possible to the recording. It turned out to be many people's favorite, and it still runs through my head occasionally."

Watson: "I remember well when Ken and Richard came over to the house I shared with Gwenno. We had a fine visit and recorded Stones, and probably the Baron of Eastmarch song as well. B of E ended up years later as the opening tune for SOTA [Shroud of the Avatar], though the recording they used as a basis was done in our friend Truly Carmichael's closet recording studio years later... and still years ago. Both were good songs that came from the heart and I am very pleased that Richard chose them for his games." Although both pieces of music were proposed by Watson, the one chosen for Ultima was Stones. Watson: "Stones is a bit simpler and the game in question allowed/en¬cour¬aged the gamer to play the tune in order to open a locked door. Perhaps RG and the designers decided it would be easier in that way."

Arnold's visit would not remain an isolated incident. Watson's house, and later his laboratory, would be an essential step for the staff involved in the following chapters of Ultima.

The Apple II's graphics capabilities were now obsolete but the versions on other hardware did not undergo any radical improvement apart from the one on the C64/C128, entrusted to Dr. Cat: "Unlike previous Ultima conversions, I started working on it before the Apple version was complete, so that the Commodore version could ship soon after it was done."

The choice made sense considering that by 1988 the installation base of the C64 was ahead of any other gaming computer. According to Dr. Cat: "The Commodore 64 sold more units than any other model of personal computer — the company claimed it sold 20 million C64s, but people researching it more recently have found out they were exaggerating, and the true number is more like 12.5 million."

The workhorse wanted by Tramiel, moreover, was a machine used mainly for games, as opposed to the Apple II which was often used in offices and schools. The population of players, therefore, was much higher on the Commodore platform.

As with Moebius, Dr. Cat set to work with a lot of effort: "Origin didn't insist that I do extra programming to take advantage of the Commodore 128. But I wanted to, so they purchased a 128 and I had it in my office to work with in addition to the Commodore 64."

The Commodore 128 had been on the market since 1985 but sales didn't meet expectations. Commodore had tried several times to interest the consumers in more powerful models but none replaced the C64. By 1989 the C128 was retired after selling almost six million units, less than half of its younger brother, but still more than all Apple II models together.

Taking advantage of the C128's backwards compatibility, Dr. Cat created a game that could run on both machines: "When it started, it would check whether it was running on a C64 or a C128, and do some extra things if it was running on a 128."

With more memory at his disposal, he used the extra 64K of RAM for music (absent on the C64) and caching the combat and dungeon data. Even the 16Ks of the additional video chip were used to reduce the loads from the 4 floppy disks the game came on.

Such a high number of floppy disks (double sided!) not only imposed more disk changes but also cut into the potential profits. Dr. Cat: "Richard had some big arguments with Robert about the game going from 2 disks, to 3 disks, to 4 disks, as each additional disk added around a dollar to the manufacturing cost & thus stripped a dollar per unit from the profits. But Richard was adamant about making the best possible game he could". The problem would arise again later and more urgent.

Arnold helped Dr. Cat to solve a problem with the SID (Commodores sound chip). For the rest of the porting Dr. Cat had a great time using all the 16 colors of the C64 video chip, again improving the version compared to the original one. Also, because of this upgrade, he was well rewarded: "With Ultima V they were fairly generous with me — when production packaging was designed, I got the nice surprise that instead of the usual 'C64 Version' sticker to put on the box, they had made a special 'C64 version by Dr. Cat' sticker that would go on every package! That was some nice additional exposure for me."

The programming work was done mainly in the New Hampshire offices, where Dr. Cat had remained together with most of the programmers when Richard and 'the rebels', as Miles called them, set sail for Texas. Towards the end of development, Dr. Cat, along with many others, also left the old premises to move to Austin: "My office in New Hampshire was given to John Romero, who had been hired to work on the PC versions of Origin games. I had an Imagewriter printer that I owned but didn't need any more, and I had one less Amdek color monitor than I needed, so I left my printer in that office and took one of Origin's monitors with me instead. They cost about the same amount of money at the time, so I thought it was a fair trade. John later remarked to me how funny he thought it was that I had glued a rubber toy rat to the printer. I told him I hadn't glued it, the heat generated by the printer had partly melted the rat and sealed it to the surface of the printer!"

While the port for Atari 800 remained substantially the same as the original version,except the PC version, released in October 1988 which took advantage of the new EGA graphics and was therefore more colorful. The other 16-bit ports for Amiga and Atari ST enjoyed mouse support, but were full of bugs and were never fixed.

Due to the termination of the affiliate relationship with Electronic Arts a few months earlier, Ultima V was published and sold through Brøderbund. The commercial relationship with the Carlston brothers' company wouldn't last long, but it had given Origin the opportunity to temporarily tone out of EA's orbit.

The Ultima V conversational engine included a black list of vulgarity and offensive words. Because of the rapidly worsening relationship between Garriott and EA, Richard had taken a small revenge by including the word "Electronic Arts" in the list of inconvenient words. Dr. Cat also had to deal with this small piece of code for his C64/C128 port: "I took one look at that very short list of swear words, and I said to myself 'Well, I know a LOT more swear words than that.' I took it as a challenge. So I added to the C64 version every single naughty word I can think of. Including 'gamahuche'[103] which I read in a book that reprinted some old Victorian erotica."

By 1988, the CRPG genre became overcrowded. Ultima V had to compete with important titles like Wasteland, Might and Magic II: Gates to Another World, Bard's Tale II: The Destiny Knight, Pool of Radiance by SSI and Wizardry V: Heart of the Maelstrom.

Of all the competitors, the most fearsome was Pool of Radiance. The first installment of a long series of titles using the Gold Box engine, it was strongly influenced by both Ultima and Wizardry. With Ultima, it shared the representation of the party via the top-down perspective, as well as the tactical combat, while with the latter the dungeons in 3D with its window located at the top left.

Although some reviewers noticed that Pool of Radiance had aspects already seen in other games, the mix was well calibrated and used the AD&D license. The fights had many tactics and the system of spells, skills and character development was very satisfying. Overall it sold over 264,000 copies, beating both Ultima V and the second episode of Bard's Tale, thus winning the 1988 sales record in the CRPG category.

Then there was another influential classic: FTL's Dungeon Master was released in December of 1987 for Atari's new 16-Bit wonder the Atari ST. Jack Tramiel had bought Atari to take revenge on Commodore with another low priced machine.

Dungeon Master revolutionized first-person dungeon crawlers with an unprecedented immersive experience; its real-time gameplay was supported by an excellent use of sound effects,[104] simple dynamic lighting and graphics that raised the bar for the competition. Fluid gameplay was possible due to activity-based progression and an uncluttered user interface.[105] Allowing full mouse-control to intuitively pick up, drop and throw objects in the view and managing the inventory via a new innovation: the paper-doll interface. Spells were based on combining runes, but with very

---

103   Term used to describe the practice of oral sex.

104   Dungeon Master's Amiga version was the first example of 3D-Sound, allowing the player to 'hear' the direction and distance a sound came from.

105   It later influenced Ultima's transition towards an efficient mouse interface

different mechanics than in Ultima IV. [106]

Dungeon Master was an instant phenomenon, becoming the best-selling title for the Atari ST, and was even responsible for increased sales of the computer (and later for memory upgrades on the Amiga). It was ported to other systems, even consoles and several Japanese computer systems. Dungeon Master was so well executed and feature-rich that later games in this subgenre such as Eye of the Beholder (1991) or Captive (1990), were called 'Dungeon Master clones'. It influenced other CRPGs and their developers too, including Garriott himself and his freelance collaborator, Paul Neurath.

Ultima V also clashed with a title published by Origin when it's Commodore 64 port was released. Times of Lore, Chris Roberts' side-project, was the latest addition to the long list of OSI titles which sold well enough but were not breakout successes, therefore becoming collector items.

Something about Roberts' game, however, would survive in Ultima.

---

106   The first appearance of a spell system based on magical syllables is probably linked to Oubliette (1977). This system was reused in Wizardry along with other features from the PLATO game.

False Step

"Sega and Nintendo found themselves facing a new and increasingly more dangerous opponent in the early 1990s-PC computers. Just as the Commodore computer had caught up to Atari and Coleco a decade earlier, personal computers threatened to eclipse the new generation of video game manufacturers as the era of multimedia began."

Kent L. Steven, The Ultimate History of Video Games

"Some of my technical goals for U6 are: 1,024 'tiles', shaded lighting, more NPC realism, even better-looking dungeons… This will likely require 128K minimum on the initial Apple][release."

Richard Garriott, in The Gamers' Forum on CompuServe, 1988

"But then the PC took off so fast — and Apple cratered so fast — that we realized we would have no games to sell. There would be no market into which to sell those games. We had to completely change our staff."

Richard Garriott, interview with Steve Burke for Gamernexus, 2016

The continued and growing success of his games had convinced Garriott not to change the way he worked. His latest product had still been purchased mainly by the Apple II community. For Ultima V Richard had to take advantage of all 64K of memory in his Apple II and improve the speed of disk loading.

Two years earlier, Wozniak himself had described Bill Budge's Pinball Construction Set as "the best software written for an 8-bit computer". Garriott's Ultima V was no less impressive than the software of his former CPCC colleague.

Ignoring the age of the platform, Richard had already set to working on the sequel on his trusty Apple II and announced new ambitious technical features: requiring 128K and offering more aesthetically pleasing dungeons. It would be a tragic error in judgment that would fester for several months before coming to light. Curiously, of all promised features, only the tile size of the map would remain intact.

The IBM PC was designed for the office and not a good machine to create games. Although Microsoft — commissioned by IBM for the development of the operating system of the platform (MS-DOS) and the BASIC interpreter — had launched two games: Colossal Cave Adventure and Donkey.bas. The latter was co-written by Bill Gates and included as an example of a MS Basic game and mocked mainly by Apple users for its simplicity and graphics.

The first change came with the PCjr, IBM's response to Commodore and Apple. It aimed at home users with its very interesting graphic and sound capabilities. On it, Roberta Williams created one of her most important and influential masterpieces: King's Quest; and saved her company with it.

The enthusiasm for the PCjr would be quickly doused by the machine's many flaws. Garriott: "The IBM was a big, unattractive rectangular box; instead of a true keyboard it had calculator keys in the 'chiclet' style. It had no obvious advantages; it didn't have substantially more memory and its DOS operating system was strange and difficult to use. To me, at least, by every objective measure it was either similar to or a little worse than the Apple."

The PCjr was not successful and IBM pulled the plug on the project after less than a year, forcing Sierra to bring King's Quest to the Apple II and the Tandy 1000, one of many IBM PC-clones. IBM had broken completely with its common business strategy and had freely distributed all the information needed to develop software and hardware for the platform.

The decision was driven by economics: To hit the market quickly at a low cost, software development was outsourced to Microsoft and the hardware used chips that were already available. The amazing success and speed with which the standard was adapted by the industry surprised IBM.

The platform grew rapidly, with the introduction of the EGA video card (1984), CGA and Hercules were replaced, and the availability of better sound options for PCs (Roland MT-32 and Adlib with the Yamaha YM3812 chip in 1987) made IBM PC compatible machines much more attractive for video games, finally being able to compete with the Apple II and Commodore 64. With the introduction of the analog Video Graphics Array (VGA) standard in 1987 and the marketing of Creative's first SoundBlaster boards in 1989, the PC was finally destined to take over the market.

The already shrunken market for Apple II Games was loosing ground even faster in the late 80s, similarly to the C64 and most other 8-Bit machines (except for the NES). The modern 16-Bit and 32-Bit platforms had doomed the meanwhile 13 year old veteran. Even the Apple II models that continued to sell were actually 16-Bit with a 6502 compatibility mode. The install base of already sold machines was on the verge of being abandoned for more modern devices. Robert and Richard's erroneous strategic choice had brought OSI close to the abyss: with several titles in development for platforms that would not survive long enough to see their completion, Origin faced the worst crisis since its foundation.

At this point it was necessary to completely revolutionize the company's modus operandi. Games had to be developed first for PC and almost everything else was a niche on the market. However, the staff consisted of experts for the 6502, and lacked experience on PCs. Until then, only some of the programmers had been involved in porting games to the PC. According to Dr. Cat, it wasn't just an accidental market forecast error: "Origin was founded by guys who loved the Apple very, very much and most of them only wanted to program games on the Apple".

To make matters worse, Ultima VI had already been in development for at least six months. The engine Richard had written needed to be rebuilt from scratch. Could Origin survive the time required to finish Ultima VI on PC after already losing six precious months?

Robert addressed the situation with a practical spirit and strictly numerical point of view. Considering that a large part of the staff had to be retrained and Origin would have to continue hiring new staff already familiar with PCs, the cost to keep the company running while porting the projects in progress, including Ultima VI, amounted to at least two million dollars. At a time when no game had yet reached the 1 million dollar threshold, this was a substantial sum. The completed games were intended to yield enough revenue to repay the investment, but considering that until then most of their non-Ultima games were not smash hits, OSI once again relied on Richard's saga. He had to score another hit, this time on a platform he wasn't familiar with, and had to do so within a tight deadline as Origin could not afford to postpone Ultima VI.

After six years of activity, the Garriott brothers had earned enough to be able to divest safely from the business while the alternative was to invest in the company and hope that everything went well. Richard had just bought a house in Austin, the Britannia Manor Mark II (Britannia Manor Mark 1, the first version of his haunted house, had been his temporary residence in New England), placing most of his savings into it. Considering Origin's assets, the Garriott brothers realized they were unable to recoup the fateful two million dollars. By borrowing from banks and mortgaging Britannia Manor, they might be able to make it. Yet, they could not so without risking everything, including potential bankruptcy and insurmountable debt in the case of failure.

In a market where many products could not make returns on their investments, keeping what they had earned and perhaps selling off licenses and IPs to one of the many electronic entertainment giants seemed a sound option. Richard and Robert made it a matter of principle that they would make it: "If we failed, not only would I lose the house, but my brother and I would lose the company and be millions of dollars in debt. We would be left with less than nothing. But we bet on our capabilities. The race was on to get my next Ultima game out with acceptable quality before we ran out of cash."[107]

They took the gamble, giving Origin the required oxygen to re-train staff, hire new technicians and managers, and convert projects onto the PC. Not only that: they raised the stakes by dissolving the affiliation agreement with Brøderbund in a spectacular announcement at the summer CES in 1989. Brøderbund announced that they had lost OSI, but earned Distinctive Software Inc. (a short-lived affiliation as in 1991 EA would purchase DSI turning it into EA Canada, their oldest and largest studio, currently still active).

The Austin office was a branch created with the sole purpose of providing Garriott with the logistical support to program Ultima while all other Origin workers remained in New Hampshire. At the head office, in addition to the administrative sections and Robert's office, there were still developers working on Ultima projects and programmers responsible for ports.

With two separate locations the communication between the employees in New Hampshire and Austin was difficult. The team in charge of porting Ultima V worked in the old New England office relying on receiving code from Richard's team in Texas from time to time. Origin had bought an AT&T 3B2 Unix based Minicomputer, but communications still had to go through Robert's hands. Lacking a direct internal e-mail system, which would arrive only a few years later, necessary communication passed through too many operators before being sorted to the right offices and this would create delays and even loss of information.

One of these mishaps occurred when Kenneth Arnold, from Texas, decided to propose one of many skill contests to engage Origin's staff. Dr. Cat: "Ken Arnold set up some logic and programming challenges just for fun. One of them was to use a made-up CPU he defined, and find the fastest code to swap the contents of two registers. Us programmers in New Hampshire were to give our answers to Robert, who would use the 3B2 email to send them down to Ken in Austin."

John Miles won the competition by handing Arnold the best solution to the puzzle using only 16 CPU cycles. Dr. Cat and Paul Neurath had remained in New Hampshire and entrusted their candidacy to Robert who had forgotten to send it to Texas. Dr. Cat: "Paul Neurath [...] had found a solution that only took 15 cycles. I submitted one using a similar coding trick but a slightly different method, which also took only 15 cycles."

107   Garriott, Richard (2017) Explore/Create, Chapter 5

In the second half of 1988, when Richard realized this serious error in judgment, the entire company's focus shifted towards the required transformation. The video game industry was about to shift away from the old 8-Bit Computers Richard had grown up with and accordingly, customer expectations grew as well, which Origin would push to new heights.

Adolescence was over. Origin had to change quickly, or it would perish.

Change of Guards

"Richard and I got shiny new 25 MHz 386 boxes that neither of us knew how to use. He got busy on the design side, and I started reading books on C and x86 assembly programming."

John Miles

"There was less of a division between programming and game design in those days."

Herman Miller

At the end of 1988, Ken Arnold left Origin to become a Systems and Hardware Engineer at Dell, while Dallas Snell finally abandoned his role as programmer to become an Executive Producer, responsible for the development of projects in New Hampshire and Austin. John Miles and Richard Garriott, who were behind a large part of the programming work for Ultima V, took a step back and abandoned the programming of the sequel due to unfamiliarity with the new platform. With the "old guard" of Apple II programmers out of the game because they had been transferred, promoted to management positions, or were temporarily unavailable, the technicians who had until now been in charge of porting became the company's most important resource; and the only workforce able to operate immediately and prevent the assembly line from stopping irrevocably.

Herman Miller and Cheryl Chen were then transferred from New Hampshire, where they had previously worked on porting for the IBM PC, and were put to work under Richard's leadership, forming the backbone of the new team.

Xiao "Cheryl" Chen was a young programmer from China who came to the United States to study computer science at Boston College and recently arrived at Origin after responding to a job advertisement in the local newspaper. Prior, she had converted games such as Chris Roberts' Times of Lore, Chuck Bueche's 2400 A.D. and, of course, Ultima V to IBM PCs but she had also shared her knowledge of Chinese culture with Paul Malone for the game Windwalker, Moebius' sequel.

Herman Miller had also recently joined Origin's staff having sent his curriculum vitae to several software houses. He was passionate about role-playing, eager to apply his knowledge of the IBM PC platform and Assembly on the MOS 6502, and wanted to make a career in the video game industry. Origin was looking for someone to take Ultima V to the IBM PC and John Fachini was in charge of leading the team of programmers. Miller's candidature arrived at the right time as the young man was immediately hired.

Freshly recruited, Chen and Miller, along with Ed Nelson, were placed to work on Ultima V, on different pieces of the code. The programming was executed simultaneously with the development of the Apple II version done by Garriott's team in Texas. Miller: "We would periodically get updates of source code from the game, written in 6502 assembly language. Then we'd make printouts of the code, and translate them into the C programming language or 8086 assembly language. The PC port was mostly written in C, with assembly language for graphics or anything that needed to be optimized to run faster. We worked in adjacent offices and shared code by carrying 5 1/4" floppy disks from room to room; we didn't have a file server or version control software in those days. We just divided up the tasks between us so that each of us was working on a different part of the game at the same time".

Thanks to the efforts of the entire team, the port of Ultima V was a success. Also, because the game used the newer EGA video standard which was superior to the old graphics capabilities of the Apple II, Ultima V on PC was much more colorful. But what was still missing on IBM machines was support for custom sound cards such as the Apple II's Mockingboard used by Kenneth Arnold for Exodus years earlier.

In addition to Chen and Miller, Dr. Cat joined the Ultima VI team as well. Along with a growing number of developers, Dr. Cat had already been transferred to Texas towards the end of the porting of Ultima V to the Commodore 64/128, a move that had allowed the version to be released at the same time as the original version for Apple II. In fact, the headquarters in New Hampshire was emptying and would soon be permanently closed in favor of Austin. Even Robert Garriott would eventually have to capitulate and return to commute and visit the headquarters in Austin a couple of times a month, as well as direct it from a distance.

Employees who were unfamiliar with the IBM PC were trained or moved to projects where their skills could be put to best use. For example, John Miles, after "digging a furrow along the way to the offices" of Chen and Miller, had "to ask one stupid question after another" in his effort to master x86 Assembly. He felt prepared enough to go back to programming, but did not deal with game development anymore: rather, he was hijacked to create tools and middleware.

Miles: "The segmented architecture in use by MS-DOS in those days was miserable to live with, so I started working on general-purpose libraries that would allow us to use C whenever possible".

With the exception of the intro and end sequence of Ultima VI, Miles would no longer be directly involved in the development of a video game. However, the tools he created before leaving Origin would earn him numerous accreditations for many of the most successful titles OSI would produce in the years to come.

One of the most important recruitments of the '88-'90 period was that of Warren Spector.

Born October 2nd, 1955, Spector was six years older than Richard and one of the oldest employees among OSI staff. He had a bachelor's degree in Communication Science from Northwestern University, Illinois, and a master's degree in Radio-TV-Film from Austin University. Here, looking for a way to pay the rent, he came across Steve Jackson and started working with SJG.

Spector quickly made a career at Jackson's company, starting as a simple editor and becoming responsible for the magazines. His career had made a turn for the better, when he left SJG and managed to jump on the diligence of TSR, the publishing house that owned the rights to D&D, one of the most influential companies in the world of table games and role-playing, and had managed a great product: Top Secret/S.I. (1987).

Spector's first meeting with Garriott took place in Richard's "black period", and Warren had not failed to notice the conspicuous Mitsubishi from which the programmer had come down to visit Steve Jackson, but on that occasion the two had not even spoken. The second, decisive meeting took place in 1987. Spector: "I was working at TSR in Lake Geneva, Wisconsin in the late-80s. I returned to Austin, TX to be on a panel at a science fiction convention called Armadillocon and found myself on a panel with Richard. He was working on Ultima V at the time and, as he and I each talked about games on the panel it became apparent that we were sympatico on a lot of things."

Upon returning to Lake Geneva, Warren began to feel homesickness and dissatisfaction with his job. Denis Loubet's phone call came at the right time: "He said Origin was looking for an Associate Producer and asked if I was interested. I said yes because I was obsessed with video games back then and because it was an opportunity to get back home to Austin."

Knowing him since SJG, Loubet had probably talked with his colleagues about the new candidate because it didn't take long for Spector to get an appointment. Nevertheless, winning a place at Origin was not at all easy: "The guy [Dallas Snell] who headed up production put me through the wringer — a nine-hour interview! — and then handed me off to Richard, Chris Roberts and some of the other creative types there at the time. They must have liked what they heard because they offered me a job (at a substantial pay cut!) and next thing I knew I was making computer games."

Always animated by a great passion for cinema, Spector tried to bring some cinematography into the video game industry, reorganizing the structure of OSI according to a hierarchical scheme very similar to that of Hollywood productions. His innovative idea would quickly take hold in the whole industry, as this form of entertainment is not substantially different from a sort of interactive cinema. The introduction of the CD-ROM and pioneers like Night Trap (1992) and, above all, 7th Guest (1993) would soon make it clear that Warren was not wrong.

Consistent with his understanding of the creative process of video games, he carved out the role of producer for several Origin titles under development and helped Richard design Ultima VI. Already accustomed to administering day-to-day operations, Spector would soon take over Origin's productions and allow the various development teams to express their full potential, leading the company to its creative peak.

With renewed energy, Richard and the Origin staff got to work with the goal of completing Ultima VI with a dead line set for early 1990.

It was without a doubt one of the most demanding periods for Garriott. Deprived of sleep by work and worry, Richard began to fear for the worst possible scenario, a delay in completing Ultima VI or a poor reception by the public. The company's remaining days were numbered and Richard, who had generally never been on time, first with the delivery date imposed by CPCC, then by On-Line Systems, could not afford to miss the deadline in March 1990.

Despair, he wrote, motivated him a great deal.

Carefully balancing time and available resources without giving in to the temptation to cut content, features, or keeping the overall quality of the product down in order to finish earlier, Richard still had to abandon the engine he had written and improved from version to version since 1978, to start his project from scratch on a new platform. Luckily, Origin's first published Chris Roberts game, Times of Lore, had bequeathed a much more user friendly interface than the Ultima V one, and the team used it as a starting point. Just as he did with D&D 1 for the first time, Richard first created the software technology and then, realizing its potential, began to develop the game.

The choice he had in front of him was decidedly complex. Until then, OSI's prototypes were specific to machines with highly standardized hardware and the software that had been written for Apple II, due to the design of Wozniak's platform, was compatible on all subsequent revisions, except for requiring memory expansions for the most complex programs. The choice to implement a soundtrack and advanced audio functionality was in fact the only feature dedicated to those who had enhanced their hardware with optional sound cards such as the Mockingboard.

Developing on such machines, or bringing the software to platforms such as the Commodore 64, which had a CPU fully compatible to Apple II's 6502, was relatively simple, mostly because the programmers had to deal with machines that had standardized hardware. With the transition to the PC, everything was destined to change because the market was made up of users who had PCs equipped with peripherals and components produced by different companies, and very diverse specifications. While the avant-garde was perhaps equipped with Hard Disks and dedicated sound cards, there was also a large market of older machines, relying on cheap processors, older versions of MS-DOS, floppy disk drives (51/4" or 31/2") and the PC speaker as audio device.

Faced with the choice of how to develop PC games, some software houses focused on products that were compatible with most of the available PCs at the time, to reach the largest possible share of the installation base. This strategy required a great deal of sacrifice: Games were being developed to work on the least performing as well as the most advanced hardware and, as a result, they risked spending money on publishing and marketing while appearing to be already outdated by the end of the whole process in comparison to the products of competitors who operated with a different approach. Other software houses, such as Sierra On-Line, decided to produce games for more advanced systems by counting on the "wow" factor, superior graphics and audio to amaze, as well as getting high sales and counting on the fact that their product would still be bought even by those who would update their hardware later.

Garriott and OSI decided to follow this strategy. Rather than looking for the lowest common denominator in the market to reach more users, they focused on developing games for cutting-edge hardware, creating games specifically aiming at the new VGA video cards and computers equipped with sound cards. This strategy, as we will see, was not without risks. In order to create a game for the most advanced technology available, Richard needed technically capable and above all, more numerous teams than what was standard at the time. The first four chapters of Ultima were written personally by Garriott, who resorted to the help of friends and collaborators for some special features such as the tiles engine and the soundtrack by Arnold. The fifth chapter of the series was largely written by Miles and Garriott, with the help of Arnold for the music and Loubet for tile graphics. However, with the sixth chapter, everything had changed. Richard's temporary exemption from programming, instrumental in giving him the time to learn the new x86 Assembly language, had become definitive. Reluctantly, Garriott ended up leaving the entire programming to others, devoting himself exclusively to the game's design.

The development team grew considerably in a few months to include four programmers (Cheryl Chen, John Miles, Herman Miller and Gary Scott Smith), who dealt with different aspects of the code and sharing tasks. Other new additions to the team also included many technicians, musicians, designers and writers. The transition of the video game industry to more maturity was underway, but not yet complete, at least at Origin. Development teams had grown to involve people with different skills but staff were not yet completely specialized. Dr. Cat, for example, although joining Origin as a programmer, entered the Ultima VI project as a plot and dialogue writer. In the same way, Miller, in addition to programming a considerable part of the game, ended up taking care of the soundtrack.

One of the main obstacles to the specialization of roles, besides the economic factor, was the almost total lack of suitable tools to create games without having strong programming knowledge. Miller: "Sound on the PC was very primitive in those days and typically involved programming. Most PCs just had a speaker that could play a single tone at a time, and you needed to do rapid pitch changes with careful timing in order to get more interesting sound effects."

In the absence of suitable instruments, writing music on a PC was more of a programming job than composition work, and excellent musicians would have been completely disorientated when lacking good computer skills, while being faced with the complex technique necessary to allow PCs to emit sounds and melodies.

The same problem also afflicted all those who were in charge of writing the dialogues, deciding the interactions between the NPCs and the player, implementing interactivity with the world and integrating the plot into the game world, which they had to draw piece by piece. For them too, powerful development tools were not available and therefore a certain programming competence was required to make the code for managing NPCs or dialogues work. The roles of programmers, designers and writers were therefore blurred, without a clear and defined line of demarcation. Cheryl Chen, for example, was mainly in charge of the UCS, the Ultima Conversation System, the code for managing dialogues with NPCs, while others had to learn the scripting language in order to implement the conversations as planned in the design.

Among the latter, there was another new enlistment in Origin. Manda[108] had recently joined the company. In 1988, when she gave in to three invitations from her acquaintances, Denis Loubet, Jeff Dee and Dr. Cat, she submitted her candidacy and was hired mainly as a graphic designer. Her first assignment was with Greg Malone's Windwalker, for whom she did some small graphic work "like pandas and bamboo", but her technical skills were remarkable and allowed her to create a small software for scanning images, connecting a fax machine to the Commodore 64.

It's no surprise in the Ultima VI team, Manda ended up playing two roles at once: as a graphic designer, drawing different portraits of NPCs, and as a writer, using Chen's UCS to implement characters dialogues. This was not an isolated case.

Cheryl Chen's creation was much more user friendly than the parser implemen-

---

108   "My whole name is Manda, no name. There's actually someone else called Amanda Dee, and she's a video game producer."

ted in the previous chapters. Instead of forcing the player to use the usual terms such as "name", "job", "health" or guessing the keyword with which to activate an NPC response, the new dialogue engine highlighted the sensitive words that the player could use in dialogues. In truth, at least in the first versions, the useful words were not immediately recognizable. Manda: "The scripting language let me introduce more keywords, which I had it highlight. In the very very first version, there was no highlighting. Highlighting keywords came in later, which made it less challenging– less like an actual conversation. The trade-off was that it guaranteed players wouldn't miss anything important."

In line with Richard's habit of including characters inspired by real people in his games, Manda was invited to meet and get to know them, in order to be able to represent them in the best possible way with her portraits. Therefore, to be able to make the portrait of Iolo, Manda went to David Watson's workshop, where the craftsman taught her how to build real crossbows and would later repair a curious object from Dr. Cat.

Watson: "Amanda, the Origin artist came to my house on numerous occasions, usually accompanied by Dr. Cat Shapiro. I repaired a traditional-style Japanese doll house for her and we worked on crossbows. Manda was great company, always full of enthusiasm, and quick to learn woodworking skills."

Manda: "Oh, I remember that! He's too kind. And the house is Dr. Cat's. It wasn't a toy. It was his dad's. His dad was a soldier in WWII, stationed in Japan in 1944. The tiny building is a scale model of a house they really built. They didn't do blueprints, they made models!"

Watson: "Yes, I had forgotten Manda's story about the house be a model of her father's place in Japan. It makes sense that builders of traditional Japanese houses wouldn't need plans if they stuck to traditional forms… all the joints and details would be established. Making medieval crossbows is a lot like that too. Anyway, Amanda was a sweetie and lots of fun to visit or work with."

When Manda met Sherry, whose nickname was "Mouse", a girl Richard was seeing at the time, she was very impressed with her ways and character: "I thought she has such a big heart, the little portrait has to have a heart-shaped patch on her front."

This is how the image of the character of Sherry the Mouse was born, even if the shape of the mouse, apart from the stain, was actually inspired by Peanut a.k.a. Hamsterball Lecter, the hamster of Dr. Cat, a very adventurous animal, who used to escape and was recaptured in one way: the owner, or Manda, had to lie down on the ground and keep a hand open with some sesame seeds, until the hamster approached to eat.

Even some programmers ended up in the game. Manda's virtual alter ego is Penumbra: "I'm into herbs and gardening, and Richard created the character as the resident of a cottage with a naughty garden full of sleep and poison patches that the Avatar has to cross". Penumbra's drawing was a self-portrait of Manda, who granted himself a small license and disregarded the rule of Richard who had decided to make the world of Ultima different from other fantasy populated by the usual dwarfs and elves. Manda: "If you look carefully, you might notice she has pointed ears. Perhaps there are still elves in Sosaria, after all."

The team of writers was very large and, in addition to Manda, obviously included Richard and Warren Spector, Greg Paul Malone II, John Miles, Herman Miller, Todd Mitchell Porter and Dr. Cat. The latter, in truth, had a leadership role on the team, although not official at the level of accreditation. On the cover of Ultima V he was given the credit for the game's port, which had never happened before. He didn't do as well as the writing manager, and the episode remained in Dr. Cat's memory with a hint of disappointment: "On Ultima VI, the in-game credits only listed me as one of the writers rather than give me the Head Writer title they used for me at the office, they said they hadn't decided to credit head writers."

Miller, besides dealing with a generous portion of the Ultima VI code, implemented the monster "spawn" system and named it: "I also came up with the idea of monster spawners, which we called 'eggs' as the icon in the map editor looked like an egg."

Since Ken Arnold, the programmer/musician who had dealt with the previous titles had left Origin, it was Miller's turn to write the code necessary for the chosen soundtrack to be played on the most popular sound cards: AdLib Music Synthesizer Card, Creative Labs Sound Blaster and the cards based on the industry standard for music hardware, the Roland MT-32 synthesizer module. The music itself was composed mainly by a new recruitment of Origin: Todd Mitchel Porter.

The history of the latter's entry into Origin says a lot about Origin's recruitment policy and informal culture before the 1990s. Porter's dream in the drawer was to enter the video game industry and he had devoted much of his free time from work to write a role-playing game called Knights of Legend. When Porter felt he was ready, he asked a friend at Penguin Software, the software house from which many of Origin's first generation of programmers and managers had come, for help to get in touch with OSI executives.

Fortunately, the contact between Porter and Origin was established just when Richard was visiting Austin to arrange accommodation for his company's detached headquarters. It was thus relatively easy for the candidate to arrange a meeting with Garriott.

Porter: "I could not believe my luck! I drove to Austin and met Richard who was looking at properties to open up an office of Origin in Texas. Richard was unbelievably nice. He spent the entire day with me and I showed him my game. We talked for many hours and I think it was around midnight when he said – 'Let us publish your game' and literally wrote out a quick contract on a napkin. I could not believe that a random call had led (not 24 hours later) to a publishing contract."

Knights of Legend was released in 1989, just before Ultima VI, and was supposed to be episodic in nature, prompting its buyers to buy the next expansions to complete the adventure, a bit like the Apshai saga. Unfortunately, sales were not good, although the reviews were positive. This put an end to the series, but Porter's career in Origin lasted a little bit longer, before he left the company for California, landed at SSI and worked on the series of D&D games well known as the Gold Box series.

For Ultima VI, Porter proposed some pieces he had composed on his guitar. As the great-grandson of the famous Chet Atkins, Todd Mitchell had learned to play since he was a child, even though he had never learned to write music: his way of composing was instinctive, by ear, and translating his productions into machine code was a challenge. Porter: "I did so by ear using some software to lay in the notes. I'd play a sequence on guitar and then note by note (listening to the tones) transcribed them to the computer. Funny note, many years later I was playing one of the songs at a Game Developers Conference and some guys came up to me and said – 'Oh my gosh that is so cool, you transcribed an old Ultima VI song to the guitar!' I laughed and told them that actually the song started on the guitar and I translated it to the computer!"

Miller's work of rearranging the music written by Ken Arnold for the previous episodes of Ultima and those written by Todd Mitchell Porter and lent to Ultima VI, did not prevent him from creating an original track, "Audchar Gargl Zenmur", which in the Gargoyle language means "Song of the Gargoyle people". Miller's track had a very interesting peculiarity: it was designed to be played for the first time alone and, at the end of the game, at the same time as "Rule, Britannia", the readjustment of the famous British patriotic song, written by Ken Arnold for Exodus and later become the hymn of Ultima and the solemn accompanying music of Lord British.

The reasons for this curious choice are explained below.

For the second time, the ballad Stones, the piece written by David Watson and his wife Kathleen Jones, returned to the 12 tracks chosen for the published version.

Among the team of writers there was another new entry: Siobhan Beeman, then known as Stephen, was a student at the University of Texas in Austin. Passionate about role-playing, she attended a center called Hexworld, led by a freelance game writer named David Ladyman. At Hexworld, Beeman had the opportunity to meet the man who would set her career in the gaming industry in motion: Scott Haring, the head of Car Wars' line at SJG.

Siobhan was a fierce Car Wars player and the meeting allowed her to participate assiduously in the testing sessions of the game designed by Jackson. When Haring left SJG in 1987, Beeman was immediately hired to replace the game designer and in Jackson's company had the opportunity to meet and get to know Warren Spector and Jeff George[109]. A little less than two years later, in the summer of 1989, Origin was looking for staff, mainly writers, to join the team working on Ultima VI. Beeman applied and thanks to the assurances of Spector and

---

109   Jeff George made important contributions to the development of Bad Blood, Wing Commander and Ultima VII Part 2, covered extensively in Volume 2

George, who had been able to work with her, got the job and was put to work on the characters of the Gargoyle race.

It wasn't a simple task because, it was necessary for Beeman to find a way to make the individual Gargoyles special and unique. Beeman: "We were painting with a broad brush, I'm afraid, but the results were fun". The only human character that Siobhan had to create was Pridgarm, who guarded Yew's cells, and to characterize him was inspired by the advertising of a company of biscuits named "Pepperidge Farms", depicting a twentieth-century Yankee old style.[110]

The team of artists also collaborated with all the programmers and writers, but first and foremost, Denis Loubet. According to an internal structure that would survive for a short time until 1992, the year of the Electronic Arts acquisition of Origin, designers and artists were a resource shared by the whole company, organized into a group of autonomous work, whose services could be requested by the teams, working on different projects. For Ultima VI, Loubet touched an important part of the work: the cover of the box, several portraits and a large amount of tiles. The new graphics engine, in addition to having a higher resolution and a wider palette, was able to draw the world using an unprecedented tileset of 2,048 pieces, creating a huge mosaic.

It was too onerous a job for anyone and Loubet, looking for helpers, suggested that his superiors hire an old acquaintance of the paper-based gaming industry, Jeff Dee. The latter had long been looking for a job and had sent his curriculum vitae to several companies, forgetting OSI. The call from Origin came as a surprise, but the interview went well and Dee was hired and immediately put to work on a Paul Neurath project, Space Rogue. Once finished helping the programmer, Jeff was hijacked for Ultima VI and then for Worlds of Ultima: The Savage Empire.

In addition to Loubet and Dee, the team of artists consisted of Keith Berdak, Daniel Bourbonnais, Glen Johnson and, of course, Manda. All contributed to varying degrees to the completion of the graphic part of Ultima VI, by far the most ambitious of all Origin projects to date.

In a hurry, Richard was convinced that the game would be published exclusively for computers with VGA video cards, the best available at the time, without the backward compatible features on older cards such as EGA and CGA. It was Gary Smith's turn to write the code needed to readjust the graphics and scale them to lower resolutions with fewer colors. Not without a great effort, the programmer surprised Garriott by managing to implement in time a driver that automatically converted the images to 256 colors in a palette of 16, 4 and even monochrome, for those who had only a Hercules Monochrome.

Given the huge number of NPCs (202 were counted by fans, but Dr. Cat remembers that he included almost 250), Richard also had doubts as to whether it was

---

110   The advertising character of "Pepperidge Farms" will then be the subject of a tribute from the animation series Family Guy and will become a widespread Internet meme.

possible, for each of them, to write the daily activity chart, dialogues and even draw portraits in tight times. Dr. Cat set to work on at least one-third of the dialogues, assigning to the team of writers those whom he could not follow personally, and supervising the work of his colleagues. Also Manda, who was already engaged with portraits, gave a hand with the dialogues. Beeman had been hired for the Gargoyle dialogues and focused on them, while Todd Porter, who had just finished lending his music to the soundtrack, offered to populate the cities that had been drawn, but were still deserted by inhabitants, all to be created from scratch.

It was a tour de force, a "death march" in Porter's words. Portraits were the most critical phase. With the artists available, each designer would have to make six portraits a day in order to finish on time. Dr. Cat: "The other 5 artists in the company finished 1 to 4 a day, depending on how fast they were. Manda lowered her usual art quality level to turn up her speed, and finished 6 a day. Since she hadn't done much other art at the company before (just converting the Windwalker art from Apple 4 color to the 16 on the C-64 for me while I was programming it), some people at Origin on her next project were concerned she wasn't a very good artist. Then they saw the work she was doing on that one, and realized that she was."

The Gargoyle portraits, to have the same style, were entrusted to a single artist, Berdak, while Jeff Dee took care of the fortune-teller.

With so many characters, even naming each one of them was a challenge. Richard had always been inspired by friends, family, colleagues and members of the SCA. Dr. Cat started with the characters who had already appeared in Ultima's universe, but discovered that they weren't enough.

At that time he attended, together with Manda, a group named Amtgard, later known as High Fantasy Society, an association of fans similar to the SCA. With the exception that the latter had as its purpose the recreation of the medieval world, while the members of Amtgard were interested in the fantasy world. Dr. Cat and Manda, decided to get help from Amtgard's friends and to create NPCs based on the members of this association.

The idea was successful and the NPCs were completed on time, but the most entertaining consequence, without a shadow of a doubt, came when Richard was invited, along with other SCA members, to participate in an Amtgard event. Dr. Cat: "Various members of the group came up to the head table to bow and greet our visiting noble. And a number of them thanked him for the privilege of having a character named for them in his game. So multiple times that evening I got to watch the expression on his face briefly betray his bewilderment as he tried to be polite and friendly, but was clearly thinking 'What's going on with all these people I never met and heard of being in my Ultima?' An experience he'd clearly never had before! I found it quite amusing."

Without the staff knowing, it was a race against time that had as its prize not only the success of the game, but the salvation of the company. Richard and Robert, deciding to move forward, had put everything they had on the plate, in the biggest bet of their professional lives.

Dr. Cat: "They didn't tell any of us staff, but the company was running out of money & couldn't get any more bank loans, so if Ultima VI wasn't finished by the beginning of March, the company would go bankrupt. Richard Garriott loaned the company all the money he had at the time, except he kept just enough that if the company went out of business, he could pay everyone one month's pay to tide them over while they looked for new jobs. Of course since they didn't tell us about this, we weren't worried and could just concentrate on making a good game and trying to finish by March 1st as they asked us to."

Extraordinarily, Garriott's staff managed to complete the work on time and send it to print. As usual, the staff celebrated the completion of the project, but did not get time to enjoy a deserved rest because Warren Spector, believing he had a particularly interesting product in his hands, almost immediately moved all the resources available to a project that Chris Roberts had been carrying out for over two years, a simulation game of space fighting with the temporary name Wingleader.

Happy with the work done, and confident that he had saved his company, Richard was still exhausted from the tour de force that led to the completion of Ultima VI, when some users reported a problem with the game's operation. Attempting to reproduce the malfunction, Origin engineers concluded that Ultima VI could not work properly if played directly from the 51/4" or 31/2" floppies, while the problem did not arise for users who had the game installed on Hard Disk.

Investigating the matter, OSI's managers soon came to the conclusion: the game had been programmed on advanced hardware, i.e. PCs equipped with Hard Disk, a device that, in 1990, was not yet standard, although it began to be relatively popular. Since no one had tested the floppy game, the defect had escaped everyone and the game had gone to press with a very serious bug that prevented it from being used on PCs not equipped with HD.

Richard Garriott: "It turned out that if you tried to play the entire game on floppy-disc drives and did not have a hard drive, it failed. That wasn't true only for the person who called or for our programmer, it was true for every person on earth who did not install this to a hard drive. And at that point less than 10 percent of consumers owned a hard drive".[111]

When the bug was finally found and reproduced, Origin had already printed and shipped hundreds of thousands of copies and Richard and Robert found themselves having to seriously consider that, in spite of everything, Origin would fail, taking all their savings with it. With nothing left to do, the two prepared for the worst, but to some surprise, the reports soon indicated that the percentage of users who had reported malfunctions, and made the game, was substantially unchanged

---

111   Garriott, Richard (2017) Explore/Create, Chapter 5

from that expected for printing errors and defective magnetic media. So it was then that Richard had discovered that the choice to create games for the most advanced hardware was a good one and that, indeed, the first to buy Ultima VI were those who had, for the most part, platforms with latest generation components and hard disks. As Garriott had to remember later, even though only a minority of PC users had hard drives, almost all Ultima VI purchasers didn't notice the bug, not using the game directly from the floppy, they didn't run into the fateful crashes that made it impossible to complete.

Origin was saved and, indeed was about to publish a masterpiece that would make it known throughout the world, dispelling forever the myth that OSI was only the company for the Ultima series.

Ultima in the East and the birth of JRPGs

"Created by Yuji Horii, Dragon Quest combined the overhead movement of Ultima with the first-person, random battles of Wizardy, and effectively created the Japanese RPG subgenre."

Kurt Kalata, The History of Dragon Quest, Gamasutra, 2008

"Both Wizardry and Ultima have huge followings in Japan. The computer magazines cover Lord British (Ultima) like our National Inquirer would cover a television star. When Robert Woodhead, of Wizardry fame, was recently in Japan he was practically mobbed by autograph seekers."

Roe Adams III, CGW, Vol 5.4, September/October 1985

Early developers and entrepreneurs in the world of video games had been players first. Nolan Bushnell experienced Spacewar! during his college years and became inspired to make the Computer Space arcade game. It wasn't a success but he didn't give up and continued trying until he commissioned the Pong project from Allan Alcorn. Games like dnd and Moria for PLATO or Colossal Cave Adventure for PDP-10 born in university environments and played by students and technicians, would soon inspire the creation of MUD,[112] adventure, dungeon crawler and RPG games on mainframes and the emerging microcomputers. Ideas and concepts of what made a game good were still maturing.

In 1983, two young Englishmen, John F. Humphreys and D. A. Briskham, wrote the CRPG Ring of Darkness for the Dragon platform by Dragon Data, a Welsh company that went bankrupt the following year. The game was quickly forgotten, sharing the fate of countless others written for failed early 80s microcomputers.

Its introduction is reminiscent of Tolkien's Lord of the Rings, talking about four rings created by powerful magicians to stop the threat posed by Shedir, the evil and most powerful Ring of Darkness. The actual game was not just similar to Akalabeth or the first two Ultimas but an obvious collage of them. Darkness was so faithful to them that it even copied Ultima II's absurd gag to kill the court jester to free the Princess.

Roland Knight and Dave Shuwchum's Gates of Delirium (1987) for the TRS-80 was a similar take on Ultima III. The hotkey system was virtually identical and the initial screen was copied as well as the tile graphics of the outside world and cities, monsters and naval vessels.

Both were early examples of taking inspiration from Ultima to a level bordering plagiarism, but they would not be the last.

Garriott's first two publishers had no distribution channels in Europe or Asia. The void was filled by small importers but the European market was dominated by other platforms than in North America and were much cheaper than the Apple II.

In 1983, the commercial agreement with Electronic Arts gave Origin access to their distribution network in Europe, where Commodore had meanwhile gained a lot of traction. The publishing rights for Akalabeth and the first two chapters of Ultima remained with Sierra On-Line and it would take Origin several years to regain control, but Exodus was immediately sold on different platforms internationally.

There was a widespread belief that the Eastern market was unpredictable and impervious for Western products, although some American companies managed to bring successful games to the booming Japanese market. Atari's Breakout was in such high demand that it caught a Japanese mafia's attention: NAMCO's founder, Masaya Nakamura, was forced to produce unlicensed arcade cabinets rather than waiting for Bushnell to send the few unsold copies not sold in the United States. Japan was a strong and interesting market, but difficult to enter. On the contrary, Japanese products had repeatedly found their way to the West with legendary successes such as Space Invaders, Pac-Man and Donkey Kong.

Ultima and Wizardry had a difficult time breaking into the Japanese market because of a flourishing local microcomputer industry that was incompatible with Western platforms. D&D also wouldn't see its first official release in Japan until

---

112   Multi User Dungeon

1985, although unofficial self-made translations were available to a few enthusiasts.

Unsurprisingly, the first generation of Japanese CRPGs, often called proto-JRPGs, were only vaguely inspired by Western ones. In the words of Naito Tokihiro, programmer and designer of Hydlide (1984): "Back then, Japanese people didn't have a well-defined sense of the RPG as a game genre. I suspect that because of this, the creators took the appearance and atmosphere of the RPG as a basic reference, and constructed new types of games according to their own individual sensibilities. In my case, I never had the opportunity to use an Apple II, so I was completely unaware of Wizardry and Ultima. Even today, I essentially know nothing about these games. I was inspired by AD&D and fairy illustrations in books from the West, and developed my own idiosyncratic view of the genre."[113]

Early Japanese games were unburdened by Western RPG rule systems and explored a wider variety of settings: from fantasy to science fiction, from espionage plots to erotic themes in modern settings. A particularly important development was the mix of RPG and action games, as shown in one of 1984's most crucial titles: Dragon Slayer, the first installment in a series from Falcom, a publisher which would soon cross paths with Ultima and Garriott.

The first to bring the mechanics of Western role-playing games to Japan was a thirty-year-old Dutchman named Henk Rogers. Born in Amsterdam, Rogers grew up in New York then moved to Hawaii where he came across D&D for the first time at university. His father had to move to Japan again for work — he was in the gems industry — and Rogers ended up following him to stay close to a girl he would later marry.

The first generation of microcomputers was a battle of numerous incompatible models for dominant market share. In 1979, NEC's PC-8001 was an early successful competitor, causing important players such as Fujitsu and Hitachi to enter the market while other Hi-Tech companies waited on the sidelines.

Its successor model, the PC-8801, impressed Rogers enough to buy one. He could not know that other manufacturers would join forces and create a compatible standard (MSX) in response, which would later take over the market.

Having played The Temple of Apshai, Ultima and Wizardry, and being a D&D enthusiast, in 1983 Rogers decided to create a CRPG, a niche category in the Japanese market. Inspired mainly by Wizardry, Rogers built a first-person dungeon crawler using semigraphical characters as Escape! did years earlier. He founded Bullet Proof Software (today Blue Planet Software) to publish it under the name The Black Onyx (a reference to his father).

Without a magic system and limited to one class (the warrior), the game was inferior to Wizardry in most aspects. An interesting feature of Rogers' game was the changing appearance of party members reflecting worn equipment.

Otherwise, Black Onyx was a very simple game by any standard.

Rogers' first marketing choice taught him a lesson about the cultural differences that caused other entrepreneurs before him to fail: Attempting to market the game using a "Frank Frazetta-style"[114] Conan the Barbarian on a pile of corpses didn't work. Nobody in Japan understood the reference and in the first month, his wife, the sales representative of their enterprise, did not receive a single phone call.

This didn't stop Rogers, a salesman at heart, who would later become famous for landing the most lucrative business deal in the history of video games: securing the rights to Tetris.[115] Accompanied by an interpreter, he visited all the editorial offices of magazines that dealt with video games offering journalists an accelerated course in role-playing games.

Rogers: "I sat down with each editor and asked them for their name. I typed this in and then asked them to choose the head that looked most like them. In this way I taught them how to roll a D&D character. Then I left them to play".[116]

The plan worked perfectly. By March, the enthusiastic magazine reviews pushed the sales and his game became the number one hit of 1984, falling to second place a year later. Black Onyx helped pave the way for RPGs and was soon ported to other platforms.

It successfully sold 150,000 copies on numerous platforms (NEC PC-8801, MSX, Sega's early SG-1000 console and Nintendos FamiCom and Game Boy Color) showing that RPGs had an enormous sales potential.

Rogers didn't innovate further to improve his game and the sequel ended up offering a very similar product. In such a fast-paced market this was a guarantee for failure as Japanese developers had already set to work with much greater skill and resources.

The competition quickly became very productive, replacing Black Onyx with a new big hit: Koichi Nakamura's Dragon Quest (1986). The Japanese staff had a much better understanding of what their market would love: Nakamura hired Akira Toriyama as artistic director, entrusting him with the task of creating the characters and art work.

Toriyama was already one of Japan's most famous and appreciated comic book artists. Since the first half of the 80s, he had achieved two great successes: Dr. Slump and Dragon Ball. With Dragon Ball he created characters that entertained Japanese readers of all ages and would later cross the ocean and doing the same across the world.

Nakamura was lucky with the musical score: Koichi Sugiyama, a famous televi-

---

114   Influential American illustrator specializing in fantasy and science fiction drawings

115   The creator of Tetris, Alexey Pajitnov, had ceded the rights to the Soviet authorities. Rogers bought it from them and made a fortune licensing it, including the famous Game Boy version

116   Parkin, Simon (2013) The Dragon Invasion, The Magazine September 2013

sion score composer had written fan mail to the company and someone recognized his name. After confirming that it was really the acclaimed Sugiyama, Nakamura contacted the composer and was able to hire him for the Dragon Quest soundtrack. Sugiyama would become the historical composer of the series and earned the reputation of being the so-called "great head of the music of the game" from Nobuo Uematsu, composer of the Final Fantasy soundtrack.

The creators of Dragon Quest took no inspiration from Black Onyx, but instead directly from its roots: Wizardry and Ultima. The game used a party system and the action happened in a top-down tile view.

"Horii was sent to the 1983 Applefest in San Francisco, where both he and fellow Enix contest winner Koichi Nakamura first saw Wizardry running on an Apple II. Woodhead's computerized version of Dungeons and Dragons left Horii and Nakamura awestruck and the two became obsessed with RPGs upon returning to Japan.Over time, Horii began to gravitate towards Ultima-inspired RPGs with their emphasis on exploration, while Nakamura remained obsessed with Wizardry and its menu-based combat. When Horii insisted the two begin working on a new type of RPG together, they decided to combine the best of each game along with Portopia's heavy emphasis on storytelling (at least, in the context of game storytelling at the time) and the result was the RPG that would finally set Japan on course to rival the West's mastery of the genre: Dragon Quest."[117]

This style turned out to be predominant until the first consoles with 3D graphics capabilities entered the scene.

Dragon Quest was such an immense success that it made Square reconsider a prior decision. Hironobu Sakaguchi had wanted to create an RPG for Square for quite some time but management rejected the idea, assuming that the potential market was too small. Dragon Quest's sales proved them wrong and Sakaguchi was given the green light. This would be the birth of the next famous JRPG: Final Fantasy. Along with Dragon Quest it went on to dominate the Japanese market and, from 1991 on, also conquered the West with the introduction of it's fourth installment.

The last important contribution in shaping the RPG genre in Japan was supplied by famous designer Shigeru Miyamoto (father of Donkey Kong and the Mario series) and Takashi Tezuka: The Legend of Zelda (1986). Although lacking

---

117   Messner, Steve, The forgotten origins of JRPGs on the PC, PC Gamer

RPG elements, their game became the archetype[118] of Japanese action-adventures in which the player can explore worlds, enter dungeons, defeat monsters and find hidden treasures.

The game's success significantly increased FamiCom's sales in Japan[119] and popularized the addition of RPG elements into the action-adventure genre which had developed independently around the world. The resulting mix created the genre of Action RPG and it's influence can be traced even to famous Rogue descendants like Blizzard's Diablo (1996).

Chris Roberts loved the fusion of genres and especially Legend of Zelda, influencing in turn OSI with Times of Lore, which then inspired Garriott in Ultima VI. The exchange of ideas between Eastern and Western game industries had started at the dawn of arcades in the early 70s. In fact, JRPGs ended up winning a large share of Western players, more than their Western counterparts had done in Japan.

Having regained the rights to the first Ultimas, Garriott's company began to publish all installments on Japanese computers and consoles such as Ultima I for NEC PC-8801 in 1988. The packaging was also adapted to the audience and Ultima III was sold by Starcraft in two boxes: one containing the game and the other a copy of the world map as a puzzle with 550-pieces.

Yoshio Kiya had already presented himself to the public with Dragon Slayer and went on to create Xanadu. It was published in 1985 by Nihon Falcom for all major platforms in the country. The gameplay was a curious mix of real-time action, platform elements and role-playing, partly inspired by western RPGs, adding many novelties.

Xanadu was very successful in Japan and sold 400,000 copies, attracting the attention of OSI. Richard Garriott flew to Tachikawa himself, where Falcom's offices were located. He hoped to acquire the rights to localize and market it in North America and have Falcom do the Japanese conversion of Ultima I. Falcom repre-

---

118   "While America has been concentrating on yet another Wizardry, Ultima, or Might & Magic, each bigger and more complex than the one before it, the Japanese have slowly carved out a completely new nickel in the realm of CRPG. The first CRPG entries were Rygar and Deadly Towers on the NES. These differed considerably from the 'action adventure' games that had drawn quite a following on the machines beforehand. Action adventures were basically arcade games done in a fantasy setting such as Castlevania, Trojan, and Wizards & Warriors. The new CRPGs had some of the trappings of regular CRPGs. The character could get stronger over time and gain extras which were not merely a result of a short-term 'Power-Up.' There were specific items that could be acquired which boosted fighting or defense on a permanent basis. Primitive stores were introduced with the concept that a player could buy something to help him on his journey. When The Legend of Zelda burst upon the scene in fall of 1988, it hit like a nova. Although it still had many action-adventure features, it was definitely a CRPG." Roe Adams III, CGW, Issue 76, November 1990

119   sold as NES abroad

sentatives were delighted to show Garriott the product. Garriott shared their enthusiasm until he saw the in-game merchant screens and an embarrassing silence filled the room. Xanadu had seven shopkeeper screens copied directly from Ultima III manuals, redrawn with few changes, and colorized.

The blatant plagiarism didn't go down well with Garriott, the deal fell apart and was replaced with threats of legal action.[120] To remedy this, Falcom had the incriminated screens modified and the dispute was resolved outside the courtroom, yet Xanadu was never sold in the West despite being deprived of Loubet's drawings. The Japanese version was already mostly in English so copies still spread abroad.

The fiasco with Xanadu also killed the Ultima I conversion agreement, which was then entrusted to another company. The resulting delay made the Japanese audience wait until 1988 for the release on PC-88, three years after the misadventure with Falcom. The programming was done mainly by Toru Hidaka, a contractor for Pony Canyon. He explains the difficulties Western companies were facing when bringing their products to Japan: "At that time the job, like this game conversion for example, was often subcontracted from Pony Canyon to other little companies, but those subcontractors had no skill for doing the job either and so subcontracted the project again to other little companies. And those little companies often lack a professional level for developing. This would degrade the quality as well as the process. So this conversion of Ultima was also an example of this phenomenon... Some subcontractor of a subcontractor of Pony Canyon asked me, 'There is no staff who can manage the machine language in our company, so please help us with it!' "[121]

---

120   Addams, Shay (1990) The Official Book of Ultima, Chapter 7

121   Szczepaniak, John (2014) The Untold History Of Japanese Game Developers

Ultima VI: The False Prophet

"Ultima VI, as a matter of fact is the first Ultima in a while in which one of the principal design criteria was that the story be both easy to follow and relatively easy to grasp. While at the same time providing you a rich world to explore and experiment with. And, you will note that ULTIMA VI has a MUCH easier to use interface than its predecessors."

Richard Garriott, in conference with The Gamers' Forum, 1990

"Ultima VI is notable for its single-scale world, in which cities blend seamlessly into the overworld, its strong moral sense, and its unstructured, non-linear gameplay — a harbinger of what would later be called sandbox games."

Data sheet of Ultima VI, Giantbomb

"I remember spending weeks at Richard's house where we plotted the game from start to finish. Richard showed me how he planned games using what he called his 'black book.' All of his games started out as hand-written notes in a black looseleaf binder. Every character, location, quest, spell, object... everything was captured in that black book."

Warren Spector

Starting with a clean slate for the sixth installment, Richard decided to completely revolutionize his game, which included a new interface and other important design choices. This made Ultima VI the first 'modern' chapter of the series. Although still placed in the second trilogy, it pioneered many changes: being written for PC first, dropping the hot-key system for an icon-based interface and leaving the Apple II community behind.

Clearly inspired by Roberts' experiment Times of Lore, Ultima VI kept the top-down perspective and the creation of the world with tiles, but added a slight tilted angle to give a sense of depth. The graphics library, which in previous titles was composed of a handful of objects redesigned in multiple frames to give a rudimentary impression of movement, had meanwhile grown out of proportion, thanks to the PC's generous 640K of RAM. Loubet drew the 2048 tiles, giving the designers a rich visual vocabulary to create the world, filling cities and castles with objects such as chairs, tables, paintings, statues, ornamental weapons, food, torches, furnishings and household goods, which were often interactive and movable.

Since the beginning, Garriott's games were rightly classified as open world, allowing the player to roam freely. The game world could be visited immediately in its entirety and without limits. Until Ultima V, however, the game world had been divided into two sections: the first-person view dungeons and the top-down view overworld.

With Ultima VI it finally came together: the game world would be created from a seamless single 1024x1024 tiles world map and no transitions from overworld to cities or dungeons. Cities, dungeons, castles, stables, streets, houses and mountains would all be the same scale, built from the same components designed by Loubet, with the single exception of a few dungeons being divided into several levels.

Richard had dropped the exploration of 3D dungeons. This choice allowed continuity of gameplay and made the development easier. This was a great relief for the work of developers who, until Ultima V, had to maintain two independent engines in one game. Richard had often come up against technical limits due to the initial choice to create dungeons via the first-person view. This led to never having implemented a saving option during the exploration of dungeons, and the lack of NPC encounters and limited actions in the dungeon left the player without a consistent experience.

Garriott: "Everything that you can pick up and use has to be able to function in 3-D and also in 2-D. That meant I had to either restrict the set of things players can use to ones that I know I can make work in 3-D or 2-D, or make them sometimes work in 2-D but not always work in 3-D or vice versa, or they will do different things in one versus the other. None of those are consistent, and since I'm trying to create a holistic world, I got rid of the 3-D dungeons."

This gain in consistency came with other gameplay drawbacks. The most obvious one was losing the expressive possibilities of the first-person view, which was missing in top-down setup. Another was the loss of fast traveling. The one scale overworld required giving the settlements proportionally more space on the map to avoid long uneventful trips through vast empty spaces in between them. At the end of the day, Lord British's castle was bigger than a mountain range, while Britain, the capital of Britannia, occupied a significant fraction of the entire planet. Cities were mainly represented only by a handful of houses, seemingly separated from one another by a few hundred meters.

The day and night cycle from Ultima V was extended: the sun began to rise in the morning to the east and set in the evening to the west, changing the illumination as the day went on. Combat remained substantially unchanged, now taking place in the seamless game map (thanks to the 'eggs' created by Miller to instruct the game on the spawn points of the monsters), with a simpler mouse interface.

The player could now set the mode of companions ('Front', 'Rear', 'Berserk', 'Retreat', etc.) in combat and let the AI manage them. This reduced the time spent in battle significantly, which had grown with each installment and had become an exhausting part of gameplay in Ultima V. Hardcore fans could still control every detail in the classic mode.

Similarly the spell casting had been simplified, dropping the long and complex process of mixing ingredients (a feature cherished by Garriott who would bring it back in Ultima Online) prior to the actual casting.

Although in some cases the simplifications had been requested in the letters to Origin, they were not welcomed by all. Devoted RPG fans who loved managing statistics, fighting, life points and advancement were displeased and came to call Ultima VI an adventure with RPG elements. On the other hand, this opened the game up to a larger audience.

In fact, the path taken by Garriott was the most effective to propose a product for everyone, where tenacity and perseverance were no longer required but the game adapted to the player.

Garriott tried to create problems, puzzles and obstacles and allowing the players to choose their preferred approach, whether by muscle and brute force, strategic craftiness, or pure innovation. The dialogues were again of great importance to one's progress and in providing the user with clues to find the best way to overcome obstacles.

In previous Ultimas, the keyword system in conversations had players occasionally resort to trial and error if they could not guess the right one to use. Ultima VI made this process much easier: keywords that could proceed the dialogue were highlighted in the text. The challenge dropped eminently from having to try out all the known keywords on NPCs to a mere collecting of dialogue fragments, matching the pieces of the puzzle and finding the solution.

The world had grown with each episode and players could now interact with hundreds of characters, each with a name, a story, and much to tell in the dialogues written under the guidance of Dr. Cat. Creating the world with such a level of detail, was not an easy task. It was an absurdly complex process according to Spector, who locked himself up in a room with Garriott for two whole weeks to accomplish this feat while eating Chinese food. Every character and place, including those from previous episodes which players expected to find again, was a small piece of the puzzle that served to complete the game and that the developers had to implement in the world of Britannia.

In previous episodes players had to wander around the world, talk to all NPCs while trying all possible keywords and noting everything down. Reflecting on the logical thread linking together the pieces of information collected, they would discover holes in the narrative and conclusions drawn that had seemed obvious to Garriott, but not to all his fans.

In Ultima VI, Garriott and Spector's world design was improved and the plot and clues were better woven into the game experience. To get to the end of the game, the player still had to collect all the hints, but how to piece them together was more comprehensive, thanks to Origin's rigorous testing.

A few months after the imperative deadline for Ultima VI's release, and with possible bankruptcy looming, the plot of the new chapter was still not ready. Garriott's approach had not changed much: Focusing first on technology and programming, then working on the setting and plot. The latter emerged during the two weeks of work with Spector.

In Ultima V not only did Blackthorn's actions, though intended to do good, have disastrous consequences, but the act of killing Mondain to save the world had created one of the most serious threats Britannia would ever experience. In the new chapter, Garriott continued with this theme. This time, the Avatar's descent into the Stygian Abyss to retrieve the Codex of Ultimate Wisdom at the end of Ultima IV, created unexpected havoc.

It's been five years since the Avatar's last trip to Britannia the animated introduction explained. The Stranger from another world was sitting on his couch in front of the television, unable to enjoy his well-deserved rest, he remained immersed in the memories of battles fought and fellow adventurers lost along the way. Outside the window, the wind was picking up speed: there was thunder and lightning. It was a sign that a portal was opening in the circle of stones behind the house. Aware of the danger overshadowing Britannia, the Stranger, now the Avatar, was ready to enter the portal and answer the call of duty.

The initial screenshot of the Avatar sitting on the couch was published for the first time in a special issue of ACE magazine, issue 31 of April 1990, one month before the game's release. In the upper left corner, just above the Avatar's head, there was an image of a woman clearly inspired by American artist Patrick Nagel's 'Woman in Jacket'. On the contrary, in the final version of the game there was a bizarre image of a centaur woman near a lap dance pole. Since Origin failed to obtain the rights to publish Nagel's work shortly before the release, the image of the woman had been replaced with a piece by Keith Berdak, 'Zebra, Too'.

Manda: "After it was pointed out that the Nagel poster wasn't public domain, Keith used his own art, the centaur girl. Keith was using Dpaint[122] at the time, which meant it was essentially done like needlepoint: dot by dot by dot."

---

122   The Photoshop of it's time for Pixel graphics

Curiously, the first edition of Ultima VI went to print with the original screenshot displaying Nagel's work on the box. Another novelty is the initial screen showing the player with some physical features (haircut and hair color), reducing the user's ability to self-identify with the hero they embodied in the game.

Entering the portal, the Avatar ends up chained to a sacrificial altar and surrounded by demonic figures similar to Loubet's drawing of Exodus, the demon who had inadvertently triggered a public relations firestorm between Garriott and conservative religious groups. These beings, also referred to as 'Gargoyles', attempted to kill the Avatar, but were thwarted when fellow adventurers Iolo, Dupre and Shamino intervened. The Avatar then learned directly from Lord British that the world of Britannia was once again in peril. The renaissance world of Ultima IV was only a memory as the Gargoyles had risen up from the depths of the earth and started a war, plundering and destroying the sanctuaries of the virtues and threatening to steal the Codex.

Soon, however, the player realized that not everything was as it seemed; the Gargoyles were not monstrous and evil creatures moved by the thirst for blood and destruction. A cataclysm triggered by the descent of the Avatar into the dungeon Doom at the end of Ultima V was threatening to destroy their home, the Underworld. From their point of view, the Avatar had stolen the Codex first, causing the Underworld to begin sinking and condemning their species to extinction. One of their prophecies foretold that the world would come to an end through the work of a 'False Prophet' who would steal the Codex; bringing ruin. The Gargoyles were in fact trying to prevent the fulfillment of this prophecy and were simply engaged in a struggle for their own survival. Equipped with a system of virtues similar to that of Britannia, the Gargoyles were driven by despair and considered the inhabitants of Britannia and the Avatar as mortal dangers.

The mission of defeating the Gargoyles soon transformed into one of building a bridge between the two civilizations, breaking down misunderstandings, and creating peace together. The aim of the game suddenly became more noble than initially presented via this brilliant plot twist. The final track "Unity" was symbolic of the harmony achieved between Britain and the Underworld at the game's conclusion. It is an amalgamation of the Gargoyle anthem written by Miller, and the song "Rule, Britannia".

The Gargoyle's language, Gargish, had its foundations in Garriott's passion for languages. Miller: "Richard came up with the initial idea of the Gargoyle alphabet, which reminded me of Alexander Melville Bell's 'Visible Speech' when he described it to me. But I think he came up with the idea on his own. Each of the strokes that make up the letters of the alphabet represents a phonetic feature of the sounds of the language. So I took that basic idea and designed an alphabet around it."

Like Richard, Miller had always enjoyed creating new languages and alphabets. Garriott's passion had given rise to the system of runes used in the world of Ultima, but privately, Richard had been working extensively on a new phonetic alphabet. The meeting between the two was very fruitful: using Garriott's alphabet, Miller created Gargish, the language of Gargoyles.

Miller: "I've long been interested in constructed languages like Tolkien's Quenya and Sindarin from 'The Lord of the Rings', or the Klingon language from Star Trek, so I took the Gargish alphabet a step further and began to develop a language. I wrote the Gargish dictionary which was included in the 'Ultima VI Cluebook', along with enough rules of grammar to translate the Gargish text in the game."

The music was not the only card played to underline the plot twist. Miller's language was also a useful tool for this purpose and Beeman, in charge of characterizing Gargoyles, could play on some linguistic ambiguities by using Herman's grammar rules. "Gargish is an expansion of the language used for spells, so like spells it consists of syllables representing concepts. A sentence is, like a spell, a string of syllables put together to communicate one coherent thought. The indication that a word is a verb, adjective or noun is done with tone and gestures, and doesn't appear in writing. Syllable order doesn't really matter and is mostly chosen to make the word sound smoother", explained Siobhan Beeman.

"Before the player completes the quest to learn the language, the Gargoyles' speech all appears in raw Gargish... and since they view the Avatar as a demon, mostly consists of their panicked screams as they run away. The Gargish for 'false prophet' is An-bal-sil-fer, which is literally 'not-evil-prediction-bringer'. A more fluent translation of 'bal-sil-fer' would be 'doomsayer' rather than 'prophet'. The Gargoyles' concept of 'prophet' or 'doomsayer' was 'person who delivers a dire warning' — in other words, an essentially good person. Adding the 'an-' negation syllable to that makes it 'person who fulfills a dire warning'. Which of course is what the Avatar winds up doing in the story. The plot of the game hinges on confusion in translation, and the very word the Gargoyles use to refer to the Avatar is itself an incorrect translation."

To Robert's relief, Ultima VI was released on schedule in March 1990, two years after the previous installment. The game was positively received by the press, who praised its technical qualities, while also noting that the performance tended to become sluggish when too many NPCs were on the screen, even on high-end systems. The replacement of random encounters with planned fights, the open world exploration, and the plot were judged very positively. Some critiqued the quests, judging them as inconsistent in difficulty such as in the middle of the game's narrative during the pirate map quest (in which Richard had the satisfaction of mocking Trip Hawkins and Electronic Arts).

With over 200,000 copies sold, Ultima VI put Origin Systems Inc. back on track. The generous package included a cloth map, the book Compendium, a black gem (the Orb of the Moon, the stone responsible for the passage of the foreigner from our world to Britannia during the intro of the game), a postcard with the Immortality Contest (a competition to have a proposed character included in subsequent titles)[123] and, in some boxes, a rune.

Ultima VI was also sold in special edition format, containing a 45 minute long audiotape with Garriott talking about the creation of the game and autographs from Richard and Denis Loubet.

Programmed on PC, the new installment was ported to several platforms, but only for a single 8-bit one: the still very popular Commodore 64. Due to the complexity of the game and limited memory, the game had very long loading times and required continuous disk swapping of three 51/4" double sided floppy disks.

The initial version had bugs, including some serious enough to ruin the gaming session. For example, there was no check for NPC resurrections. If a player resurrected a dead companion after filling the eighth slot in the party, a ninth companion was created and able to follow the party, but was not controllable via the interface. This glitch caused the game to crash very quickly.

Origin immediately put a part of the staff at work on a patch, which was distributed to retailers or sent by mail to customers on request. The company's fame was about to become equally marked by both the amount of bugs in its games and the ambition behind the titles it was about to release.

Origin's golden age had begun.

123   The 17 winners were included in Ultima VII and Ultima VII part 2, http://wiki.ultimacodex.com/wiki/Immortality_Contest

Ultima Worlds

"Fewer disks and smaller teams"

Siobhan Beeman

"They never really told us what the final sales were. I thought it was terribly short-sighted to end the Worlds project, because they were SO cheap to produce, compared to the AAA budgets of the main-line games."

Philip Brogden

Since the beginning of his career, Garriott had an unwritten rule to implement better engines with every new Ultima. The complex and expensive work on the engine for Ultima VI challenged his view: rising costs with each iteration made reuse a good idea. Already with Ultima IV, Garriott had imagined writing a second part rather than going straight for the next chapter but changed his mind; creating a tense situation with Electronic Arts. To keep the affiliate relationship alive, certain sales numbers had to be reached, therefore it relied heavily on the release of an Ultima installment every year.

The Ultima VI engine, in 1990, was one of the most sophisticated of its time. That year RPG fans also enjoyed Eye of the Beholder, a derivative game of Dungeon Master, with a spectacular intro capable of showing the dungeon with VGA graphics.

Another competitor was SSI's Champions of Krynn, part of the Gold Box series which was released two years after Pool of Radiance. However, it didn't keep up well with other RPGs due to its simple graphics.

Old rival Wizardry arrived with Wizardry VI: Bane of the Cosmic Forge. Since Wizardry IV: The Return of Werdna (1987) the series was a commercial disaster, having lost many of its fans. With the fifth installment development had finally arrived in the hands of David W. Bradley. Faithful to the dungeon crawling formula, Bradley completely rewrote the engine, added a graphical mouse-interface and colorful art work, regaining some of the fan base. Unfortunately, the game was still using the old EGA standard which was much less capable than VGA.

In addition, Ultima VI shared shelf space with two sci-fi RPGs from Electronic Arts. The first, produced internally, was the unofficial sequel to Brian Fargo's Wasteland: Fountain of Dreams. It fell short of fans' expectations and made them wait for the 'real' sequel, which arrived in 2015 from inXile Entertainment. The second, Hard Nova, mixed space and planetary exploration with RPG phases during landing on the ground or in space stations. Both games had modest success, partly due to their sub-par technical qualities. Fountain of Dreams was also considered too short compared to its predecessor. Hard Nova was a little better, managing to improve some aspects of the gameplay already seen in the previous title Sentinel Worlds I: Future Magic.

Ultima VI competed against RPGs with inferior engines and out of those only Eye of the Beholder tried to address the VGA market. The western CRPGs of 1990 were mostly derivatives or sequels of the established Wizardry, Ultima and Dungeon Master theme. Ultima VI stood out clearly targeting users owning high-end computers with its engine and VGA support.

The advantage had to be capitalized on and expenses for developing the advanced engine had to be paid. Even if Garriott didn't appreciate the idea of creating a new chapter without introducing substantial advancements, many people began to consider the idea of creating a game with the name of Ultima and with the Avatar as the main protagonist, but not directly integrated in the series.

One of the supporters of this idea was Jeff Johannigman.

His career in the video game industry started early. While still at Cornell University, Johannigman began writing games for the Atari 8-bit platform. Two of them, Rabbotz! (1982) and Snark Hunt were submitted to the Atari Program Exchange, a software distribution circuit for Atari 400/800 directly created and maintained by a division of the company founded by Bushnell.[124]

Once he graduated, thanks to his experience with Atari's microcomputers, he

---

124   Authors could propose their software to Atari's program management division, which included the titles in a catalog for customers. Programmers were remunerated according to the units sold and every four months, the most deserving games were further rewarded with bonuses from 1,000 to 25,000 dollars. Among APX's most successful titles were the strategy game Eastern Front (1941) and the shoot'em up Caverns of Mars (unusual because it scrolled from top to bottom). Both games were so successful that they were also sold in cartridges as well

was hired by Brøderbund and put in charge of managing the port of The Mask of the Sun and The Serpent's Star, two graphic adventures by Ultrasoft, before moving on to Epyx, where he would program, along with Ray Carpenter, G.I. Joe: A Real American Hero, a popular action game based on the series of toys by Hasbro.

The next three years he spent at EA, first implementing anti-copy systems, then as a technical director and finally as an associate producer. Johannigman gained a lot of experience and worked on several titles for the popular platforms, namely Apple II, Atari 8 bit, Commodore 64 and the future market leader: the IBM PC.

In 1989 Jeff Johannigman received an offer from Origin as a producer. It was a promotion from his current role as associate producer, but OSI was clearly a less important and less well paid opportunity than EA. Any doubts about his decision would quickly vanish. Johannigman: "We had just started packing up our home for the move when the Loma Prieta earthquake[125] struck in October, convincing me it was the right time to leave California."

Johannigman's reluctance was also due to the fact that he expected Texas to be a hostile and hot environment dominated by cacti and oil wells. Jeff: "Austin was nothing like I had envisioned, full of green hills and great book stores. To seal the deal, the day after the interview, Warren Spector drove us around Austin to show us how affordable houses were compared to California."

Britannia Manor mkII, the Texan residence of Richard, built and equipped to be simultaneously a museum, astronomical observatory and haunted house, had claimed another victim: "And Richard gave me the grand tour of Britannia Manor, including the observatory dome, secret passages, hidden dungeon, and human-sized gyroscope. I was sold."

As soon as he arrived at Origin, Johannigman discussed with Spector and Snell the possibility of reusing the engine of Ultima VI: "Since Origin had invested so much money in the U6 engine, Dallas, Warren, and I started to discuss affordable ways to reuse the technology around the time U6 was nearing completion. We wanted to leave the 'swords and sorcery' RPG setting to Lord British, and brainstormed several other genres that the U6 engine could support. Warren was a big fan of the Edgar Rice Burroughs 'Lost World / Jungle Romance' stories. I had always dreamed of mashing a bunch of Victorian-era characters into one story. We decided the Lost World genre was the better idea to start with."

Even though Robert had four producers at his fingertips, he hadn't yet put his hand to Origin's organization. The result was that projects were not assigned on the basis of producers' capabilities, inclinations or tastes, but simply on the basis of availability. Johannigman had just been hired and was therefore free from other commitments, while Spector was already busy with other games.

---

125   On October 17 at 17:04 local time a devastating earthquake of magnitude 7.1 on the Richter scale struck the state of California. 63 people died and thousands were injured, while the damage was measured in billions of dollars.

Johannigman: "Since I had more free time on my schedule, I was the one who got to be Producer on Warren's idea, which became 'Savage Empire' (and he later took on mine, with 'Martian Dreams'.)"

As will be seen later, this inefficient system of allocating producers would have created a number of problems.

The idea behind the Ultima Worlds project was simple: economies of scale. Savage Empire could guarantee additional returns to Origin without much effort. The idea that the Avatar could travel between worlds was present from the beginning of the series, so it was clearly possible to place adventures in a wild world or even on Mars.

Siobhan Beeman was hired as a writer because of her experience in SJG board games but unbeknownst to all, her arrival at Origin provided the company with a more important resource than expected. Beeman: "While working on U6, I mentioned in casual conversation that I was a programmer, not just a writer. I'd learned programming at the age of 9 — my father was a programmer at NASA, so we had home computers pretty much from the first year they were available. I'd also worked as a programmer in C during my last summer of high school. Warren and Richard were flabbergasted that I hadn't told them this right off the bat, and quickly took advantage of my skills: I was made the project director on the U6 spin-off Worlds of Ultima: The Savage Empire."

Origin had started with young, skilled and enthusiastic developers full of great ideas, but still learning techniques for streamlining and optimizing the development process. What works in a small team doesn't always scale well with larger groups and often requires new, more effective approaches. At the same time, more powerful machines allowed for trading in — which were extremely expensive prior — performance penalties for a shorter development time. Deadlines and evolving new engines made it even more difficult to find time for those improvements in such a rapidly changing environment. The resulting lack of comfortable tools was felt and badly missed by some, but not a show stopper as most staff were programmers; even some Project Directors were hands-on. Beeman: "Effectively this role made me the team lead, much the same way a movie director guides the crew of a film; I did a lot of programming and project management, some story editing, and a little writing and game design."

Despite the initial intentions of a low cost production, Beeman had in mind using her programming skills to add some features to Savage Empire and, above all, she needed someone able to conceive an adventure worthy of the Ultima brand. She thought of involving an old acquaintance from SJG, Aaron Allston. Beeman had entered the gaming industry thanks to Car Wars and Allston had been a point of reference, having written the book Autoduel Champions (1983), a crossover between Steve Jackson's car game and the role-playing superhero Champions. Aaron Allston's skills and experience even led him to write a D&D RPG module for TSR, The Grand Duchy of Karameikos supplement (1987), with 64 pages of detailed information about Karameikos, maps and tips for creating adventures and campaigns.

The two had met for the first time at Ladyman's Hexworld. Allston was a DM and by watching him Beeman learned a lot about how to set up and run an adventure. "Aaron was a delight to work with," Beeman remembered years later, after the premature death of the game designer in 2014. Similar feelings were also shared by Johannigman: "I will say that 'The Savage Empire' was by far my favorite experience. Not because of any specific creative contribution I made to the game, but more because I got to work with such a phenomenal team. It turned out great primarily due to the talents of [...] Beeman as lead designer/programmer, and the late (and dearly missed) Aaron Allston who crafted a truly wonderful story and set of characters."

Using a new engine for the animated sequences, Daniel Bourbonnais designed the introduction, consisting of a long camera movement from left to right to show a wild panorama with dinosaurs and other prehistoric creatures. Manda also joined the team, helping with the scenarios, created with a new tileset including creatures in line with the lost world theme of Savage Empire, while Jeff Dee took care of helping with the tiles.

The game was ready by fall 1990. Technically very similar to Ultima VI, Worlds of Ultima: The Savage Empire had in addition the Origin FX Engine,[126] which gave the role-playing game a more cinematic edge from the start, showing a conductor and the Earth on the horizon in its introduction.

The setting created by Johannigman, Spector and Snell's brainstorms, Allston's pen, Garriott's suggestions and Beeman's contributions, was a mix of Tolkien, D&D and SCA, with strong inspiration from Victorian adventure novels such as Arthur Conan Doyle's The Lost World, Jules Verne's Journey to the Center of the Earth and H. Rider Haggard's King Solomon's Mines. Quotes to all these works were countless in the dialogues written by Aaron and another new hire of Origin: Philip Brogden.

The story of Savage Empire begins with a failed experiment involving the obsidian moonstones, teleporting the Avatar to the valley of Eodon, a primitive world inhabited by a civilization fragmented into different tribes. They too were transported from different times in world history and were now torn apart by an enduring state of war. The mission of the Avatar was to learn the tribal magic and cultures with the aim of restoring peace in the world of Eodon by bringing together the thirteen tribes in a war against a species of giant insects, called Myrmidex.

The gameplay of Savage Empire was very similar to Ultima VI, with the exception of the spells system: it had been replaced with a more rudimentary tribal form of magic. Ultima's spin off was equipped with a highly interactive environment filled with numerous objects that the player could take or use. The dialogues were very well maintained and varied to the point that even secondary characters, not involved in the main quest, had been provided with interesting stories and lines. Sava-

126   See the chapter Eclipse in volume II

ge Empire staff decided to include characters clearly inspired by those of Garriott: Triolo instead of Iolo, Shamuru instead of Shamino and Dokray instead of Dupre. Spector had the honor of giving his face to a key character, Dr. Johann Spector, the first antagonist of the Avatar and then an ally, confirming a trend at the time that each Origin game contained a virtual alter ego of the new producer.

Contrary to the last Ultimas, in Savage Empire it was not possible to select the character's sex. When the management team considered it, the decision seemed obvious: adding the option of a female Avatar would have severe consequences for the game's development. It would require drawing templates and rewriting dialogues, ending up most likely with additional floppies. At a time when available space was scarce and floppies expensive, it could potentially reduce profit margins. The aim of the project was to take advantage of an available engine and keeping costs to a minimum. Not only that: it would lengthen the development time and add complexity to a project expected to be finished quickly.

Johannigman: "While we could have made the Avatar a female character, we would have then had to rewrite much of the storyline and dialogue for all combinations — male Avatar in love with Female Native, Female Avatar in love with Male Native, Male Avatar in love with Male Native, and Female Avatar in love with Female native. Those combinations would have added weeks of work to the schedule that, at the time, I didn't think were justified."

There was a second reason to consider. Johannigman: "First and foremost, we were trying to stay faithful to the conventions of a very specific genre — the Lost World Romance. The genre itself is a product of its time, over a century ago. Common to the genre, and central to the storyline in a fundamental way, is the trope of the strong-jawed male hero romancing the exotic native woman. Making the Avatar a lesbian would have been outside the genre in a way that would be imposing modern values on a century-old setting. It would have felt untrue to the recipe, as it were."

In a short meeting the attendees discussed the changes developers would have to work on and the costs involved. Someone pointed out that the cliché would lose momentum if there was a female Avatar instead of a heroic masculine man, and no one objected.

The choice seemed obvious to everyone that this was the easiest way to go without incurring additional costs or delays in the project plan. But Beeman regretted it: "The only thing that happened on Savage Empire that I didn't like was that we took away the option to play as a woman, something that existed in Ultima VI and in Martian Dreams. This was deliberate: In order to be true to the feel of those old 'pulp adventure' books, the story featured a romantic subplot between the Avatar and the 'jungle princess' Aiela. The decision was made as a team to limit the Avatar's gender so as to avoid the negative press a lesbian romance would have provoked. Obviously as a transgender lesbian I was not very happy with this decision, but at the time I was closeted and there was a limit to how comfortable I felt fighting for it."

Would it have been possible to do otherwise and write a story with a homosexual love between a female Avatar and Princess Aiela? Beeman: "I know Aaron would have been perfectly happy to write that story. I know Jeff Johan[n]igman and Richard would have been fine with it."

Richard had already taken heat for the cover of Exodus designed by Loubet and made fun of those who had accused him of being the satanic pervert of the American youth, by choosing '666' as his internal telephone number. However, in this case the entire company would have risked ending up in the middle of another controversy.

Siobhan: "Even if the four people in that room had all said, 'Let's just do this and be legends!', the head of the company (Richard's brother Robert), and the head of the marketing department would have talked us out of it — and I can't say that they'd have been completely wrong to do so. Society hasn't made as much progress as it needs to, but it's made more progress than people today can really comprehend."

Maybe, if someone had decided to sponsor the change, the final decision would have been different. Johannigman: "It is a fascinating artistic decision, and one that I would probably make differently today. However, in 1990 (27 years ago), I was not as aware of all the personal issues involved. [...] Had I considered it an important enough issue back then, I am sure I could have justified and fought to include those options."

Richard Garriott has no doubts :"Had we had Siobhan or anyone else champion alternative story ideas, we likely could have accommodated it. In Ultima III your stick figure was gender neutral. Later games began to incur greater and greater costs to support more art variations and story variations with any 'alternatives' we wished to include, so any additional expenses would often need a champion. Back in the day, telling a classic pulp story did not seem a problem. Fundamentally, I believe it is fine to MAKE a role playing game that makes you ROLE PLAY not yourself, but whatever the story teller WANTS you to be, a human, an elf, a dog, a man, a woman, etc. That being said, I like role playing games where the character is YOUR avatar, thus it needs to reflect all the shades of self-description people have."

During the 1980s, the theme of homosexuality was mostly absent from video games. When it was mentioned, at best it was done by trivializing LGBT characters and resorting to gender reversal stereotypes, or, at worst, by using mocking or derogatory terms. The Savage Empire, for a brief moment, would have had the chance to be one of the first CRPGs in which the player would be given the opportunity to fully embody the homosexuality of their character, with a specially written quest line and dialogues (and not simply agnostic towards the combination of sex of the player character and the NPC). But during the meeting nobody took the floor to become the champion and, to Beeman's great regret, the possibility faded. Star Ocean: The Second Story (1998) became the first role-playing game in which players could have a homosexual relationship with a male NPC (Ashton) or female (Precis). With the release of Mass Effect (2007) in the Western world, players would be presented with this feature for the first time, even if it did so only halfway: the main character Shepard could have a lesbian love affair with an extraterrestrial (Liara T'Soni) but not a gay one (that came with the third chapter of the series). The theme of lesbian love was proposed in a veiled way: The alien race Asari was an asexual species with female physical characteristics, able to unite and reproduce with any other alien creature, regardless of sex. Starting from the sequel in 2010, players were able to have a love affair not only with an Asari, but with a woman, Kelly Chambers.

Savage Empire was initially released only on PC and a few years later brought to Japanese platforms, but it didn't experience much success — according to Beeman, around 40,000 copies — yet Origin's management decided to give the spin-off series a second chance anyway: Martian Dreams.

According to the usual process of allocating projects to producers, Martian Dreams was entrusted to Spector, while Johannigman was hijacked for Runes of Virtue, the first Ultima title on a portable console.

For the new project, Johannigman could count on a small but now mature team. Dr. Cat and Gary Scott Smith designed and programmed the game for Nintendo's Game Boy, while Manda took care of the graphics and music, writing a special song, 'Cheese Song', played during the exploration of the overworld. Dr. Cat: "She wrote lyrics to go with it, which we were going to print in the instruction booklet, but we were two pages over on length and that's what got cut."

"I have a dear friend,
She is a small mouse,
She has a big heart,
And her name is Sheri.

And if you ask her,
Sheri will you help me,
She will tell you first to
Bring her some cheese.

Cheese! Cheese! How I wish I had some,
Cheese! Cheese! Where am I to get some.
Everybody wants it,
Even monsters like it,
Tell me where am I to, get me some cheese!"[127]

To draw the maps, an internal contest was held, advertised in the Point of Origin company newsletter. Herman Miller and Paul Isaac submitted some maps and

---

127   the song lyrics are courtesy of Manda

won, getting them included in both chapters and a special mention in a manual of the second chapter Runes of Virtue II.

Although Nintendo Power had made an eight-page special for Runes of Virtue, the game was not very popular with the public and critics alike, remaining obscure and quickly forgotten, even though it was the first game in the Ultima series with multiplayer support.

While Johannigman and his team were creating Runes of Virtue, Spector set to work on the other Ultima spin-off. Although the idea of putting "a bunch of Victorian characters into one story" was Johannigman's, Spector was more than comfortable as the producer of a role-playing game with this setting: "I've always been fascinated by the Victorian era. It was a time of incredible technological progress — telephones, automobiles, phonographs, movies — all sorts of stuff we take for granted today started in the late-Victorian era. It was also a time when people like Jules Verne were starting to think about the future."

The original design was very different. Jeff George had many ideas when he was appointed director of the project Martian Dreams and was looking forward to working on it: "I was super excited to be doing a near-future, possibly slightly-cyberpunk adventure with the Ultima VI engine. At the time, I was very inspired by the foreseeable future and the exploration and colonization of our own Solar System. This was right at the height of the cyberpunk era in science fiction."

Spector's plans were quite different: "Combining futurism with Victorian tech seemed like an obvious idea. And including real historical figures in the game was just me forcing a team led by a guy named Jeff George to indulge me in my mania for all things Victorian."

In truth, George wasn't so enthusiastic about the Victorian setting desired by Spector: "Don't get me wrong — I had a great opportunity working for Origin as the director of what was at that time a huge game using an amazing engine, and I am grateful for it. But on that project, I always felt like I was an employee carrying out someone else's vision. Bad Blood was very much my baby, and I'd been all in on Squadron/Wing Commander, but in all honesty, when Worlds of Ultima 2 became the Victorian adventure Martian Dreams, I found myself leading the development of a game that in all honesty, I probably wouldn't have been very interested in playing."

The plot and setting of Martian Dreams became an original mix of Victorian science fiction and technology, spaceships and steam engines, as well as telegraphs and rockets, in one of the earliest examples of what we call steampunk. In a way, the cyberpunk imprint George would have liked to give the game survived Spector's move to Victorian times. If Savage Empire had drawn heavily from Victorian adventure stories, Martian Dreams was clearly inspired and evocative of early science fiction, especially the works of Jules Verne and Herbert George Wells, with particular reference to the literary classic The Time Machine.

The game started with the usual FX Engine presentation but in homage to Mars, with a red planet. It was a continuation from the previous installment: The Avatar and the virtual alter ego of Spector received a book from a strange visitor, which was written by Spector himself. In the book, the two discovered how to use moonstones to travel through time and decided to return to the Victorian era, just as a manned rocket was about to leave for Mars with historical figures Sigmund Freud, Nikola Tesla and journalist Nellie Bly on-board. It was a rescue mission of the world leaders, who had been mistakenly sent to the red planet. Percival Lowell[128] had built a giant cannon to send explorers to Mars, when through an act of sabotage it flew off into space right as the aforementioned world leaders were on board. The avatar and his famous fellow travelers were soon sent to the red planet to investigate, discovering the mysterious secrets of an alien civilization on Mars and stopping the diabolical plans of the monk Rasputin.

Jeff George led the team, slightly smaller than that of Savage Empire, and Philip Brogden was drawing the world and populating it with monsters, secrets, places to discover and characters.

The latter had begun his experience at Origin with Savage Empire, writing some dialogues and programming NPC actions. As usual, lacking specialized editors the work turned into a programming task. Brogden: " 'UseCode' was the internal scripting language that handled everything from branching conversations to interacting with objects like doors and bombs."

UseCode was a scripting language developed by Herman Miller for Ultima VI to automate describing objects for the game engine or make NPCs talk . It was not overly complicated but without tools, the scripts had to be created manually in text editors, requiring a lot of patience and copy&paste.

For Martian Dreams, Brogden was in charge of drawing the world and began work on a real map of Mars from NASA's archives. Working with transparent plastic sheets on it, he first drew the legendary Mars channels and then the points of interest, finally dividing the map into sectors. Accepting input from colleagues, the designer had slowly drawn the general map, and the writers added specific quests, meetings or objects. It was a team effort and everyone could participate according to the attitude that "Nothing at Origin was ever really complete until it shipped — not the story, maps, art or programming. We always worked on everything right up to the last possible second", Brogden recalls.

Manda, Steve Cantrell, Karl Dolgener and Mary Beth Miller were in charge of the dialogues but when the game was almost complete, Raymond Benson arrived at Origin and was tasked with testing the NPC dialogues.

From an artistic point of view, Jeff Dee had one of the most important tasks: he designed many of the tiles with which the designers composed the world,

---

128   inspired by Percival Lowell, an American businessman, mathematician and astronomer who lived between 1855 and 1916

made sketches of the creatures and monsters of Mars, as well as designing the spaceship in the shape of a bullet, clearly inspired by Jules Verne's From the Earth to the Moon, as was the rest of the game.

Richard's involvement was very limited because he was involved in other projects. Spector: "Richard was off working on Ultima VII and trusted me to do interesting, cool things with the Avatar while he was off making the new game in the 'Ultima number' series."

In Martian Dreams the developers once again had fun including the alter egos of Richard Garriott, Greg Dykes and David Watson, Richard Sherman, Greg Duprey and David Yellin, disguised in deliberately clumsy ways. Not only that: the character creation was reminiscent of Richard's fortune-teller, replacing her with Sigmund Freud; the well-known psychoanalyst.

In 1991, Martian Dreams was published on PC to a less enthusiastic reception than Savage Empire, convincing management to pull the plug on Ultima Worlds and cancel an already started conversion for SNES.

Johannigman: "We hoped that the 'Worlds of Ultima' games would attract a larger audience — all the Ultima players, PLUS new players who would be interested in the new genre settings. In truth, I think we only got the subset intersection — the small number of already existing Ultima fans who also happened to be fans of each particular setting. In retrospect, if 'Savage Empire' had been released a year LATER, when the first 'Jurassic Park' movie hit theaters, it might have been a much bigger hit. Maybe."

However, it would not be the last time that a spin-off project would appear at OSI, with mixed results.

Ultima VII was in an advanced state of development and the resources used for the two Ultima Worlds, rather than being diverted to a third chapter with a dubious economic return, were assigned to other more promising projects. Chris Roberts had created a resounding success, earning the role of producer and command over a significant share of OSI's resources.

His gem brought the world's attention to the Texan company known for CRPGs, a space combat simulation. Wing Commander swept the market with stratospheric sales, inspiring other companies to develop similarly expensive high-quality games. Origin itself was at the heart of this change and would be completely transformed by the challenges of a new market in a few years.

A long chain of events was set in motion that would lead OSI to become one of the most influential companies of the 90s and a technological spearhead in the North American video game industry. All of this started with something that Garriott had been anticipating for a long time: another game to ease the financial responsibility from the shoulders of the Ultima franchise. In a few months, this franchise would even eclipse Garriott's.

Acknowledgments

Writing this book was a great personal and professional challenge which gave me the opportunity to relive the birth of computer role-playing games, the Ultima series, and the history of Origin Systems Inc. All this would not have been possible without the support of many extraordinary people, first of all my wife Martina, who was always there for me and generous with advice and encouragement, even in the most difficult moments, not to give up and believe in my project.

The biggest thanks goes to Richard Garriott for helping me in my research, kindly answering my questions and even contacting former colleagues, as well as to Enrico Ricciardi, who took care of everything I could never have done and making the realization of this book possible.

For the present volume, I would like to say a special thank you to the Originites Al Nelson, Dr. Cat, Herman Miller, Ken Arnold, Raymond Benson, Robert White, Siobhan Beeman, Philip Brogden and the Kickstarter backers who have strongly supported the project with a generous donation: Fabio Pericoli and Dominik Reichardt.

A heartfelt thanks also goes to the Originites and supporters of Kickstarter Dave Albert, David Ladyman, David Watson, Jeff Dee, Jeff George, Jeff Johannigman, John Miles, Manda, Michael Beckley, Michael Sims, Paul Neurath, Richard 'Diko' Mather, Todd Porter, Vincenzo Verducci, Warren Spector and all those who contributed to the book's research while preferring to remain anonymous.

I also want to thank Andreas Przygienda and Ellouise McGeachie for their invaluable editing and translation work. Andreas' knowledge of computer history was crucial in fact-checking, and their commitment, skill and professionalism have been decisive in turning my writing into an editorial product which I am proud of.

Finally, I feel the need to thank the many supporter who provided their financial support; the small — but skillful and enthusiastic — group of Moongaters, who helped me to successfully complete the crowdfunding campaign, Gallara Dragon, Jarrod Kailef, Kenneth Kully, Pascal Welsing, Richard Pickles, Stephen Emond; Giorgio Morocutti and Carlo Santagostino of Retrocampus, who believed in the project and provided their fantastic retrocomputers for the trailer.

Index